MANGA
FOR SUCCESS

LEADING MEETINGS AND TEAMS

AUTHOR
MASUMI TANI

ARTWORK BY
ENMO TAKENAWA

WILEY

Published by John Wiley & Sons, Inc., Hoboken, New Jersey.

Published simultaneously in Canada.

For general information on our other products and services or for technical support, please contact our Customer Care Department within the United States at (800) 762-2974, outside the United States at (317) 572-3993 or fax (317) 572-4002.

Wiley also publishes its books in a variety of electronic formats. Some content that appears in print may not be available in electronic formats. For more information about Wiley products, visit our web site at www.wiley.com.

Library of Congress Cataloging-in-Publication Data is Available:
ISBN 9781394176199 (Paperback)
ISBN 9781394176205 (ePub)
ISBN 9781394176212 (ePDF)

Cover Design: JMA Management Center Inc.
Cover Images: JMA Management Center Inc.
© ShEd Artworks/Shutterstock

SKY10042728_030923

Contents

PROLOGUE

Facilitation is...?

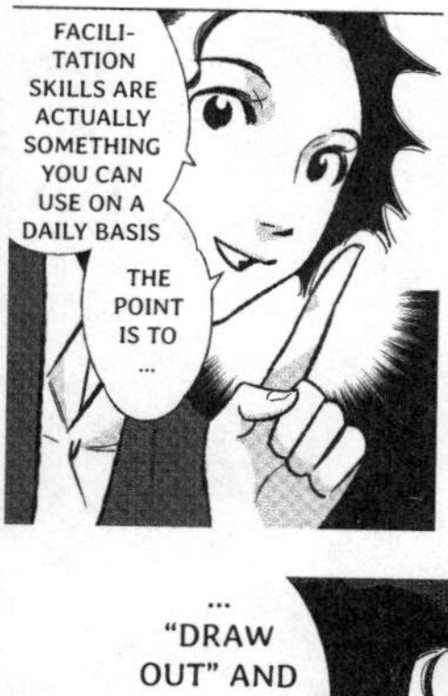
FACILITATION SKILLS ARE ACTUALLY SOMETHING YOU CAN USE ON A DAILY BASIS
THE POINT IS TO ...

PART 1

The Fundamentals of Facilitation

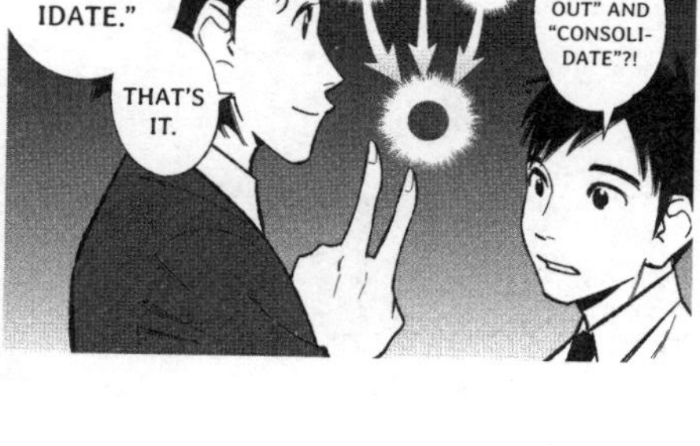
... "DRAW OUT" AND "CONSOLIDATE."
THAT'S IT.
"DRAW OUT" AND "CONSOLIDATE"?!

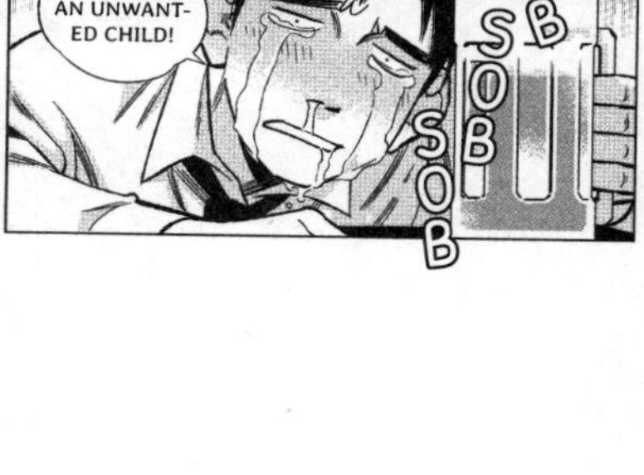
SO I *AM* JUST AN UNWANTED CHILD!
SOB SOB SOB SOB

PART 2

Putting Facilitation to Practice

PART 3

Applying Facilitation

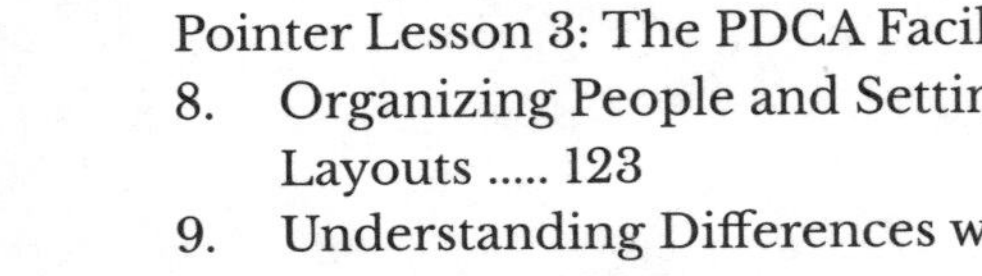

EPILOGUE

The Facilitation Mindset

Hello, I'm Masumi Tani.

My first book, *Facilitation Skills for Leaders!*, was published in 2014. I was overjoyed to receive many positive reactions saying how easy it was to understand, but along those comments, there were some that caught my attention.

"The contents of the book finally sunk in after I took part in a workshop."

"Even though I've been trying to put it into practice, it hasn't been going well in the field..."

Each time I heard such words, I thought how nice it would be if I could paint a better, easier-to-understand picture of facilitation being put into practice. It wasn't long before I was approached about writing this book, *Leading Meetings and Teams* and I still can't forget the feeling of excitement | I had.

This book, depicting the growth of the protagonist through trial and error, together with the transformative effect this has on his workplace, seeks to convey the reality of facilitation in a tangible, easily digestible fashion. It is the result of the hard work of many people, including JMA Management Center's Okada-san,* the wonderful illustrations of Enmo-san, and countless others.

A leader who has the ability to draw out and consolidate things from others, or a facileader for short, will naturally attract people and form a nice work environment and team. However, there are many obstacles on the road to obtaining these skills. Many give up thinking, "I tried, but it didn't go well" or "Yeah, it's not something I can do." A big reason as to why it may not be going well is because they do not have a successful concept of facilitation.

You probably lack any senior staff that can act as role models for facilitation in action and have never experienced the sort of ideal meeting where opinions are actively thrown out and discussed. It can be hard to find the motivation to continue grappling with the concepts of facilitation when you can't see the end result.

Also, another large source of problems is that there is a big difference between a seminar or workshop and the actual workplace.

* The honorific suffix "san" is standard in the Japanese business world.

It's natural for there to be a difference in enthusiasm between workers who have gathered with the explicit interest of learning about facilitation and regular members of the workplace. When trying to form a facilitative work environment for you and your co-workers, implementing facilitation techniques in meetings is only half the battle. It is necessary to understand each team member and apply facilitation to each of them individually, even in daily life.

There's an infinite variety of workplaces; no two are exactly alike. Things may go well or they may not. It can't always turn out exactly as we'd like it to. I expect that the facilitation skill will be a strong asset for leaders who want to turn such situations into positive ones.

Facilitation exists wherever people gather. The level-up process began the moment you flipped open this book. A journey of a thousand miles begins with a single step. Come and take your first step as a facileader, along with the protagonist.

Masumi Tani

Prologue

Facilitation is...?

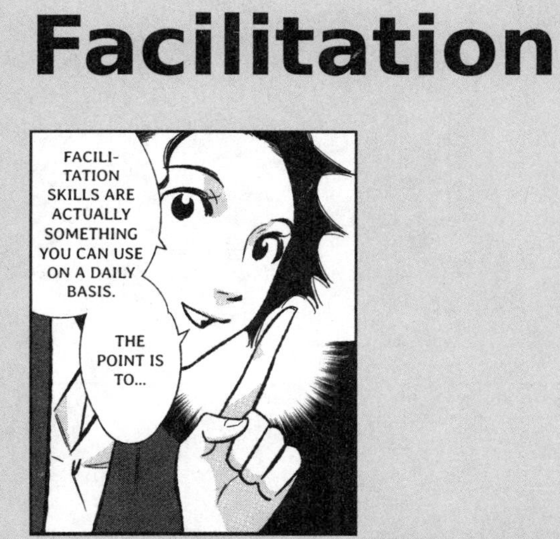

FACILI-TATION SKILLS ARE ACTUALLY SOMETHING YOU CAN USE ON A DAILY BASIS.
THE POINT IS TO...

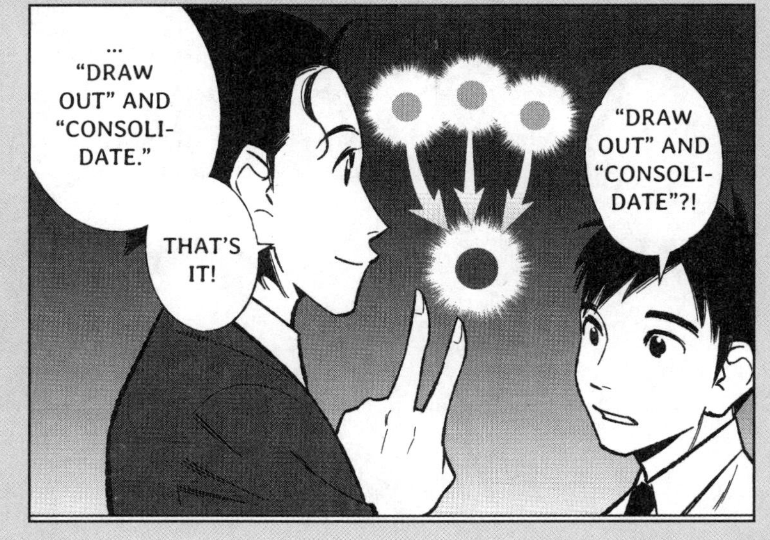

... "DRAW OUT" AND "CONSOLI-DATE."
THAT'S IT!
"DRAW OUT" AND "CONSOLI-DATE"?!

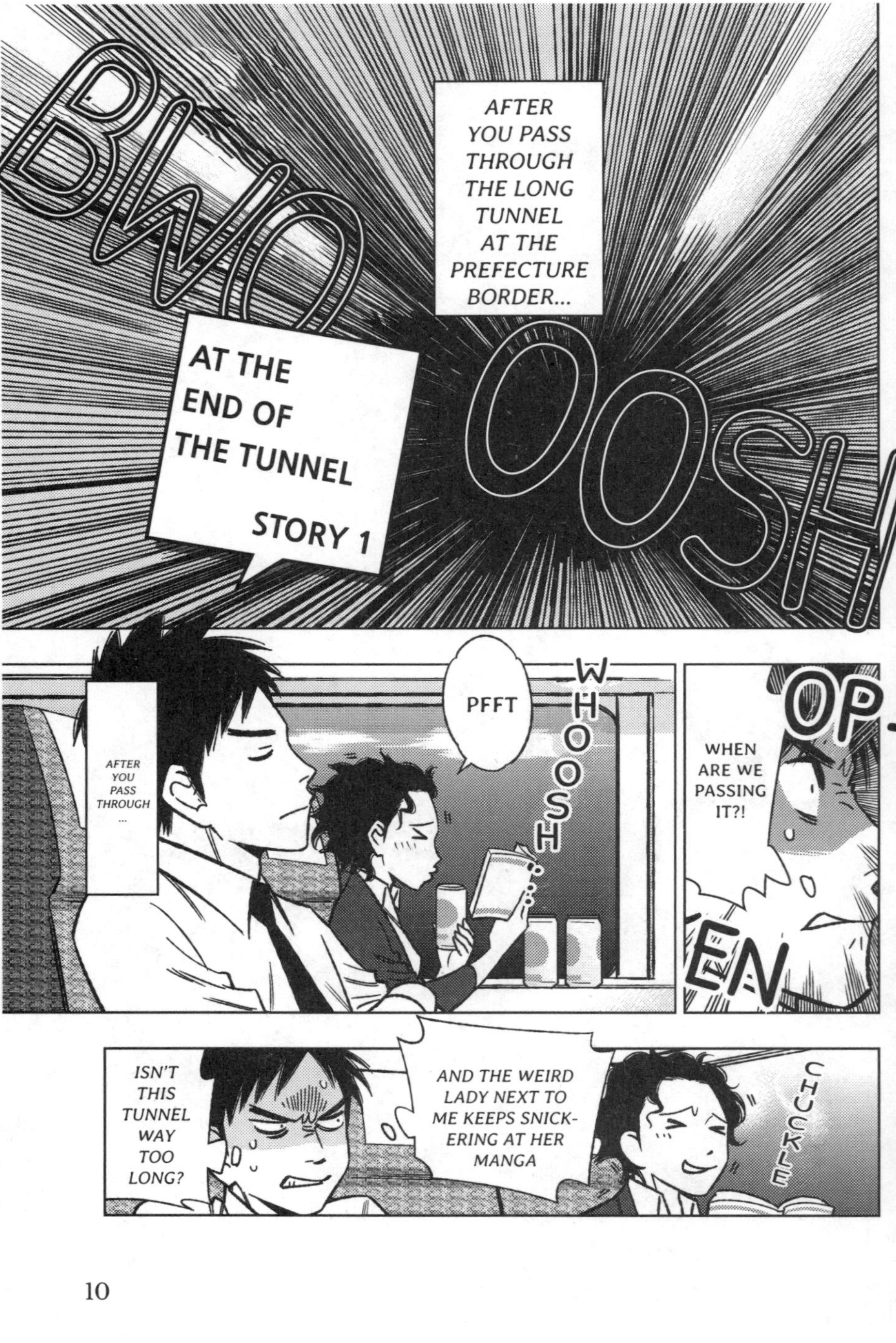
BWOOOSH
AFTER YOU PASS THROUGH THE LONG TUNNEL AT THE PREFECTURE BORDER...
AT THE END OF THE TUNNEL
STORY 1
AFTER YOU PASS THROUGH ...
PFFT
WHOOSH
OP
WHEN ARE WE PASSING IT?!
EN
ISN'T THIS TUNNEL WAY TOO LONG?
AND THE WEIRD LADY NEXT TO ME KEEPS SNICK-ERING AT HER MANGA
CHUCKLE

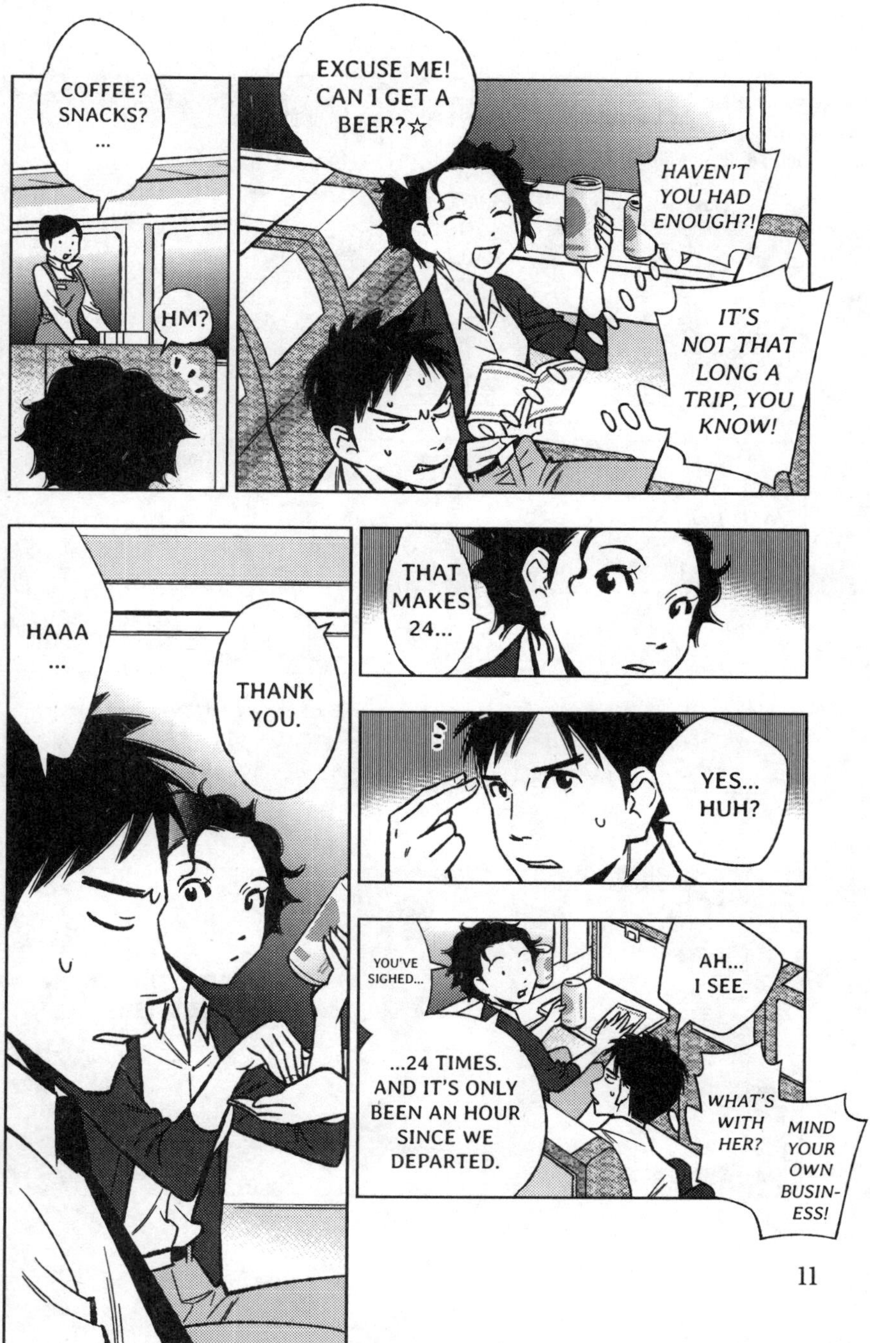
COFFEE? SNACKS? ...
HM?
EXCUSE ME! CAN I GET A BEER?☆
HAVEN'T YOU HAD ENOUGH?!
IT'S NOT THAT LONG A TRIP, YOU KNOW!
THAT MAKES 24...
YES... HUH?
HAAA ...
THANK YOU.
AH... I SEE.
YOU'VE SIGHED...
...24 TIMES. AND IT'S ONLY BEEN AN HOUR SINCE WE DEPARTED.
WHAT'S WITH HER?
MIND YOUR OWN BUSIN-ESS!

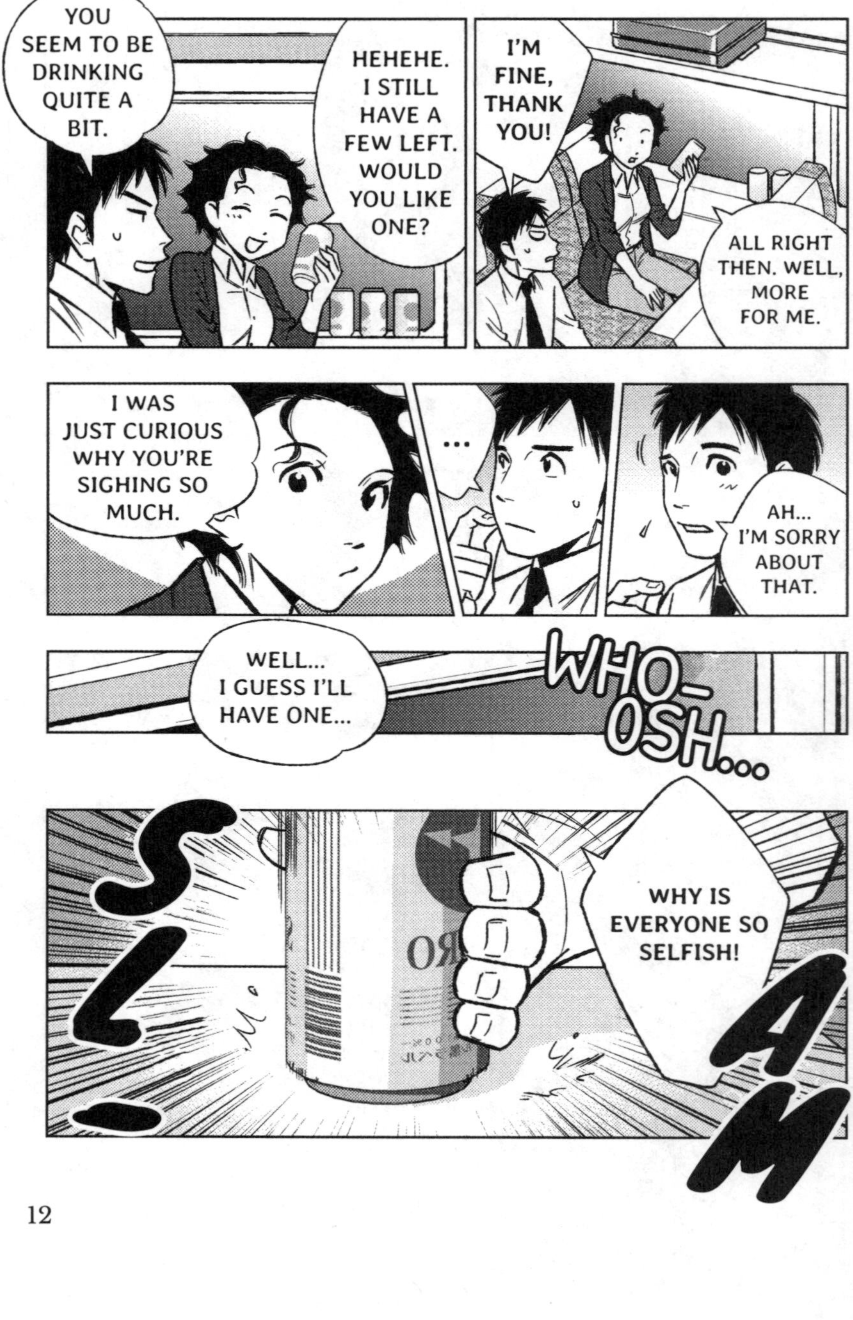

YOU SEEM TO BE DRINKING QUITE A BIT.
HEHEHE. I STILL HAVE A FEW LEFT. WOULD YOU LIKE ONE?
I'M FINE, THANK YOU!
ALL RIGHT THEN. WELL, MORE FOR ME.
I WAS JUST CURIOUS WHY YOU'RE SIGHING SO MUCH.
...
AH... I'M SORRY ABOUT THAT.
WELL... I GUESS I'LL HAVE ONE...
WHO-OSH...
SLAM
WHY IS EVERYONE SO SELFISH!

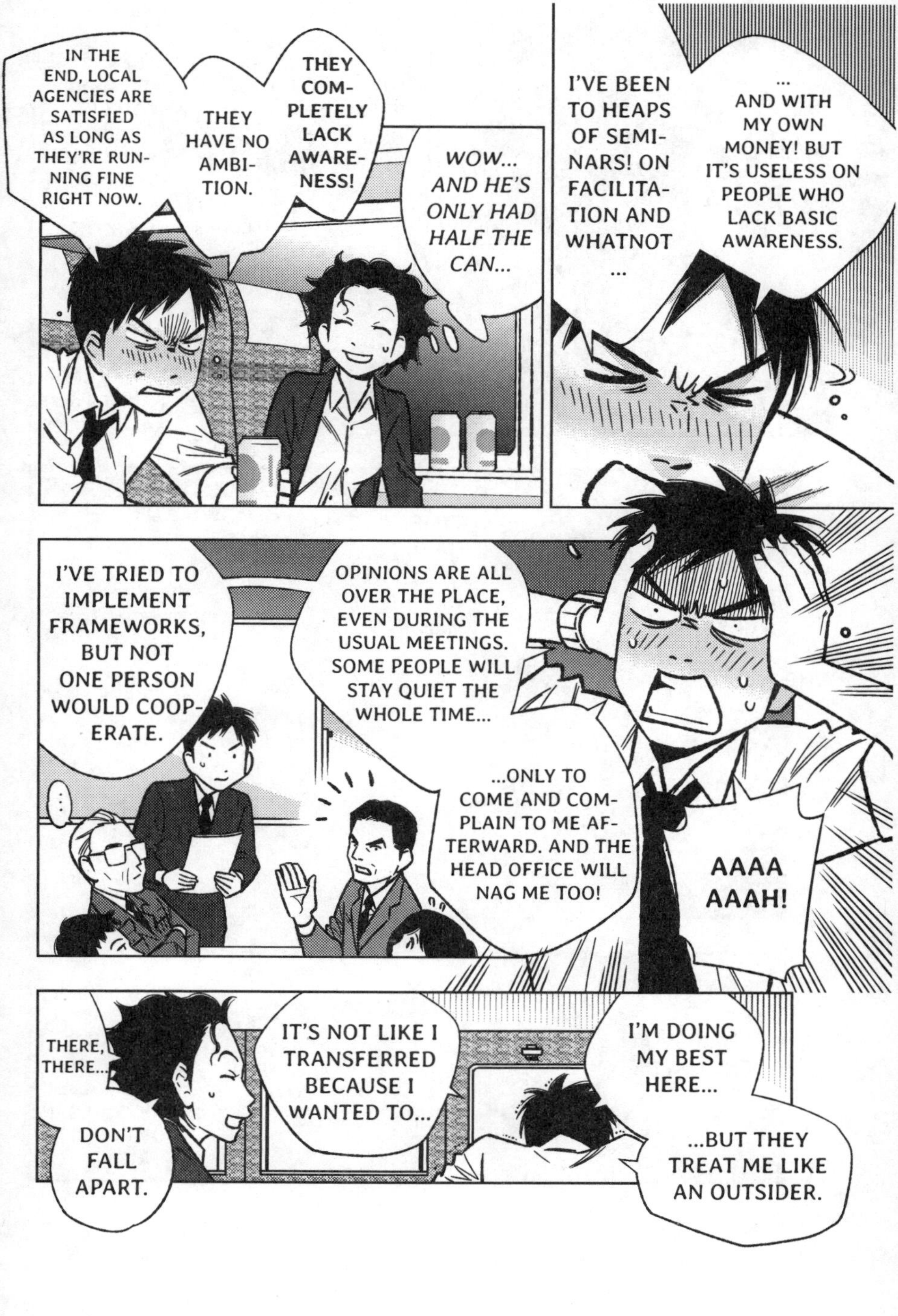
IN THE END, LOCAL AGENCIES ARE SATISFIED AS LONG AS THEY'RE RUNNING FINE RIGHT NOW.
THEY HAVE NO AMBITION.
THEY COMPLETELY LACK AWARENESS!
WOW... AND HE'S ONLY HAD HALF THE CAN...
I'VE BEEN TO HEAPS OF SEMINARS! ON FACILITATION AND WHATNOT ...
... AND WITH MY OWN MONEY! BUT IT'S USELESS ON PEOPLE WHO LACK BASIC AWARENESS.
I'VE TRIED TO IMPLEMENT FRAMEWORKS, BUT NOT ONE PERSON WOULD COOPERATE.
...
OPINIONS ARE ALL OVER THE PLACE, EVEN DURING THE USUAL MEETINGS. SOME PEOPLE WILL STAY QUIET THE WHOLE TIME...
...ONLY TO COME AND COMPLAIN TO ME AFTERWARD. AND THE HEAD OFFICE WILL NAG ME TOO!
AAAA AAAH!
I'M DOING MY BEST HERE...
...BUT THEY TREAT ME LIKE AN OUTSIDER.
IT'S NOT LIKE I TRANSFERRED BECAUSE I WANTED TO...
THERE, THERE...
DON'T FALL APART.

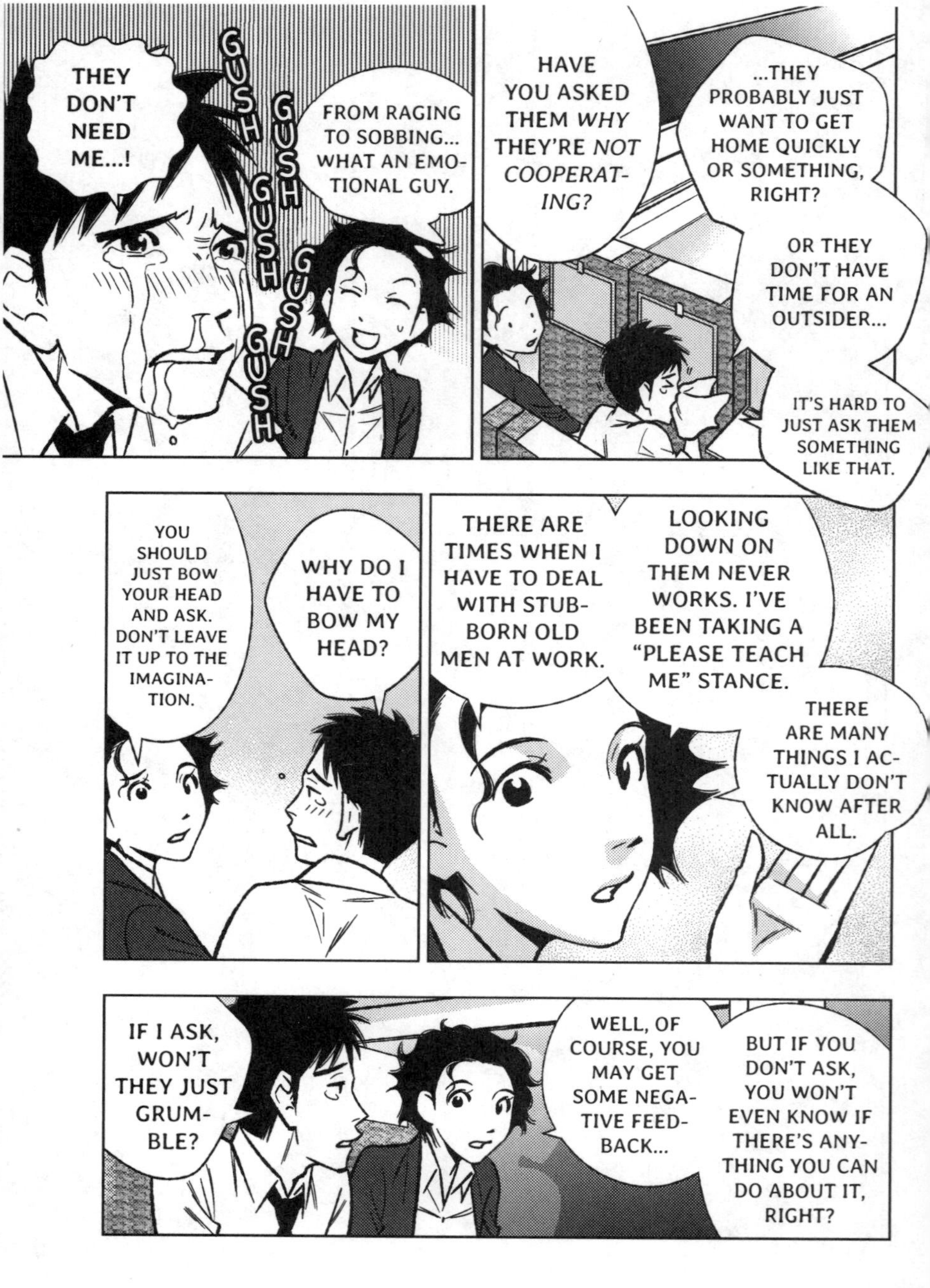
THEY DON'T NEED ME...!
GUSH GUSH GUSH GUSH GUSH
FROM RAGING TO SOBBING... WHAT AN EMOTIONAL GUY.
HAVE YOU ASKED THEM *WHY* THEY'RE *NOT* COOPERATING?
...THEY PROBABLY JUST WANT TO GET HOME QUICKLY OR SOMETHING, RIGHT?
OR THEY DON'T HAVE TIME FOR AN OUTSIDER...
IT'S HARD TO JUST ASK THEM SOMETHING LIKE THAT.
YOU SHOULD JUST BOW YOUR HEAD AND ASK. DON'T LEAVE IT UP TO THE IMAGINATION.
WHY DO I HAVE TO BOW MY HEAD?
THERE ARE TIMES WHEN I HAVE TO DEAL WITH STUBBORN OLD MEN AT WORK.
LOOKING DOWN ON THEM NEVER WORKS. I'VE BEEN TAKING A "PLEASE TEACH ME" STANCE.
THERE ARE MANY THINGS I ACTUALLY DON'T KNOW AFTER ALL.
IF I ASK, WON'T THEY JUST GRUMBLE?
WELL, OF COURSE, YOU MAY GET SOME NEGATIVE FEEDBACK...
BUT IF YOU DON'T ASK, YOU WON'T EVEN KNOW IF THERE'S ANYTHING YOU CAN DO ABOUT IT, RIGHT?

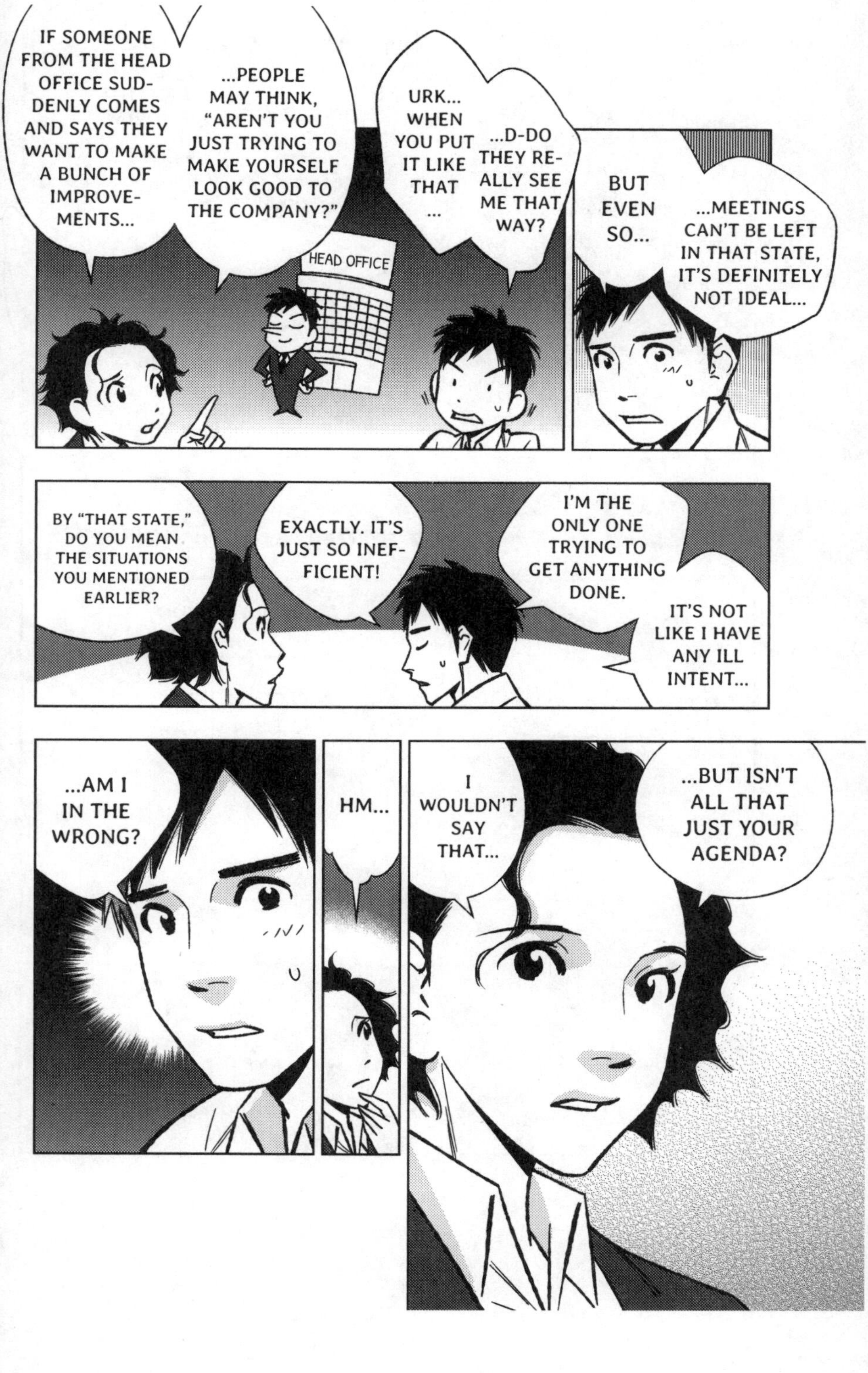
IF SOMEONE FROM THE HEAD OFFICE SUDDENLY COMES AND SAYS THEY WANT TO MAKE A BUNCH OF IMPROVEMENTS...
...PEOPLE MAY THINK, "AREN'T YOU JUST TRYING TO MAKE YOURSELF LOOK GOOD TO THE COMPANY?"
HEAD OFFICE
URK... WHEN YOU PUT IT LIKE THAT ...
...D-DO THEY REALLY SEE ME THAT WAY?
BUT EVEN SO...
...MEETINGS CAN'T BE LEFT IN THAT STATE, IT'S DEFINITELY NOT IDEAL...
BY "THAT STATE," DO YOU MEAN THE SITUATIONS YOU MENTIONED EARLIER?
EXACTLY. IT'S JUST SO INEFFICIENT!
I'M THE ONLY ONE TRYING TO GET ANYTHING DONE.
IT'S NOT LIKE I HAVE ANY ILL INTENT...
...AM I IN THE WRONG?
HM...
I WOULDN'T SAY THAT...
...BUT ISN'T ALL THAT JUST YOUR AGENDA?

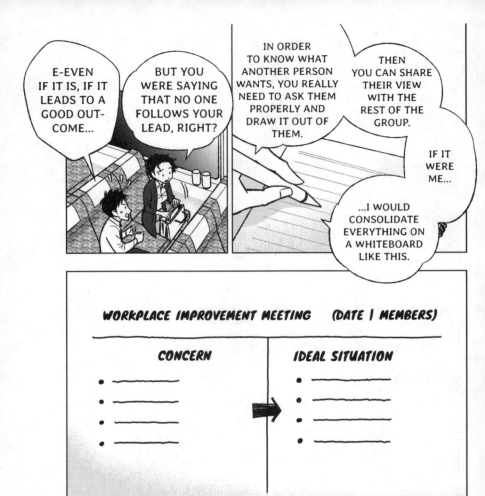

WORKPLACE IMPROVEMENT MEETING   (DATE | MEMBERS)

CONCERN	IDEAL SITUATION
• _____	• _____
• _____	• _____
• _____	• _____
• _____	• _____

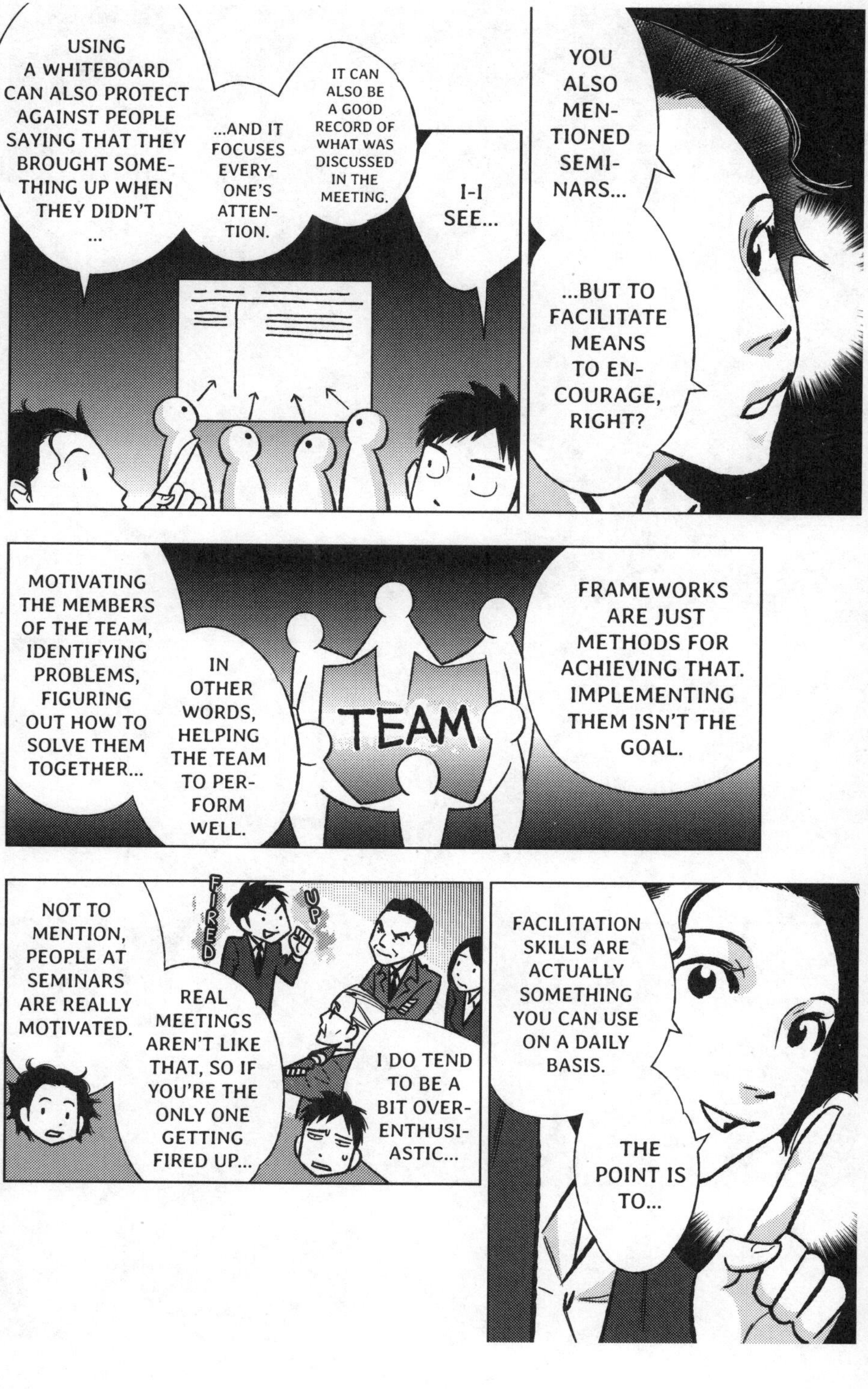
USING A WHITEBOARD CAN ALSO PROTECT AGAINST PEOPLE SAYING THAT THEY BROUGHT SOME-THING UP WHEN THEY DIDN'T ...
...AND IT FOCUSES EVERY-ONE'S ATTEN-TION.
IT CAN ALSO BE A GOOD RECORD OF WHAT WAS DISCUSSED IN THE MEETING.
I-I SEE...
YOU ALSO MEN-TIONED SEMI-NARS...
...BUT TO FACILITATE MEANS TO EN-COURAGE, RIGHT?
MOTIVATING THE MEMBERS OF THE TEAM, IDENTIFYING PROBLEMS, FIGURING OUT HOW TO SOLVE THEM TOGETHER...
IN OTHER WORDS, HELPING THE TEAM TO PER-FORM WELL.
TEAM
FRAMEWORKS ARE JUST METHODS FOR ACHIEVING THAT. IMPLEMENTING THEM ISN'T THE GOAL.
NOT TO MENTION, PEOPLE AT SEMINARS ARE REALLY MOTIVATED.
FIRED
UP
REAL MEETINGS AREN'T LIKE THAT, SO IF YOU'RE THE ONLY ONE GETTING FIRED UP...
I DO TEND TO BE A BIT OVER-ENTHUSI-ASTIC...
FACILITATION SKILLS ARE ACTUALLY SOMETHING YOU CAN USE ON A DAILY BASIS.
THE POINT IS TO...

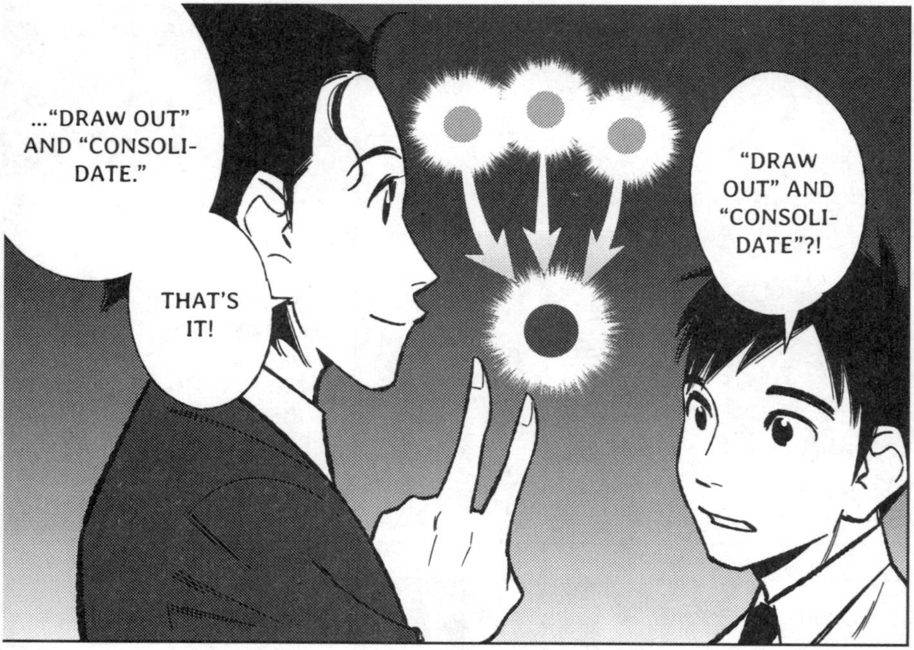
..."DRAW OUT" AND "CONSOLI-DATE."
THAT'S IT!
"DRAW OUT" AND "CONSOLI-DATE"?!

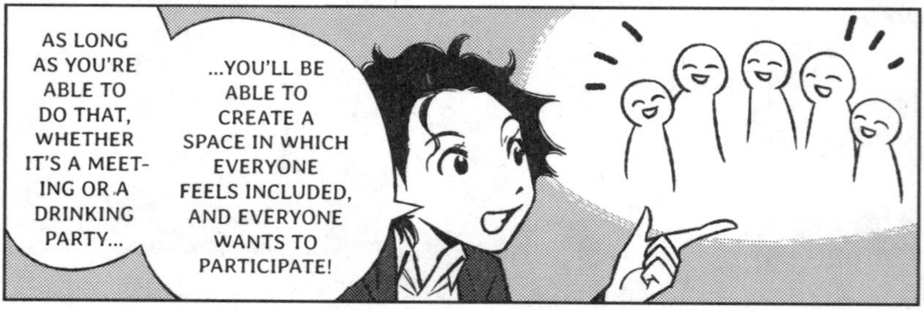
AS LONG AS YOU'RE ABLE TO DO THAT, WHETHER IT'S A MEET-ING OR A DRINKING PARTY...
...YOU'LL BE ABLE TO CREATE A SPACE IN WHICH EVERYONE FEELS INCLUDED, AND EVERYONE WANTS TO PARTICIPATE!

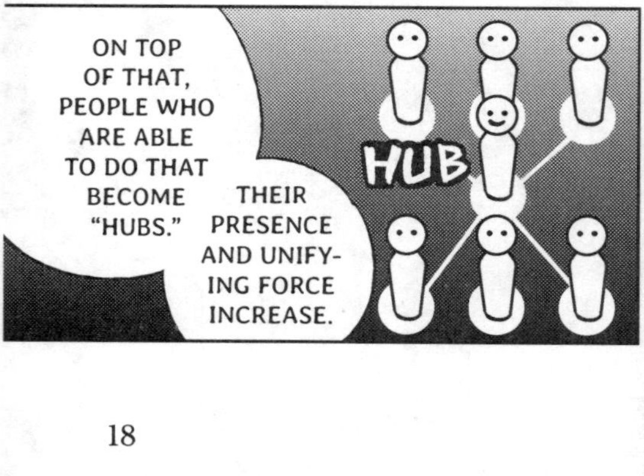
ON TOP OF THAT, PEOPLE WHO ARE ABLE TO DO THAT BECOME "HUBS."
THEIR PRESENCE AND UNIFY-ING FORCE INCREASE.
HUB

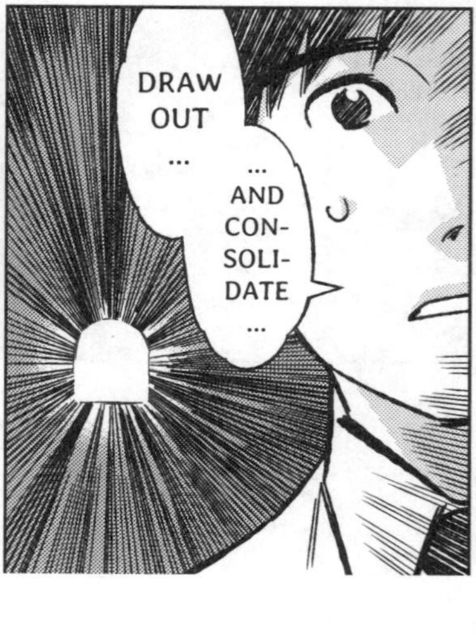
DRAW OUT ...
... AND CON-SOLI-DATE ...

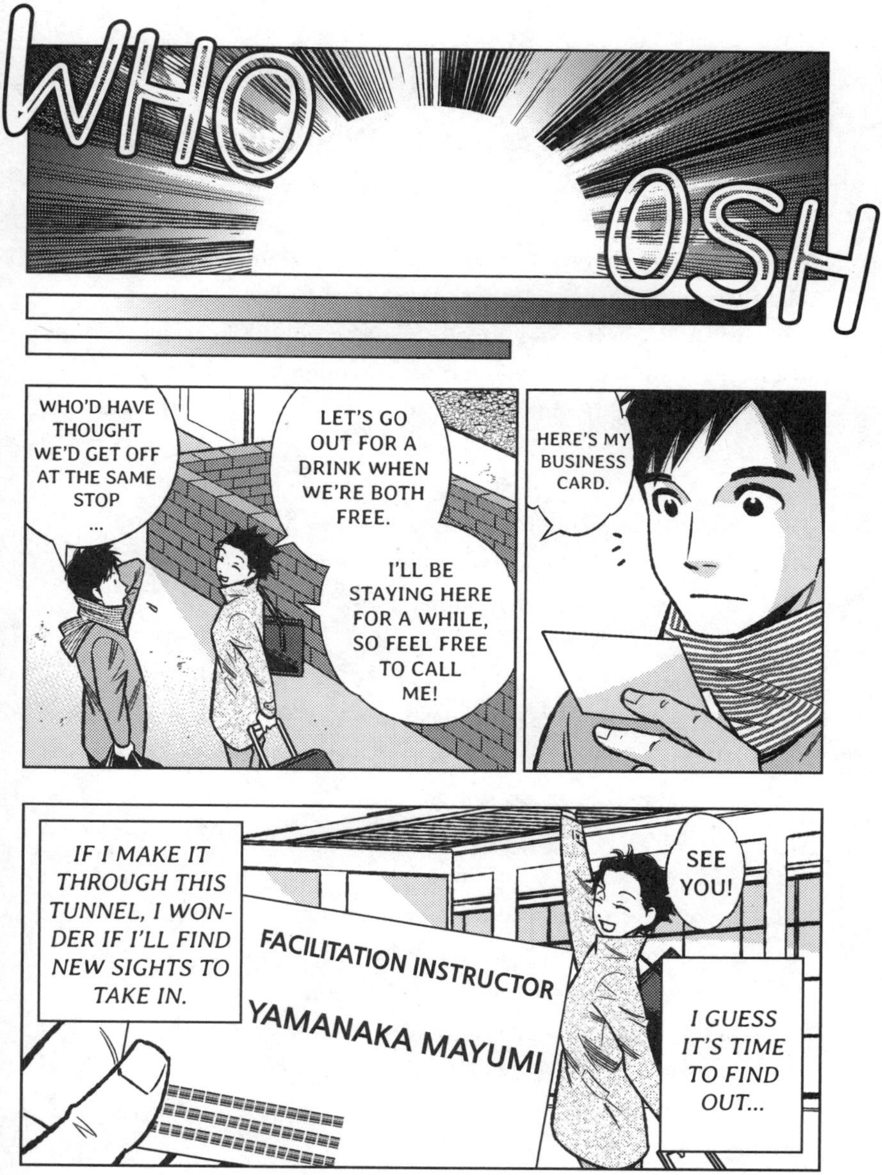
WHOOSH
WHO'D HAVE THOUGHT WE'D GET OFF AT THE SAME STOP ...
LET'S GO OUT FOR A DRINK WHEN WE'RE BOTH FREE.
I'LL BE STAYING HERE FOR A WHILE, SO FEEL FREE TO CALL ME!
HERE'S MY BUSINESS CARD.
IF I MAKE IT THROUGH THIS TUNNEL, I WONDER IF I'LL FIND NEW SIGHTS TO TAKE IN.
FACILITATION INSTRUCTOR
YAMANAKA MAYUMI
SEE YOU!
I GUESS IT'S TIME TO FIND OUT...

1 The Skills of a Facileader Who Runs Their Team Well

When they're in charge of a new team or starting something new, all leaders seriously consider ways in which their team might be improved and how it could provide better results. Rather than just sitting there worrying about it, leaders often find themselves trying out many different fixes, only to end up doing everything themselves.

Every leader is doing their best in their own way. However, there are both successful and unsuccessful leaders in this world. What might be the difference between them?

One of the answers, the one I wish to convey with this book, is the facilitation skill. Before I begin any of that, though, let's start with a quick self-check of your current facileader skills. Please answer the following questions with a yes or no.

Q1. Do you tell your team members what you need from them and what you expect of them?

Q2. Is your team equipped with the necessary tools, resources, and materials needed to properly do their jobs?

Q3. Do you provide each of your team members with the opportunity to do their best work every day?

Q4. Have you recognized or praised a team member's results in the past week?

Q5. Have you told your team members that you care about them as individuals?

Q6. Have you shown support for your team members' growth?

Q7. Do you listen to your team members' opinions and respect them?

Q8. Have you told your team members that their role is vital to the mission/goals of the company?

Q9. Have you grasped each of your team members' working styles and encouraged them to do quality work?

Q10. Are you aware of the interpersonal relationships your team members have?

Q11. Have you made the time to talk to your team members about their progress in these past six months?

Q12. In the past year, have you provided opportunities for your team members to learn about their work and grow?

Taken from *First, Break All* the *Rules: What the World's Greatest Managers Do Differently* by Marcus Buckingham and Curt Coffman.

Now, how many of these did you say yes to? If your answer is not that many, don't worry, you can only grow from here on out. Let's study, practice, and put into practice with the aim of becoming a facileader who can run their team smoothly.

2 Drawing Out and Consolidating

Facilitation is the skill of a facileader who is able to run their team well. If I had to sum it up in a single word, it would be to encourage. Just like you have seen in the facileader self-assessment, the idea is to encourage your team members in a variety of ways and help them to produce results. Broadly speaking, there are two skills required to achieve this.

The first one is the act of drawing out. You need to draw out both the positive and negative sides of any given opinion, positives such as motivation and ideas, and negatives such as complaints and criticism. Only drawing out positives, for example, would not result in a very lively discussion. A workplace in which any opinion can be freely voiced is the kind of environment that will produce a strong, flexible team.

After you draw out the opinions of your team, you need to consolidate. Consolidation is the act of gathering up something scattered, such as people's ideas in a meeting, and forming them into one single lump. By doing this, team members can align their wills, with the aim of creating a shared vision and objective for the team and making everyone's opinion clear.

A whiteboard, for example, is a useful and powerful tool for visualizing everyone's opinions.

The skill of drawing out and consolidating is indispensable for leaders managing diverse teams. In order to do so effectively, it's important to first listen to a variety of opinions while maintaining neutrality.

Of course, maintaining complete neutrality no matter what will ultimately prevent you from performing your duties as a leader. As Carlos Ghosn, former CEO of Nissan, puts it: "A leader must deal with the subtleties of people's minds. However, in terms of judgment, rationality and theory must be given priority. Subordinates will follow your lead if they think they will produce results." An important job of a leader is to make better decisions and produce results. Drawing out and consolidating the opinions of team members who are familiar with the field is a huge factor in the ability to make good, informed decisions.

Facilitation isn't just about running meetings effectively. It's actually a guideline that shows us how to be a leader.

Pointer Lesson 1

Fostering a Sense of Satisfaction. How to Set a Theme

What do you need to do in order to unify a team that isn't performing well?

First of all, there's no way people who think, "That person's weird" or "They're wrong" could all gather in one place and suddenly get along with each other. You've probably heard it a hundred times, but daily interactions and human relationships are extremely important. It's often basically impossible for things to be resolved via meetings only.

With that said, as a leader, you are often required to convince such team members within a set time frame, be it a meeting or some other such deadline. For example, when you want to convey something to your team that they have no motivation toward, or that they are opposed to, the important thing is to **listen to what they have to say** before concluding the discussion.

"What if it's difficult to draw out what they have to say?"

The trick to bringing out the true feelings of team members who are complacent or reluctant to express themselves is to **directly ask them for their input**. It's also important to discard this misconception that as a leader, you have to know everything. It's totally fine to be humble, not to be caught up with everything that's going on in the workplace, and to ask your team members to explain things to you.

"There are many things leaders don't know or understand."

Of course, as a leader, there are things I want to say or have you do. However, I don't know how those things will sit with you all. That's why I want you to tell me what the challenges are for you, and how we can make it work. Let's brainstorm together.

It is also very important to focus on the dissatisfactions and concerns that someone may have, such as the reasons for their opposition or why they refuse to go along with anything. This is because the true source of dissatisfaction for many people is that they feel their voices are not being heard.

Different departments will have different objections. Imagine, for example, that the sales department wants to increase their sales. However, manufacturing is suffering from a labor shortage. Under such circumstances, even if a project to get more prospective customers is launched, it will not be easy to create a cooperative framework that transcends departments.

"Sales always act all high and mighty because they bring in jobs, but we're the ones that end up getting thrown around when they overdo it!" It is very important to not turn a blind eye to such dissatisfaction and complaints. You must give them the opportunity to vent, and listen to them. This is because depending on how you choose to listen to these complaints, they can become excellent suggestions that lead to future improvements. For example, I think it's sometimes necessary to have people complain and talk things out at personal events outside of the work environment. Alternatively, I think it would be a good idea to hold meetings with the sole purpose of finding and raising awareness for issues like this.

"But won't the team become rather negative if I only listen to complaints?"

I think each and every one of us has both a positive and a negative side. While there may be many negative aspects such as dissatisfaction or complaints, there's a huge variety of positive aspects too. Anticipation, curiosity, and thoughts such as "I want to try that" or "Sounds fun" are common as well.

When something happens, for example, when a new project or improvement activity starts, I believe that depending on the circumstances and the person in question, both sides will make themselves known. It would be great if everyone were always in agreement and always motivated, but of course, that isn't the case most of the time.

Many workers will never say a word, as they feel that even if they state their opinion in a meeting, nothing would change. However, this only results in the negative feelings piling up internally. "We're going to have to do it anyway" or "You just want to push things in this direction" are some examples of these feelings. In situations like this, if the team morale isn't rectified, it becomes difficult to unify the team, and productivity will not increase. That's why I believe it is extremely important to draw out both negative and positive comments, as neutrally as possible.

They don't say anything at meetings, but they also don't perform their duties properly or follow directions. Wouldn't a situation like that just be a waste?

"Nevertheless, dissenting opinions won't change anything in the end, right?"

Certainly, that can ring true for many objections that differ from the views of the leader or the team as a whole. However, those team members will understand that although their views did not affect the outcome this time, in the future their ideas might be better reflected. They will begin to realize that at the very least they are being **hear**d and **understood**.

It may be true that there's no point in speaking up, but at least their view has been acknowledged and accepted by the other team members. That's the sort of way of thinking you want to promote. You want your team members to say, "Fine, I don't agree with this, but maybe we can try it my way next time." The approach of listening to your team members and trying new things, having them not go well, and figuring out what went wrong is much better than having a workplace full of people with no motivation, hiding their dissatisfaction.

"Is there a trick to bringing out negative opinions?"

What I try to do is to bring out **both the negatives and the positives, at the same time**. People tend to ask for just the negative opinions first. Only talking about the negatives will create a pessimistic, gloomy mood in the team and kill their motivation. We'd like to avoid the sorts of situations where the leader will be forced to give their team a dressing-down for their poor attitude!

In order to prevent a situation like that from happening, you need to work together with your team members to discuss the concerns (negatives), the results produced when things go well (positives), and what is important in order to succeed. After coming up with a lot of opinions for both sides, give them some encouragement. Together, come up with some countermeasures for their concerns. If there is a possibility of achieving better results, encourage them to be proactive about it.

From the leader's perspective, what is important for success is often linked to things they want the team members to do or change. Give them some encouragement here as well. Tell them that if something is important, we should do it. Let's think of ways to incorporate it.

"What exactly will that look like?"

Let's take a meeting with the theme "Participation of Women in the Workforce," for example. If it goes well, you'll get responses like "It'll revitalize the workplace" and "More people will want to join the company." If it doesn't go well, however, you might hear the following concerns: "How would maternity leave be handled?" "Would there be an increase in short-term workers?" "What will the effects of that be?" "Will there be unfair compensation?"

If you ask something like "What's important to your job moving forward?" you'll likely get a variety of answers such as "Daily communication," "good organization," and "good cooperation between team members."

If you ask, you may find that most people actually agree with what you're trying to do. You'll think, "Oh, so they do agree with me, they do understand." But if there are concerns and worries about implementing those ideas, it's important to maintain the attitude of trying to address and solve those problems together as a team.

"Is there anything else I should be careful of?"

Two of the most important factors are the setting of the topic of discussion, in the first place, and dealing with responses to that topic in a calm, flexible manner, in the second place.

Let's take the earlier "Participation of Women in the Workforce" topic, for example. If there are people who honestly don't care about the participation of women and believe there are more important matters, they may be opposed to the entire topic itself. You'd probably consider cutting them out entirely with thoughts such as, "That's an outdated way of thinking" or "We don't need people on the team who think like that." There's no need for you to treat any and all opinions with respect, after all. However, if you want to have a productive discussion that includes everyone, you may need to reconsider the theme itself.

For example, if you change the theme to "What Should Be Done in Order to Create a Better Working Environment for Everyone?" then it now applies to all workers. Another theme could be "Thinking about the Future of the Workplace." If we bring up these socially themed topics and support the discussion with a range of evidence and facts, then it can be expected that the topic of women in the workplace will be broached eventually.

Now let's use a sales department meeting as an example, as the same logic applies. If you start with a theme such as new customer development, then you'll find that people of the opinion that caring for the current customers takes priority will be opposed from the get-go.

What's important to understand here is this: if team members are easily able to see the leader's agenda via the theme, there will be people who are opposed to that agenda before discussions have even started. If you want to avoid unnecessary opposition, consider rethinking your theme. On top of that, having the flexibility to take every opinion that gets voiced and say, "I see, that's important, too," creates an open forum in which any opinion can be easily expressed.

What can be useful in these situations is to create a "derailment space" on the whiteboard and jot down any points and opinions that are unrelated to the topic of the day. It is important to be willing to write down and visualize the disagreements and misaligned opinions first, without getting emotional about them.

Pointer Lesson 2

To Draw Out or to Convey?

I haven't been able to draw out opinions very well.

Drawing out and consolidating opinions is the core of facilitation, but if you're trying to draw out the wrong thing, it's not going to go well. Let's imagine a leader who already has a solid image of what they want to do and how they want to do it. Trying to draw that exact preconceived notion out of the team, or trying to put words in their mouth, is one of the worst things that a leader can do. **Commands or instructions are something that must always be conveyed directly** and not something that should be drawn out. This includes things you *must* have them do, and conditions they *must* abide by. For example, if there are three different methods (A, B, C) for completing a task, but this time it is absolutely necessary to use method A, you must convey that information in a way that makes it clear there's no room for discussion, and you must also tell them why.

However, if methods A, B, and C are all perfectly suitable, even if the leader has a preference, by letting the team use whichever method they like, the leader is giving them the choice.

The leader may think method A is good. However, by listening to the team's propositions for methods B and C, and by considering, discussing, and having everyone agree on one method, they're conveying to the team that they want to hear their ideas, not just their own. This is another useful approach for drawing things out.

"When I ask them to do something, they won't just sit there and accept it."

I bet.

For that reason, is it not all the more important to draw out the reasons and arguments they may have for not listening? As a leader, on top of drawing out various elements such as the person's troubles, issues, comprehension of the subject at hand, recognition of the end goal, and so on, I think it's important to show them that both what you'd like them to do and their concerns **are expressly tied to finding a good solution.**

For example, you've said, "We're going to work on the 5S from now on."

I bet you can all too easily imagine the negative responses you'll receive. "Isn't there something more important to do?" "But that project's such a pain..." and so on.

What you want to consider in a situation like that is what exactly are the worries and hardships for the employees at your workplace while they carry out their day-to-day tasks. Is the deadline too tight? Do they not have enough people? What effect would the 5S* project have, and what would the merits be for your team and your company?

In addition, encouraging them to think. "Oh, this is important," or "I feel like this is worth doing" is in itself a facilitative measure.

And finally, at times I think it is important to draw out your team members' **"sense of impending danger."** That feeling of "If I don't do it, there'll be trouble." Leaders look at the whole image, including the future, and this often results in them feeling like, "If things continue as they are, it's not going to go well." Regular team members, on the other hand, are often so busy with their own tasks that they cannot see the big picture. The following questions can be helpful to see the big picture:

"How will the world change over the next 10 years?"

"How has the world changed in the last 10 years?"

* 5S is a workplace organization method aimed at making work efficient, effective, and safe. The name comes from five Japanese words—*seiri, seiton, seiso, seiketsu,* and *shitsuke*—which are usually translated to "sort," "set in order," "shine," "standardize," and "sustain." See https://en.wikipedia.org/wiki/5S_(methodology) for more information.

In order to draw useful opinions out from the team members, it is necessary **to provide them with information and data** upon which they can form those opinions. In this way, if you can use multiple perspectives to stimulate both the desire and the need to do something in your team members, you'll find you'll be able to get them involved and engaged in a variety of ways.

"If I listen to too many things, everything starts to feel disjointed and unorganized."

Make sure to properly sort out what you need to convey and what you need to draw out.

Differentiate the phases of drawing out opinions and consolidating those opinions.

If you fail to sort one from the other and let it all mix up into one big mess, I don't think it will go well for you. That's why you should start by organizing everything. If you can do that, everything should clear itself up a little.

However, every person is a little different. Each and every one of them has their own individual problems, issues, circumstances, and goals. Even so, if you want to unify your team, you need to **find the similarities.** So in some regards, everyone will be different, but there will also be similarities shared by everyone. In other words, you'll be able to sort out points in which everyone's different, and also in which everyone is similar.

On top of that, I think in the first place, the method for deciding with what purpose and toward what goal the team should be working is also very important.

Column THE FOUR STAGES OF LEVELING UP

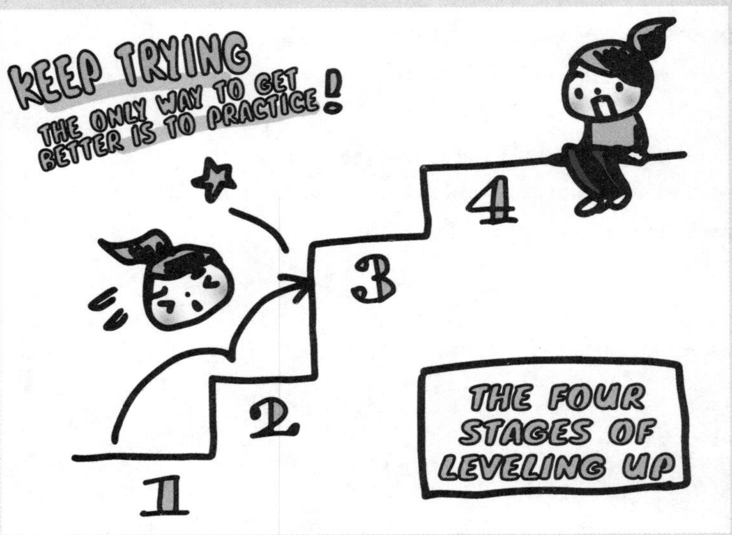
KEEP TRYING
THE ONLY WAY TO GET BETTER IS TO PRACTICE!
1
2
3
4
THE FOUR STAGES OF LEVELING UP

If you want to acquire facilitation skills, or any new skills for that matter, it's first useful to have a grasp of the four stages of competence.

This theory, which was proposed by members of the Gordon Training Institute in the 1970s, aims to show a clear, step-by-step depiction of the process of learning a new skill.

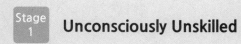

Stage 1 Unconsciously Unskilled

"Facilitation? I've never heard of it."

We are unable to work on things we don't yet know about, nor can we develop the desire to learn about them in the first place. The first stage, stage one, is where you not only are not able to perform the skill, you don't even know about its existence at all.

In order to move to the next stage, you need to become aware. You need to realize that there's a new skill, knowledge, and information. Also, you need to notice there's a challenge you face that might require that skill.

Now if you take a look at yourself and your surroundings, you may find many things that will help you start to level up. For example, before you took the facileader self-assessment on page 20, you might not even have known the issues you were facing.

Here are a few examples of people not even realizing how poorly they're performing. There's the bitter company president, complaining, "Our staff members don't greet me!" when in reality, they've just been lightly shrugging off said greetings. Or a department head who says they talk to their young team members often, but in reality, it always just turns into a lecture. We think we're doing great, but in reality... Let's just say it happens to all of us. If you ever feel irritated because you don't understand someone, or when they're failing to understand you, the first step is to take a deep breath. I recommend considering this as an opportunity to improve your communication skills, as it's very possible that you're the problem, not them.

Encountering someone for whom your usual way of handling things does not work is a unique opportunity to improve your approach—and maybe even a chance to find a new one. You should be proud of yourself for noticing such shortcomings and move on to the next stage.

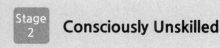

Consciously Unskilled

"I know about facilitation! But it's difficult to actually implement it at work."

This is the next stage after you come to a realization. It's the trial stage.

I know what I need to do, but for some reason, I just can't make it work...

This part of stage two can feel rather painful, as you're now aware of your shortcomings but still lack the skills to do anything about them. Maybe it would be easier to visualize if we use sports, instruments, or dancing as an example.

The dance moves seem so simple, but when you try them you fall flat. You know how it's supposed to look in your head, but you aren't able to move your body like that. Many people give up here and quit practicing altogether. They turn a blind eye, saying things such as, "I guess it's just not for me."

Some examples are the boss that realized upon reflection that he hadn't been praising his workers enough, but after trying they told him it was weird. Or the boss that was planning on listening to the young employee's story for sure this time, but before he knew it he was at it again, lecturing away.

If you want to continue reflecting and improving, what you need is comrades. When trying to work with facilitation, I highly recommend finding a study buddy, both inside and outside the company. If you have someone you can talk to about what went well, what didn't, and how you can continue to improve moving forward, it won't be long before you find your way through to the next stage.

It's natural for your first attempt to be a failure. Continue to level up with friends who can laugh off the failures with you.

 Consciously Skilled

"I'll do it if I remember, but I tend to end up doing it my way."

As your level rises, your next task is to not forget.
Even if you're able to do it now, you're not used to it, and you may find yourself falling back into old habits.

Even though you're able to use a whiteboard in meetings, you may forget to use it. Facilitation in general may even slip your mind.

Once you move up to stage 3, lay a plan out so you don't forget. Present and share the rules for running meetings. Leave a note on your desk with important tasks you need to do as a facileader.

It's important to utilize as many mechanisms as possible to force yourself into situations where you have no choice but to use the skills you've learned.

At our company, this is what made whiteboard meetings the norm. For your daily practice, involve those around you with these arrangements.

 ## Stage 4 Unconsciously Skilled

Try to involve those around you in your daily practice.

"Of course I do it, I don't even really think about it."

If you practice daily and put all the right mechanisms in place, you'll reach this stage without even realizing it.

This is the state where the facilitation skill has become yours. You're able to do it naturally, without being conscious of it. You should have reached a state where you, as the facileader, are able to make your team run smoothly and produce good results.

If that isn't the case, then that's proof that you still have some things left to learn. Here are some things I recommend doing.

Try to remember what was in stage 1. Think back about stage one, ask those around you if they can identify any problems with your approaches, take the facileader assessment again, and find new ways to grow.

If you change, your surroundings will follow.

Reviewing your own actions and attitudes and improving your level will result in better changes around you.

When you think things aren't going your way, that's your chance to train.

Climb through these stages, and level up your skills.

PART 1

The Fundamentals of Facilitation

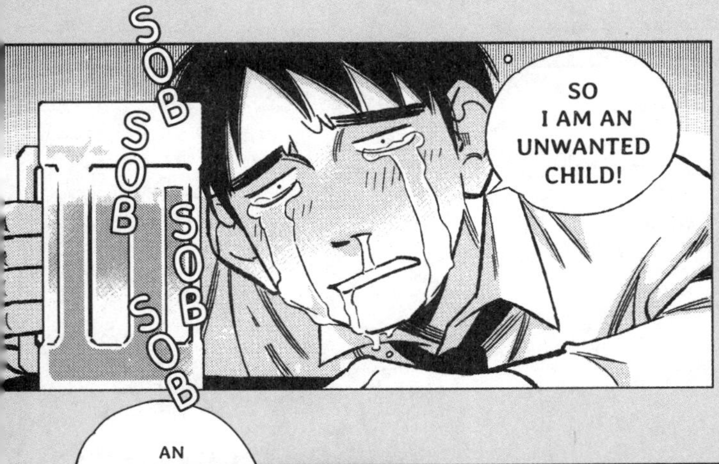
SOB SOB SOB SOB SOB
SO I AM AN UNWANTED CHILD!

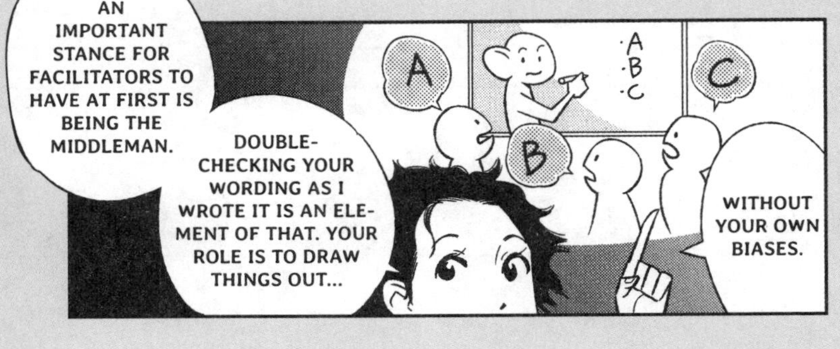
AN IMPORTANT STANCE FOR FACILITATORS TO HAVE AT FIRST IS BEING THE MIDDLEMAN.
A
·A ·B ·C
C
B
DOUBLE-CHECKING YOUR WORDING AS I WROTE IT IS AN ELEMENT OF THAT. YOUR ROLE IS TO DRAW THINGS OUT...
WITHOUT YOUR OWN BIASES.

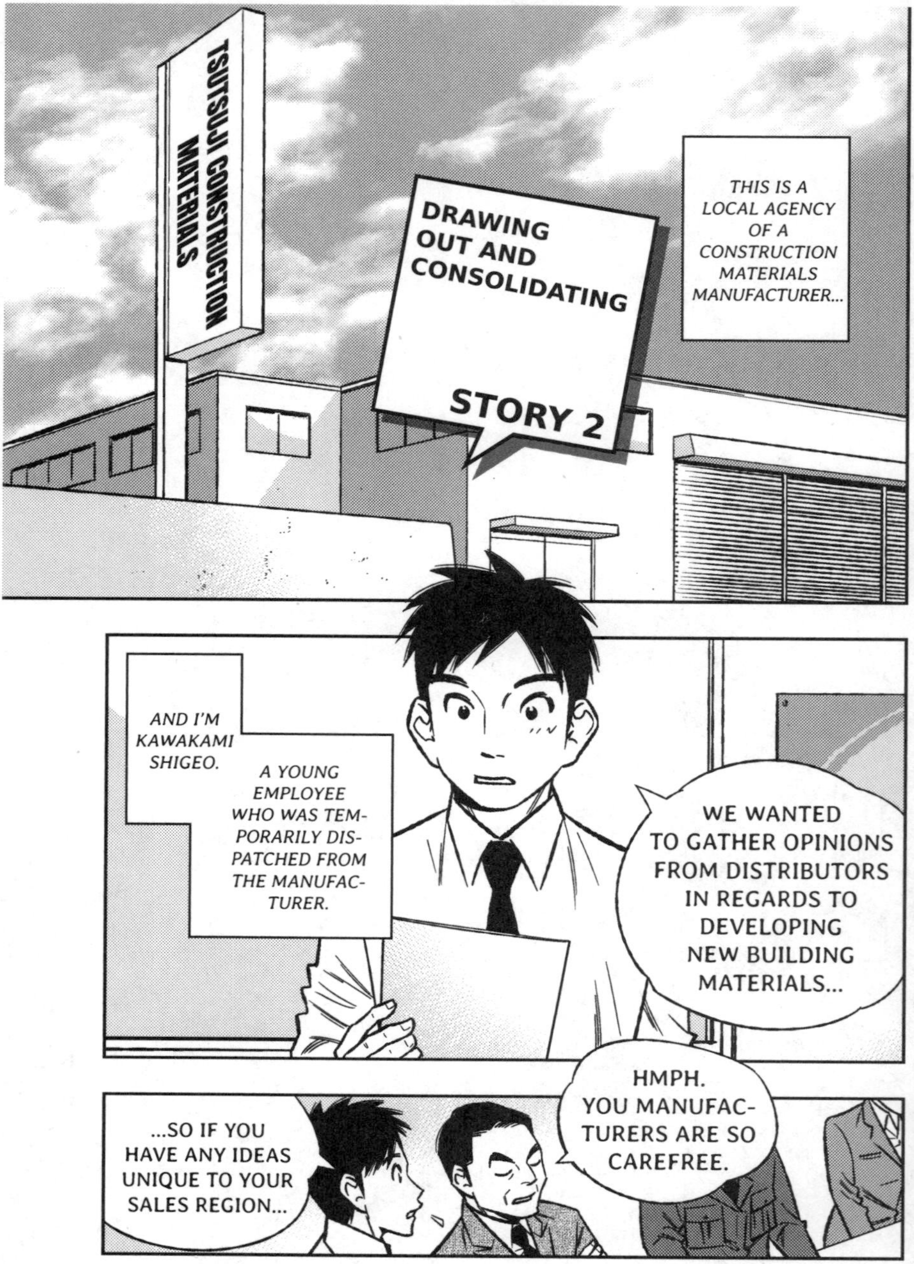
TSUTSUJI CONSTRUCTION MATERIALS
DRAWING OUT AND CONSOLIDATING
STORY 2
THIS IS A LOCAL AGENCY OF A CONSTRUCTION MATERIALS MANUFACTURER...
AND I'M KAWAKAMI SHIGEO.
A YOUNG EMPLOYEE WHO WAS TEMPORARILY DISPATCHED FROM THE MANUFACTURER.
WE WANTED TO GATHER OPINIONS FROM DISTRIBUTORS IN REGARDS TO DEVELOPING NEW BUILDING MATERIALS...
...SO IF YOU HAVE ANY IDEAS UNIQUE TO YOUR SALES REGION...
HMPH. YOU MANUFACTURERS ARE SO CAREFREE.

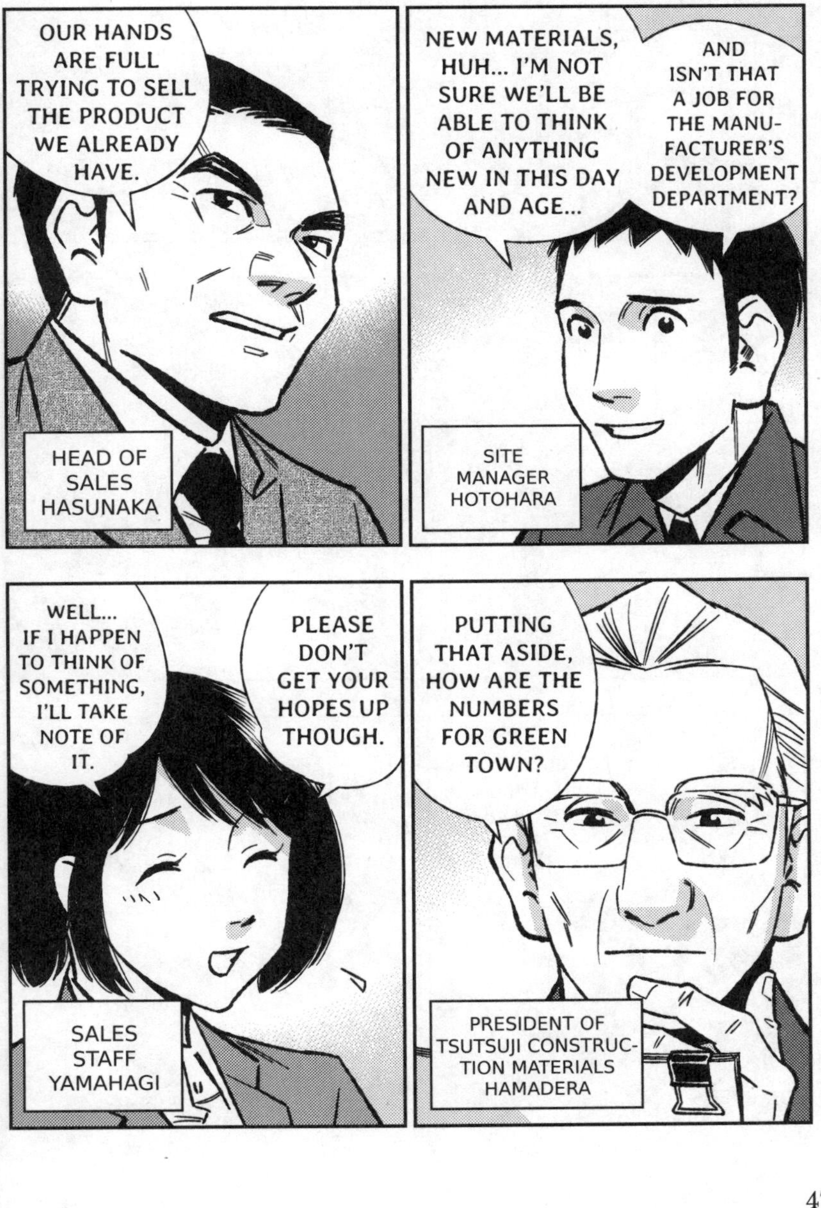
OUR HANDS ARE FULL TRYING TO SELL THE PRODUCT WE ALREADY HAVE.
HEAD OF SALES HASUNAKA
NEW MATERIALS, HUH... I'M NOT SURE WE'LL BE ABLE TO THINK OF ANYTHING NEW IN THIS DAY AND AGE...
AND ISN'T THAT A JOB FOR THE MANU-FACTURER'S DEVELOPMENT DEPARTMENT?
SITE MANAGER HOTOHARA
WELL... IF I HAPPEN TO THINK OF SOMETHING, I'LL TAKE NOTE OF IT.
PLEASE DON'T GET YOUR HOPES UP THOUGH.
SALES STAFF YAMAHAGI
PUTTING THAT ASIDE, HOW ARE THE NUMBERS FOR GREEN TOWN?
PRESIDENT OF TSUTSUJI CONSTRUC-TION MATERIALS HAMADERA

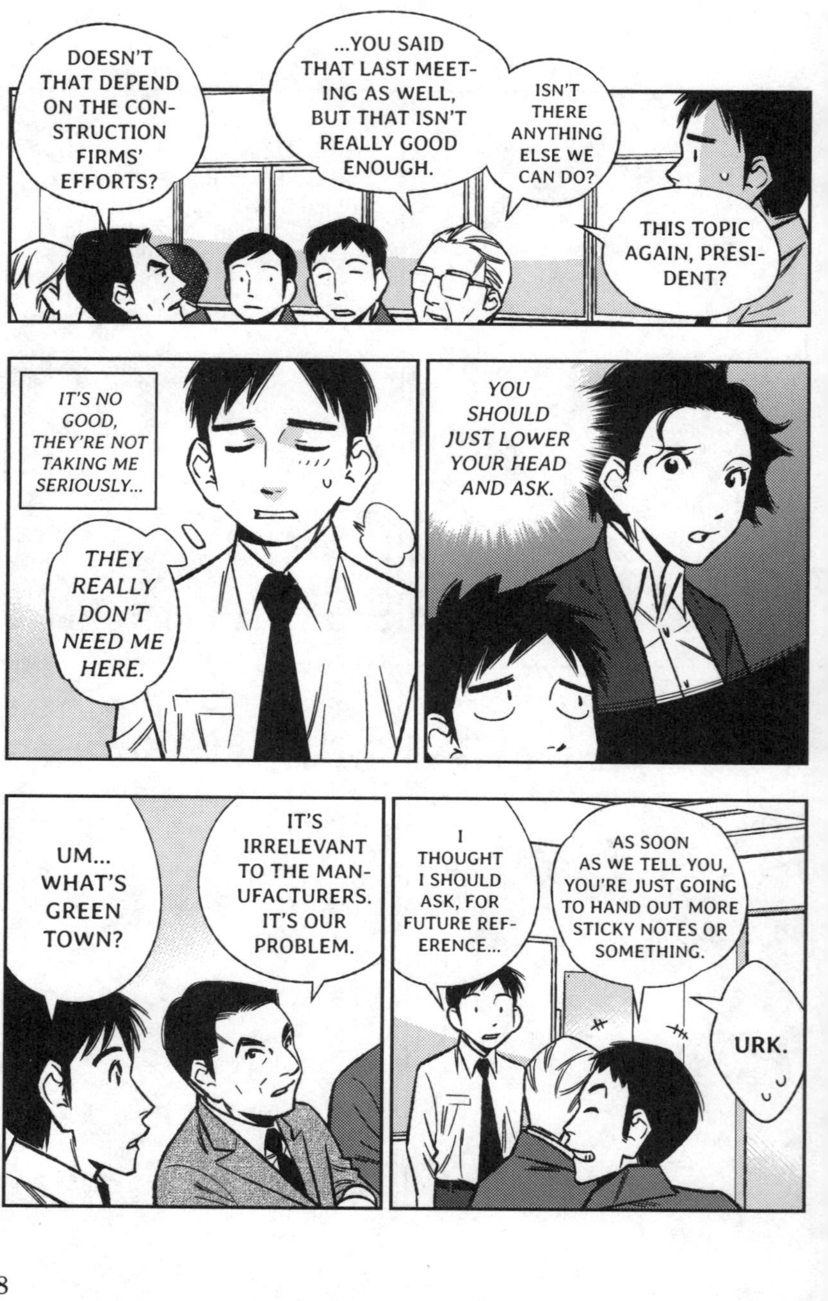
DOESN'T THAT DEPEND ON THE CONSTRUCTION FIRMS' EFFORTS?
...YOU SAID THAT LAST MEETING AS WELL, BUT THAT ISN'T REALLY GOOD ENOUGH.
ISN'T THERE ANYTHING ELSE WE CAN DO?
THIS TOPIC AGAIN, PRESIDENT?
IT'S NO GOOD, THEY'RE NOT TAKING ME SERIOUSLY...
THEY REALLY DON'T NEED ME HERE.
YOU SHOULD JUST LOWER YOUR HEAD AND ASK.
UM... WHAT'S GREEN TOWN?
IT'S IRRELEVANT TO THE MANUFACTURERS. IT'S OUR PROBLEM.
I THOUGHT I SHOULD ASK, FOR FUTURE REFERENCE...
AS SOON AS WE TELL YOU, YOU'RE JUST GOING TO HAND OUT MORE STICKY NOTES OR SOMETHING.
URK.

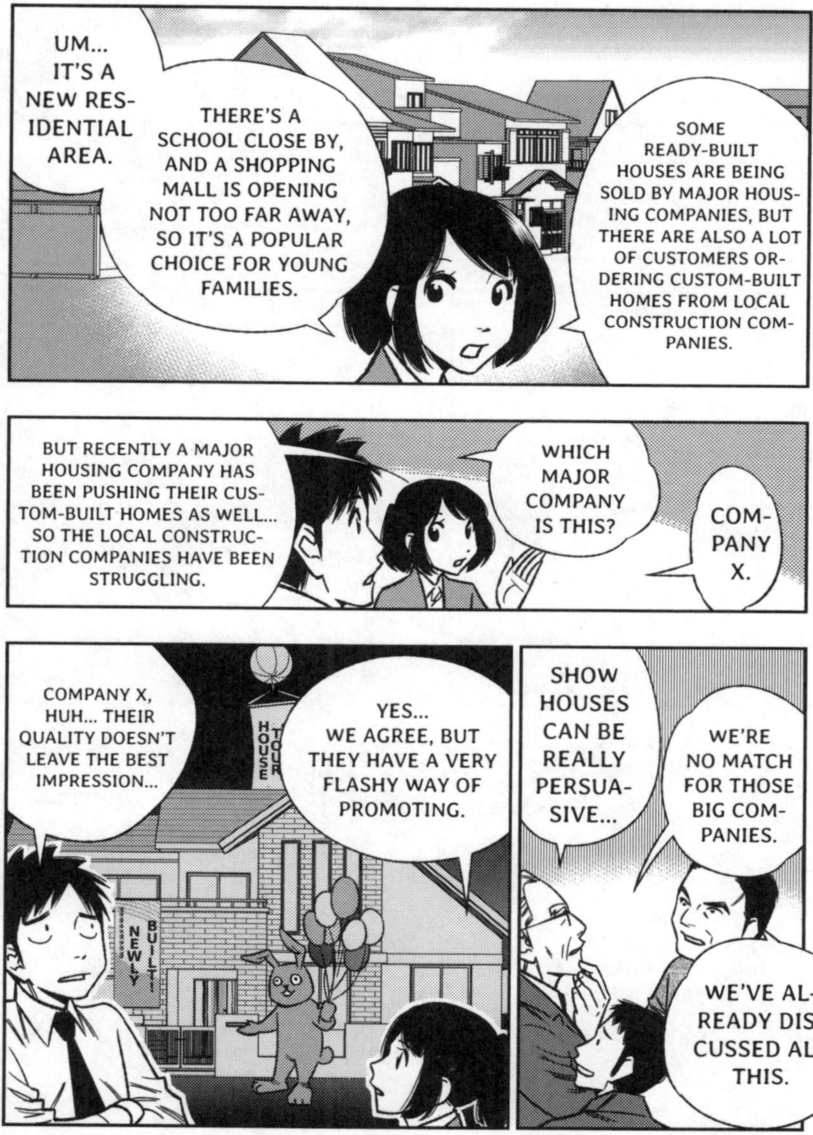
UM... IT'S A NEW RES- IDENTIAL AREA.
THERE'S A SCHOOL CLOSE BY, AND A SHOPPING MALL IS OPENING NOT TOO FAR AWAY, SO IT'S A POPULAR CHOICE FOR YOUNG FAMILIES.
SOME READY-BUILT HOUSES ARE BEING SOLD BY MAJOR HOUS- ING COMPANIES, BUT THERE ARE ALSO A LOT OF CUSTOMERS OR- DERING CUSTOM-BUILT HOMES FROM LOCAL CONSTRUCTION COM- PANIES.
BUT RECENTLY A MAJOR HOUSING COMPANY HAS BEEN PUSHING THEIR CUS- TOM-BUILT HOMES AS WELL... SO THE LOCAL CONSTRUC- TION COMPANIES HAVE BEEN STRUGGLING.
WHICH MAJOR COMPANY IS THIS?
COM- PANY X.
COMPANY X, HUH... THEIR QUALITY DOESN'T LEAVE THE BEST IMPRESSION...
HOUSE TOUR
YES... WE AGREE, BUT THEY HAVE A VERY FLASHY WAY OF PROMOTING.
NEWLY BUILT
SHOW HOUSES CAN BE REALLY PERSUA- SIVE...
WE'RE NO MATCH FOR THOSE BIG COM- PANIES.
WE'VE AL- READY DIS- CUSSED ALL THIS.

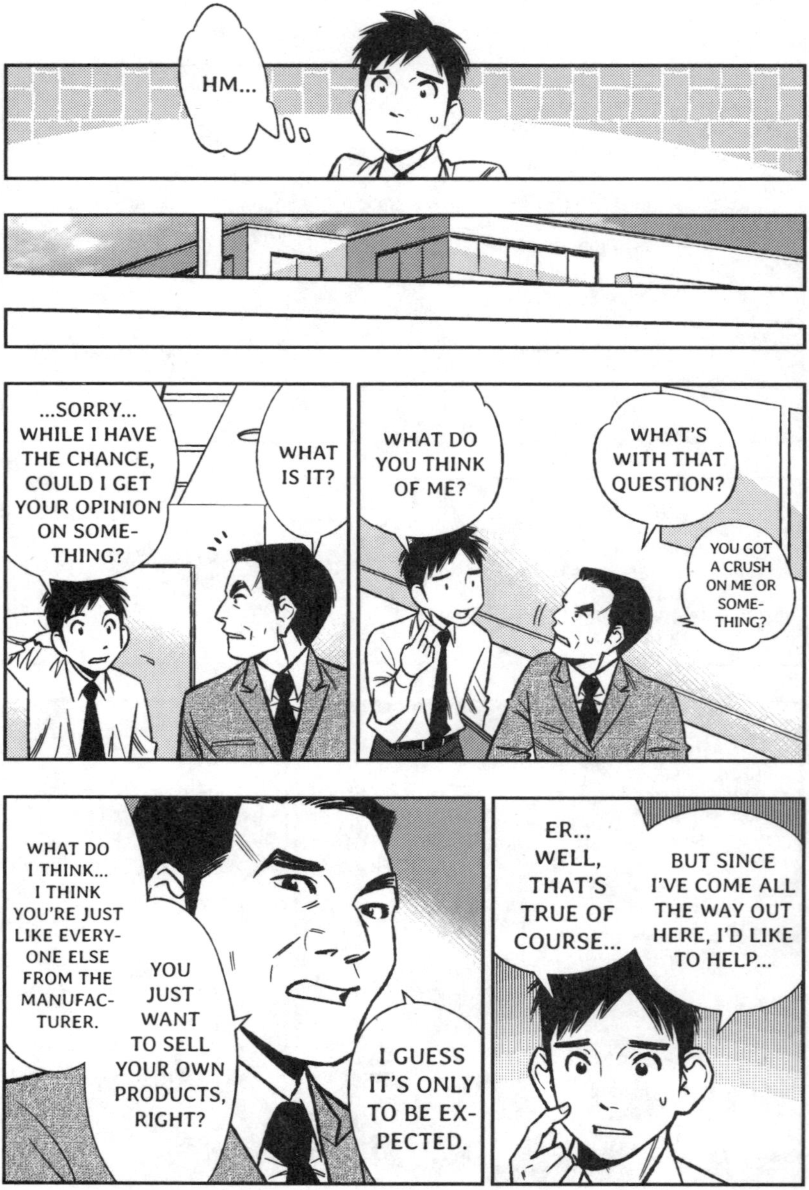
HM...
...SORRY... WHILE I HAVE THE CHANCE, COULD I GET YOUR OPINION ON SOME-THING?
WHAT IS IT?
WHAT DO YOU THINK OF ME?
WHAT'S WITH THAT QUESTION?
YOU GOT A CRUSH ON ME OR SOME-THING?
WHAT DO I THINK... I THINK YOU'RE JUST LIKE EVERY-ONE ELSE FROM THE MANUFAC-TURER.
YOU JUST WANT TO SELL YOUR OWN PRODUCTS, RIGHT?
I GUESS IT'S ONLY TO BE EX-PECTED.
ER... WELL, THAT'S TRUE OF COURSE...
BUT SINCE I'VE COME ALL THE WAY OUT HERE, I'D LIKE TO HELP...

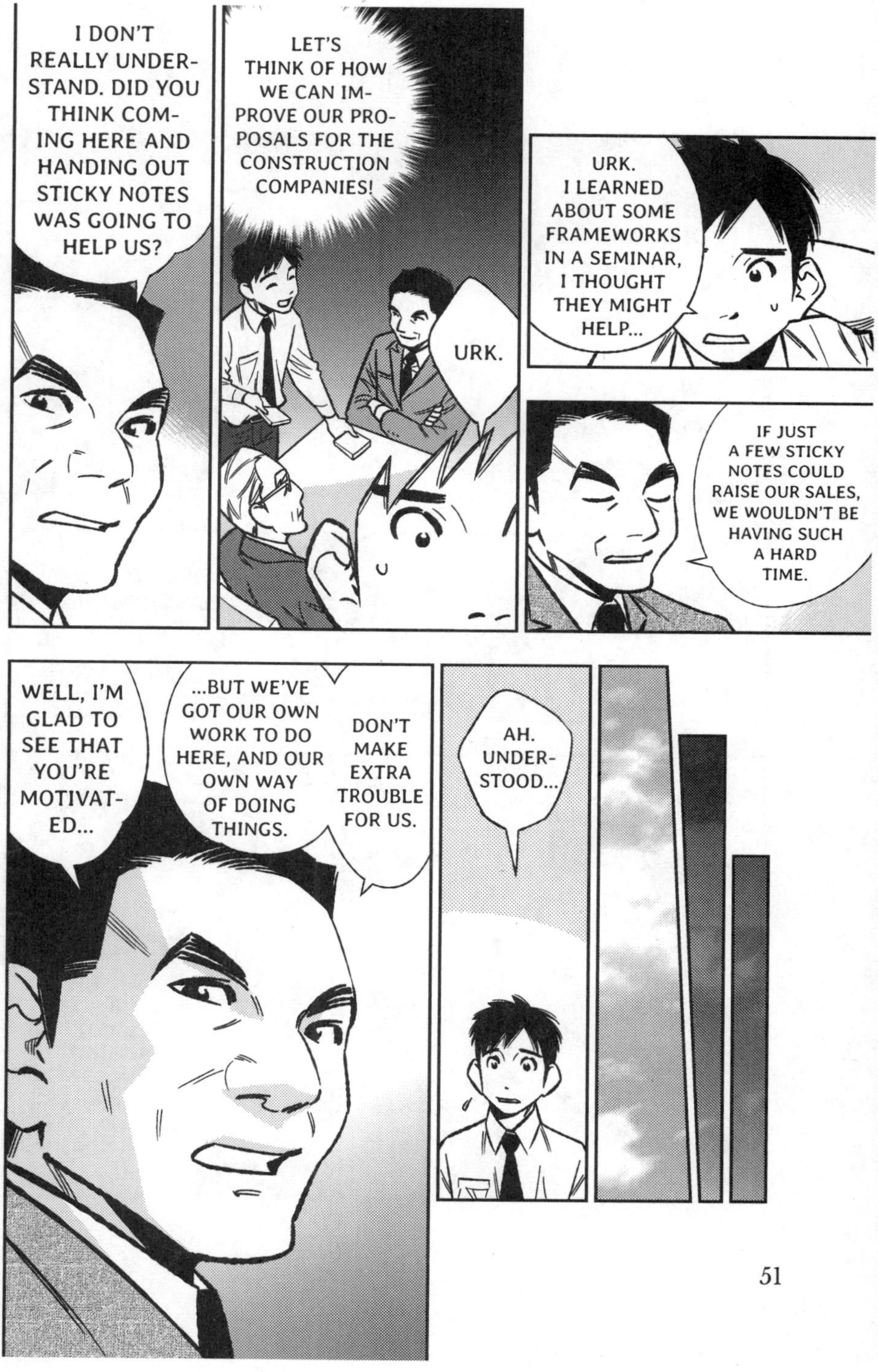
I DON'T REALLY UNDER-STAND. DID YOU THINK COM-ING HERE AND HANDING OUT STICKY NOTES WAS GOING TO HELP US?
LET'S THINK OF HOW WE CAN IM-PROVE OUR PRO-POSALS FOR THE CONSTRUCTION COMPANIES!
URK.
URK. I LEARNED ABOUT SOME FRAMEWORKS IN A SEMINAR, I THOUGHT THEY MIGHT HELP...
IF JUST A FEW STICKY NOTES COULD RAISE OUR SALES, WE WOULDN'T BE HAVING SUCH A HARD TIME.
WELL, I'M GLAD TO SEE THAT YOU'RE MOTIVAT-ED...
...BUT WE'VE GOT OUR OWN WORK TO DO HERE, AND OUR OWN WAY OF DOING THINGS.
DON'T MAKE EXTRA TROUBLE FOR US.
AH. UNDER-STOOD...

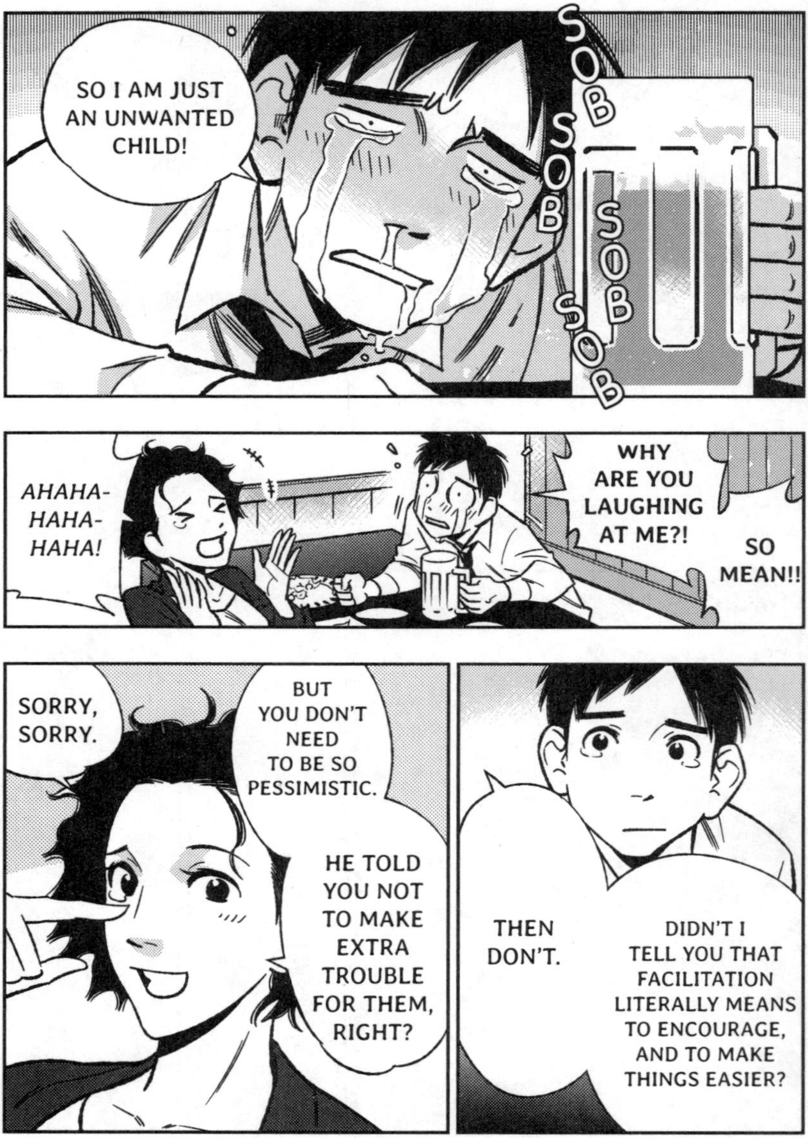
SO I AM JUST AN UNWANTED CHILD!
SOB SOB SOB SOB SOB
AHAHA-HAHA-HAHA!
WHY ARE YOU LAUGHING AT ME?!
SO MEAN!!
SORRY, SORRY.
BUT YOU DON'T NEED TO BE SO PESSIMISTIC.
HE TOLD YOU NOT TO MAKE EXTRA TROUBLE FOR THEM, RIGHT?
THEN DON'T.
DIDN'T I TELL YOU THAT FACILITATION LITERALLY MEANS TO ENCOURAGE, AND TO MAKE THINGS EASIER?

IN OTHER WORDS, SUP-PORTING YOUR TEAM SO THAT THEY'LL HAVE AN EASIER TIME DOING THEIR WORK.

THAT'S WHY YOU NEED TO *DRAW OUT...*

AND CONSOLI-DATE

HM... AND YOU SAID THAT THE BEST WAY TO DO THAT IS WITH A WHITEBOARD, RIGHT...?

EXACTLY. TO START OFF, ALL YOU NEED TO DO IS FOR-MAT IT LIKE THIS.

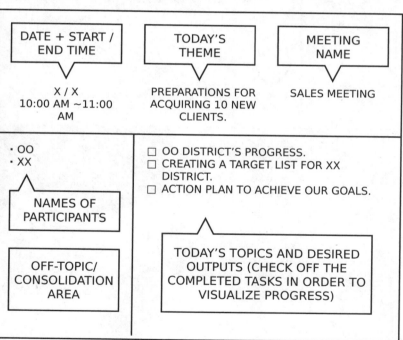

DATE + START / END TIME	TODAY'S THEME	MEETING NAME
X / X 10:00 AM ~11:00 AM	PREPARATIONS FOR ACQUIRING 10 NEW CLIENTS.	SALES MEETING

· OO
· XX

NAMES OF PARTICIPANTS

OFF-TOPIC/ CONSOLIDATION AREA

☐ OO DISTRICT'S PROGRESS.
☐ CREATING A TARGET LIST FOR XX DISTRICT.
☐ ACTION PLAN TO ACHIEVE OUR GOALS.

TODAY'S TOPICS AND DESIRED OUTPUTS (CHECK OFF THE COMPLETED TASKS IN ORDER TO VISUALIZE PROGRESS)

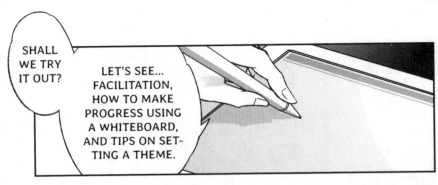

SHALL WE TRY IT OUT?

LET'S SEE... FACILITATION, HOW TO MAKE PROGRESS USING A WHITEBOARD, AND TIPS ON SETTING A THEME.

8:00 PM – 9:00 PM
20XX.X.X.

· YAMANAKA
· KAWAKAMI-KUN

FACILITATION LECTURE

☐ HOW TO MAKE PROGRESS USING A WHITEBOARD.
☐ TIPS ON SETTING A THEME.

UH-HUH.

I THINK I UNDERSTAND HOW TO WRITE IT OUT...

...BUT I GET THE FEELING THAT SINCE THEY'RE ALREADY RESISTANT TOWARD ME, THEY WON'T WANT TO PARTICIPATE IN THE FIRST PLACE.

LIKE I'D TALK TO SOMEONE LIKE HIM.

WELL... IN THE END, IT DOES ALL RELY ON YOUR COMMUNICATION SKILLS A BIT...

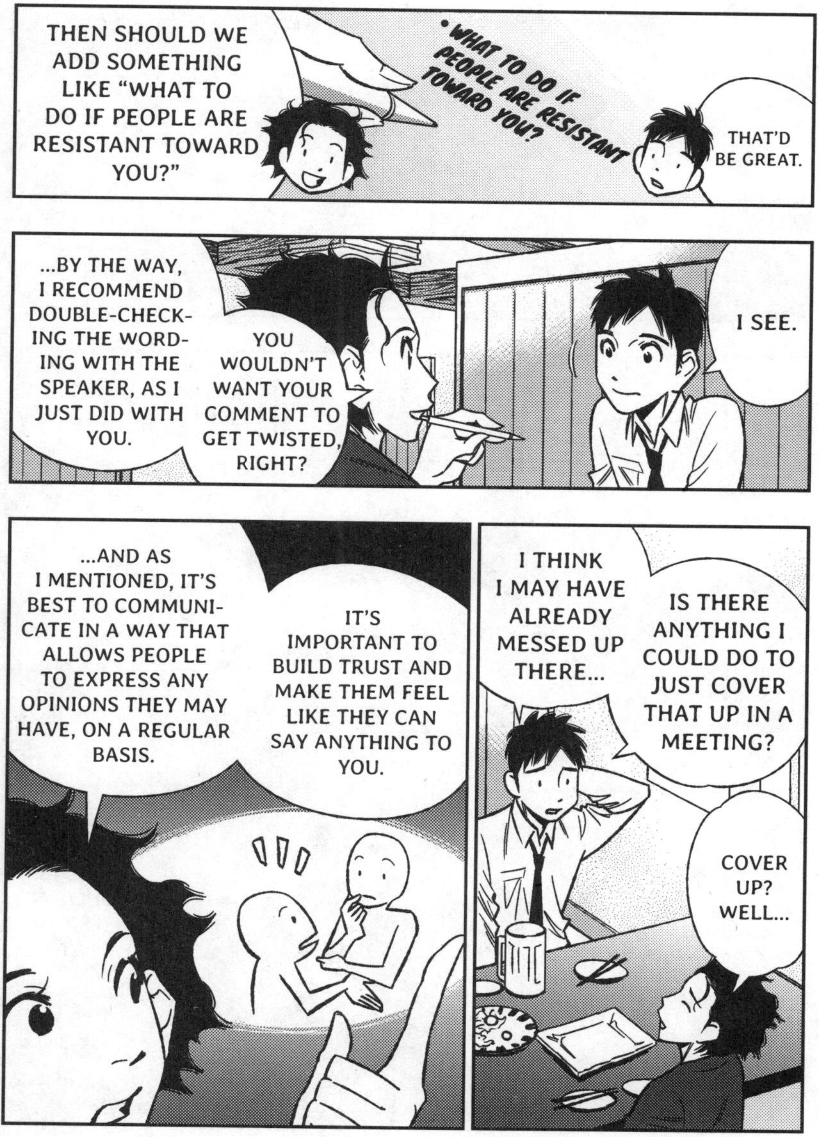
THEN SHOULD WE ADD SOMETHING LIKE "WHAT TO DO IF PEOPLE ARE RESISTANT TOWARD YOU?"
• WHAT TO DO IF PEOPLE ARE RESISTANT TOWARD YOU?
THAT'D BE GREAT.
...BY THE WAY, I RECOMMEND DOUBLE-CHECKING THE WORDING WITH THE SPEAKER, AS I JUST DID WITH YOU.
YOU WOULDN'T WANT YOUR COMMENT TO GET TWISTED, RIGHT?
I SEE.
...AND AS I MENTIONED, IT'S BEST TO COMMUNICATE IN A WAY THAT ALLOWS PEOPLE TO EXPRESS ANY OPINIONS THEY MAY HAVE, ON A REGULAR BASIS.
IT'S IMPORTANT TO BUILD TRUST AND MAKE THEM FEEL LIKE THEY CAN SAY ANYTHING TO YOU.
I THINK I MAY HAVE ALREADY MESSED UP THERE...
IS THERE ANYTHING I COULD DO TO JUST COVER THAT UP IN A MEETING?
COVER UP? WELL...

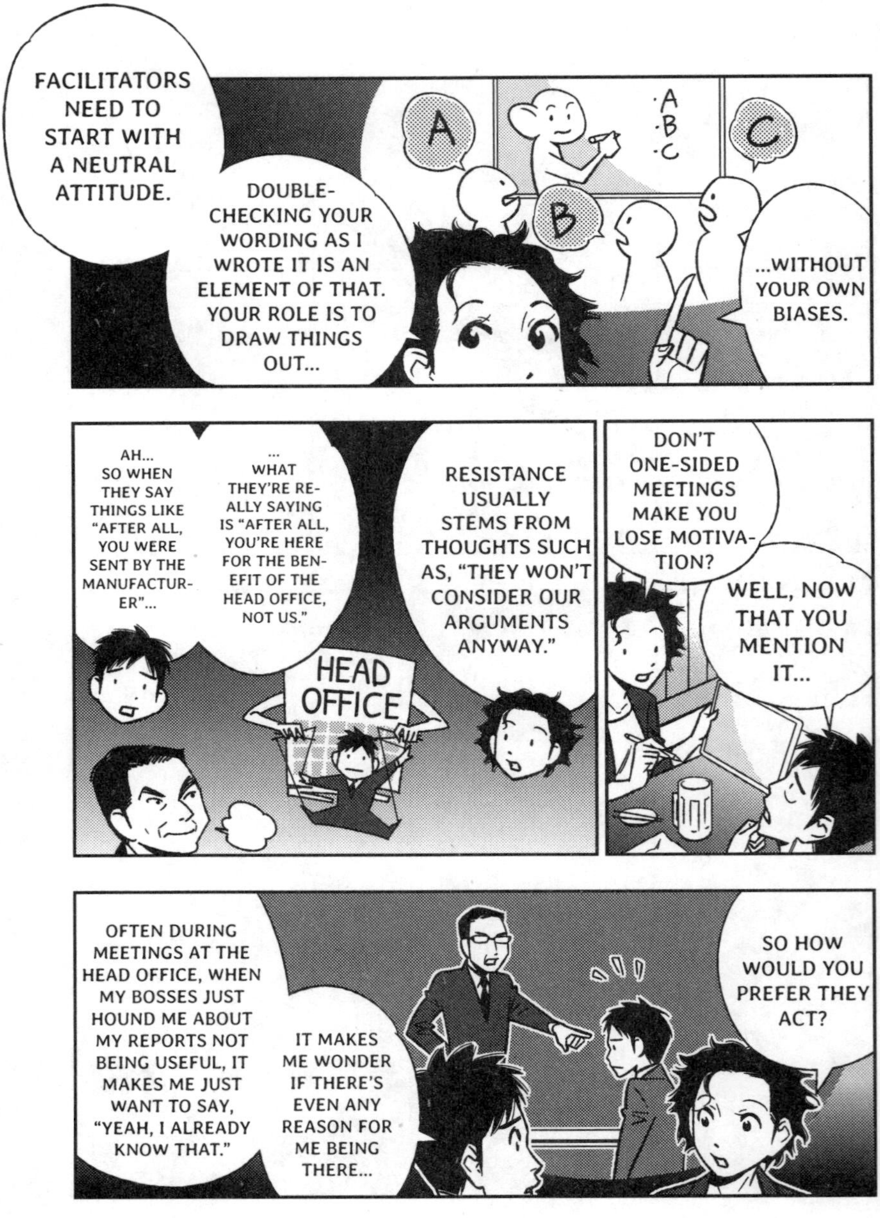

FACILITATORS NEED TO START WITH A NEUTRAL ATTITUDE.
DOUBLE-CHECKING YOUR WORDING AS I WROTE IT IS AN ELEMENT OF THAT. YOUR ROLE IS TO DRAW THINGS OUT...
...WITHOUT YOUR OWN BIASES.
AH... SO WHEN THEY SAY THINGS LIKE "AFTER ALL, YOU WERE SENT BY THE MANUFACTURER"...
... WHAT THEY'RE REALLY SAYING IS "AFTER ALL, YOU'RE HERE FOR THE BENEFIT OF THE HEAD OFFICE, NOT US."
HEAD OFFICE
RESISTANCE USUALLY STEMS FROM THOUGHTS SUCH AS, "THEY WON'T CONSIDER OUR ARGUMENTS ANYWAY."
DON'T ONE-SIDED MEETINGS MAKE YOU LOSE MOTIVATION?
WELL, NOW THAT YOU MENTION IT...
OFTEN DURING MEETINGS AT THE HEAD OFFICE, WHEN MY BOSSES JUST HOUND ME ABOUT MY REPORTS NOT BEING USEFUL, IT MAKES ME JUST WANT TO SAY, "YEAH, I ALREADY KNOW THAT."
IT MAKES ME WONDER IF THERE'S EVEN ANY REASON FOR ME BEING THERE...
SO HOW WOULD YOU PREFER THEY ACT?

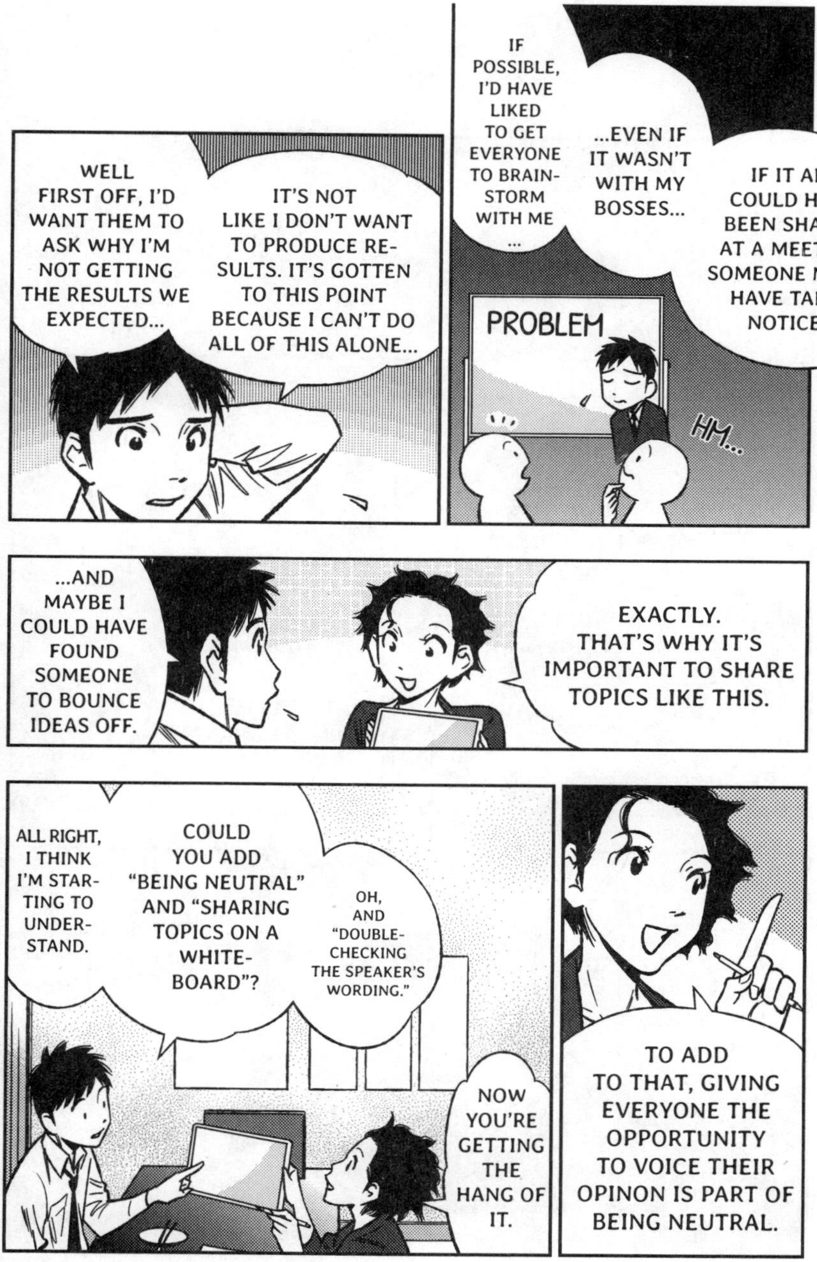
WELL FIRST OFF, I'D WANT THEM TO ASK WHY I'M NOT GETTING THE RESULTS WE EXPECTED...
IT'S NOT LIKE I DON'T WANT TO PRODUCE RE-SULTS. IT'S GOTTEN TO THIS POINT BECAUSE I CAN'T DO ALL OF THIS ALONE...
IF POSSIBLE, I'D HAVE LIKED TO GET EVERYONE TO BRAIN-STORM WITH ME ...
...EVEN IF IT WASN'T WITH MY BOSSES...
IF IT ALL COULD HAVE BEEN SHARED AT A MEETING, SOMEONE MIGHT HAVE TAKEN NOTICE...
PROBLEM
HM...
...AND MAYBE I COULD HAVE FOUND SOMEONE TO BOUNCE IDEAS OFF.
EXACTLY. THAT'S WHY IT'S IMPORTANT TO SHARE TOPICS LIKE THIS.
ALL RIGHT, I THINK I'M STAR-TING TO UNDER-STAND.
COULD YOU ADD "BEING NEUTRAL" AND "SHARING TOPICS ON A WHITE-BOARD"?
OH, AND "DOUBLE-CHECKING THE SPEAKER'S WORDING."
NOW YOU'RE GETTING THE HANG OF IT.
TO ADD TO THAT, GIVING EVERYONE THE OPPORTUNITY TO VOICE THEIR OPINON IS PART OF BEING NEUTRAL.

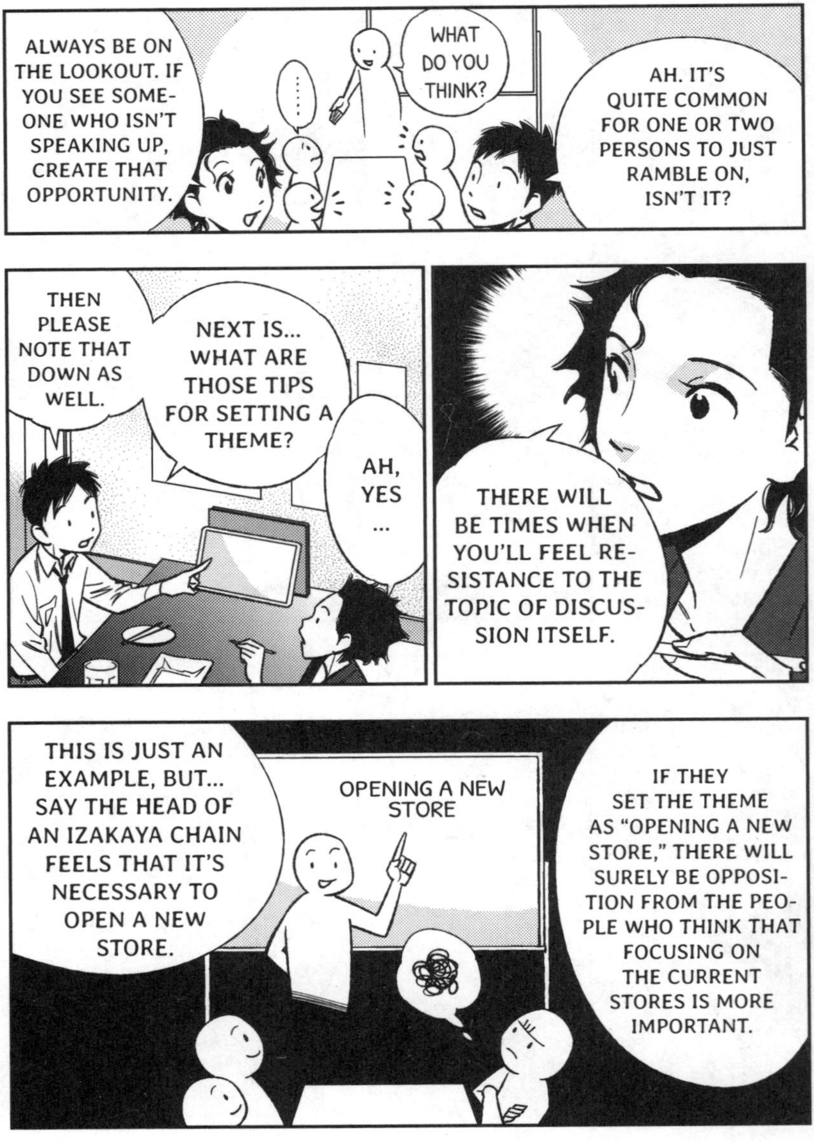
ALWAYS BE ON THE LOOKOUT. IF YOU SEE SOME-ONE WHO ISN'T SPEAKING UP, CREATE THAT OPPORTUNITY.
......
WHAT DO YOU THINK?
AH. IT'S QUITE COMMON FOR ONE OR TWO PERSONS TO JUST RAMBLE ON, ISN'T IT?
THEN PLEASE NOTE THAT DOWN AS WELL.
NEXT IS... WHAT ARE THOSE TIPS FOR SETTING A THEME?
AH, YES ...
THERE WILL BE TIMES WHEN YOU'LL FEEL RE-SISTANCE TO THE TOPIC OF DISCUS-SION ITSELF.
THIS IS JUST AN EXAMPLE, BUT... SAY THE HEAD OF AN IZAKAYA CHAIN FEELS THAT IT'S NECESSARY TO OPEN A NEW STORE.
OPENING A NEW STORE
IF THEY SET THE THEME AS "OPENING A NEW STORE," THERE WILL SURELY BE OPPOSI-TION FROM THE PEO-PLE WHO THINK THAT FOCUSING ON THE CURRENT STORES IS MORE IMPORTANT.

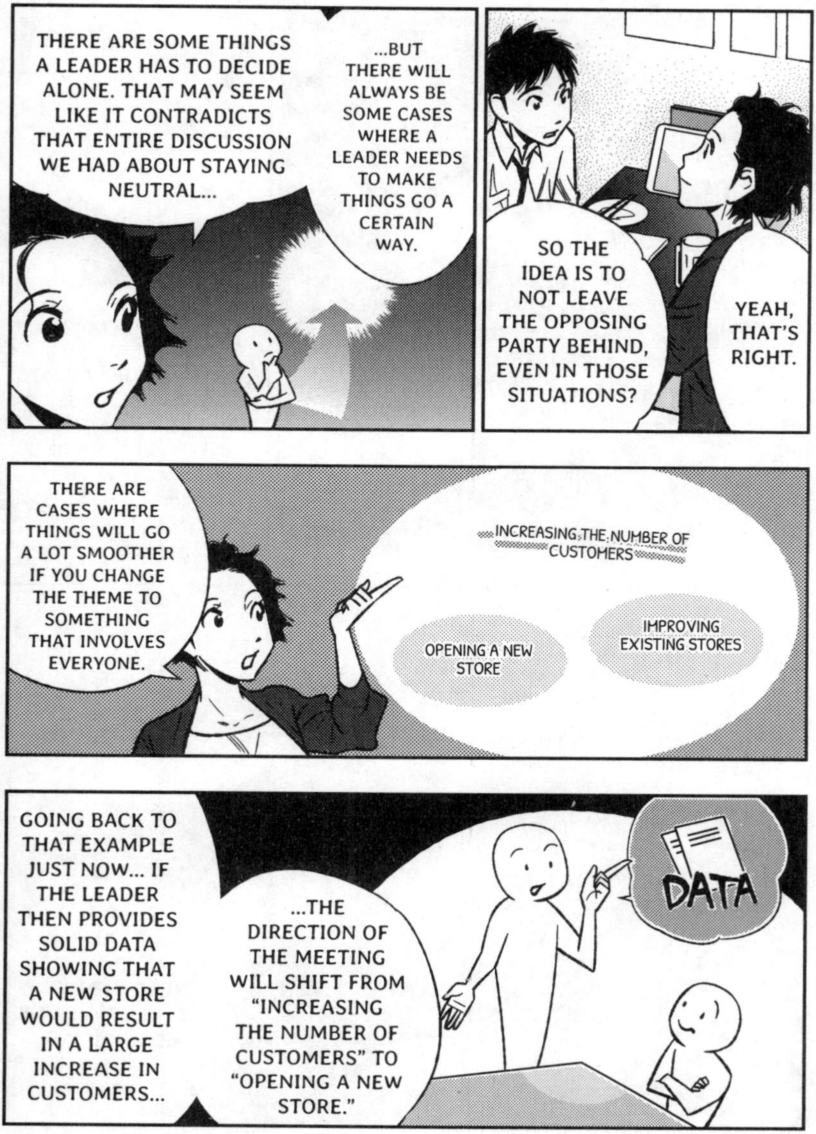
THERE ARE SOME THINGS A LEADER HAS TO DECIDE ALONE. THAT MAY SEEM LIKE IT CONTRADICTS THAT ENTIRE DISCUSSION WE HAD ABOUT STAYING NEUTRAL...
...BUT THERE WILL ALWAYS BE SOME CASES WHERE A LEADER NEEDS TO MAKE THINGS GO A CERTAIN WAY.
SO THE IDEA IS TO NOT LEAVE THE OPPOSING PARTY BEHIND, EVEN IN THOSE SITUATIONS?
YEAH, THAT'S RIGHT.
THERE ARE CASES WHERE THINGS WILL GO A LOT SMOOTHER IF YOU CHANGE THE THEME TO SOMETHING THAT INVOLVES EVERYONE.
INCREASING THE NUMBER OF CUSTOMERS
OPENING A NEW STORE
IMPROVING EXISTING STORES
GOING BACK TO THAT EXAMPLE JUST NOW... IF THE LEADER THEN PROVIDES SOLID DATA SHOWING THAT A NEW STORE WOULD RESULT IN A LARGE INCREASE IN CUSTOMERS...
...THE DIRECTION OF THE MEETING WILL SHIFT FROM "INCREASING THE NUMBER OF CUSTOMERS" TO "OPENING A NEW STORE."
DATA

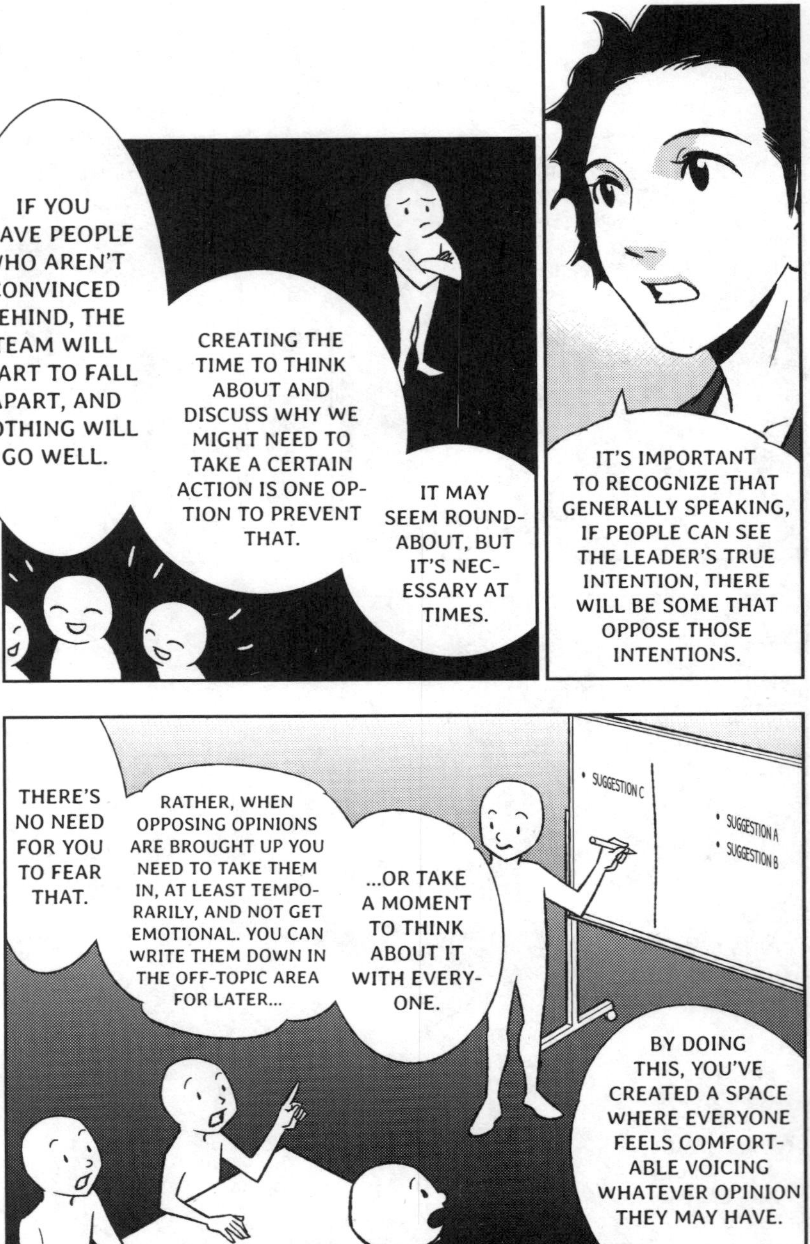
IT'S IMPORTANT TO RECOGNIZE THAT GENERALLY SPEAKING, IF PEOPLE CAN SEE THE LEADER'S TRUE INTENTION, THERE WILL BE SOME THAT OPPOSE THOSE INTENTIONS.
IF YOU LEAVE PEOPLE WHO AREN'T CONVINCED BEHIND, THE TEAM WILL START TO FALL APART, AND NOTHING WILL GO WELL.
CREATING THE TIME TO THINK ABOUT AND DISCUSS WHY WE MIGHT NEED TO TAKE A CERTAIN ACTION IS ONE OPTION TO PREVENT THAT.
IT MAY SEEM ROUNDABOUT, BUT IT'S NECESSARY AT TIMES.
THERE'S NO NEED FOR YOU TO FEAR THAT.
RATHER, WHEN OPPOSING OPINIONS ARE BROUGHT UP YOU NEED TO TAKE THEM IN, AT LEAST TEMPORARILY, AND NOT GET EMOTIONAL. YOU CAN WRITE THEM DOWN IN THE OFF-TOPIC AREA FOR LATER...
...OR TAKE A MOMENT TO THINK ABOUT IT WITH EVERYONE.
• SUGGESTION C
• SUGGESTION A
• SUGGESTION B
BY DOING THIS, YOU'VE CREATED A SPACE WHERE EVERYONE FEELS COMFORTABLE VOICING WHATEVER OPINION THEY MAY HAVE.

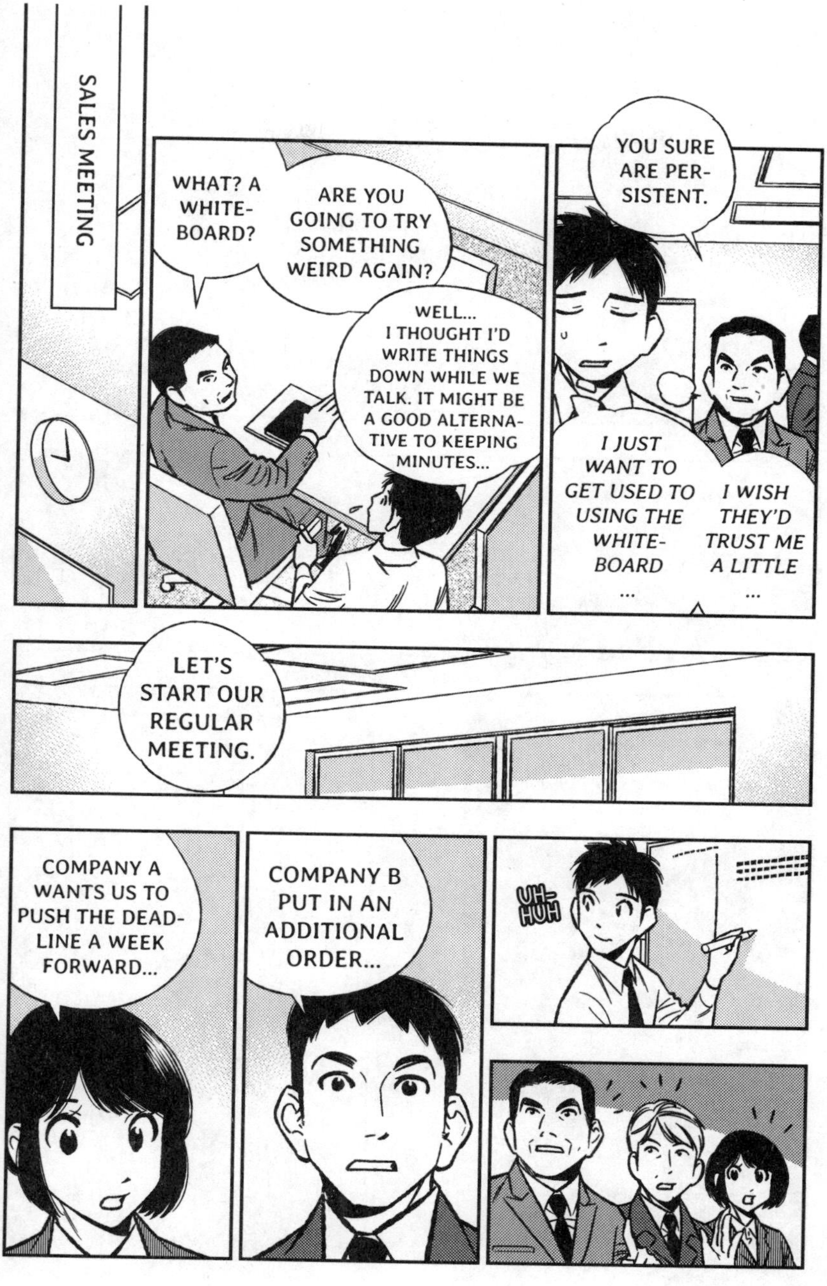
SALES MEETING
WHAT? A WHITE-BOARD?
ARE YOU GOING TO TRY SOMETHING WEIRD AGAIN?
WELL... I THOUGHT I'D WRITE THINGS DOWN WHILE WE TALK. IT MIGHT BE A GOOD ALTERNATIVE TO KEEPING MINUTES...
YOU SURE ARE PERSISTENT.
I JUST WANT TO GET USED TO USING THE WHITE-BOARD ...
I WISH THEY'D TRUST ME A LITTLE ...
LET'S START OUR REGULAR MEETING.
COMPANY A WANTS US TO PUSH THE DEAD-LINE A WEEK FORWARD...
COMPANY B PUT IN AN ADDITIONAL ORDER...
UH-HUH

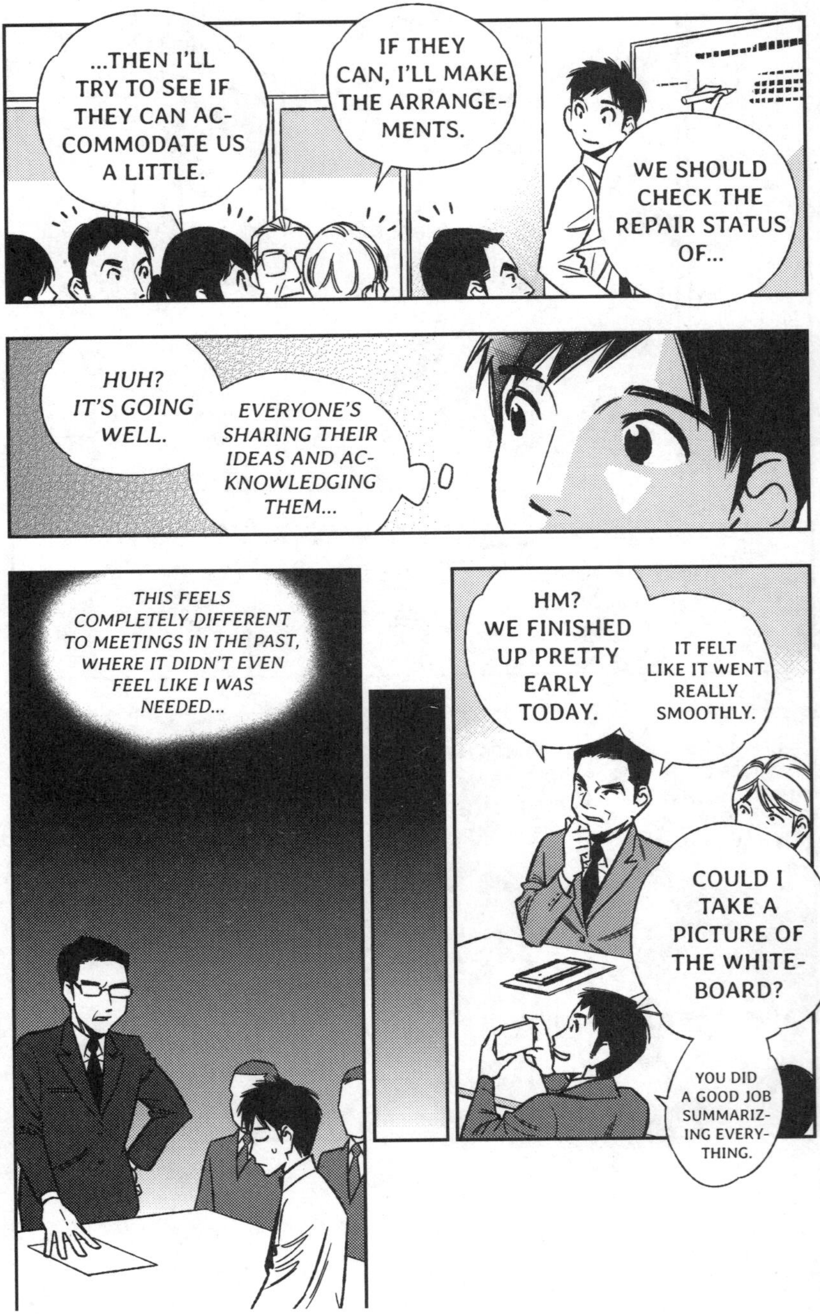
...THEN I'LL TRY TO SEE IF THEY CAN AC-COMMODATE US A LITTLE.
IF THEY CAN, I'LL MAKE THE ARRANGE-MENTS.
WE SHOULD CHECK THE REPAIR STATUS OF...
HUH? IT'S GOING WELL.
EVERYONE'S SHARING THEIR IDEAS AND AC-KNOWLEDGING THEM...
THIS FEELS COMPLETELY DIFFERENT TO MEETINGS IN THE PAST, WHERE IT DIDN'T EVEN FEEL LIKE I WAS NEEDED...
HM? WE FINISHED UP PRETTY EARLY TODAY.
IT FELT LIKE IT WENT REALLY SMOOTHLY.
COULD I TAKE A PICTURE OF THE WHITE-BOARD?
YOU DID A GOOD JOB SUMMARIZ-ING EVERY-THING.

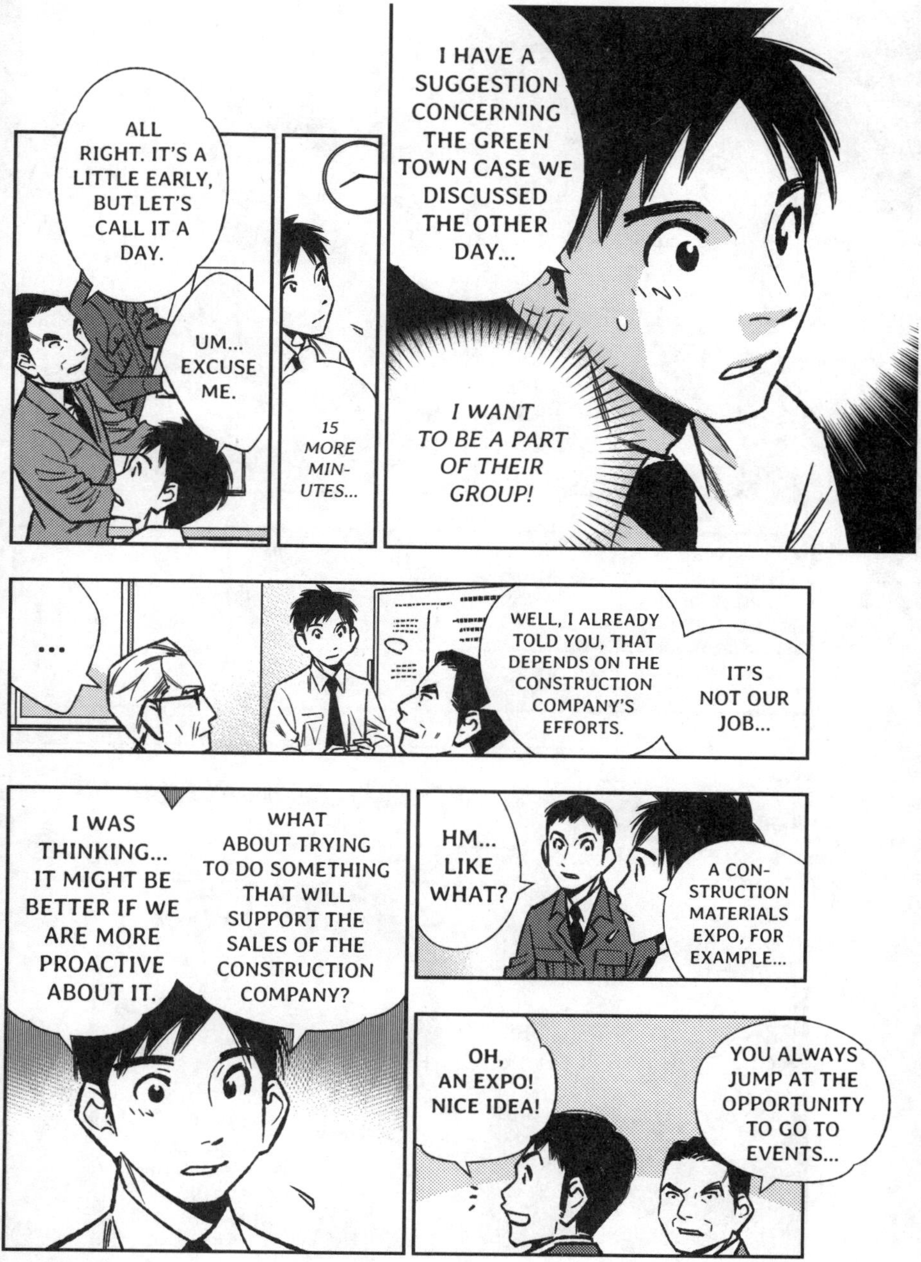
ALL RIGHT. IT'S A LITTLE EARLY, BUT LET'S CALL IT A DAY.
UM... EXCUSE ME.
15 MORE MIN-UTES...
I HAVE A SUGGESTION CONCERNING THE GREEN TOWN CASE WE DISCUSSED THE OTHER DAY...
I WANT TO BE A PART OF THEIR GROUP!
...
WELL, I ALREADY TOLD YOU, THAT DEPENDS ON THE CONSTRUCTION COMPANY'S EFFORTS.
IT'S NOT OUR JOB...
I WAS THINKING... IT MIGHT BE BETTER IF WE ARE MORE PROACTIVE ABOUT IT.
WHAT ABOUT TRYING TO DO SOMETHING THAT WILL SUPPORT THE SALES OF THE CONSTRUCTION COMPANY?
HM... LIKE WHAT?
A CON-STRUCTION MATERIALS EXPO, FOR EXAMPLE...
OH, AN EXPO! NICE IDEA!
YOU ALWAYS JUMP AT THE OPPORTUNITY TO GO TO EVENTS...

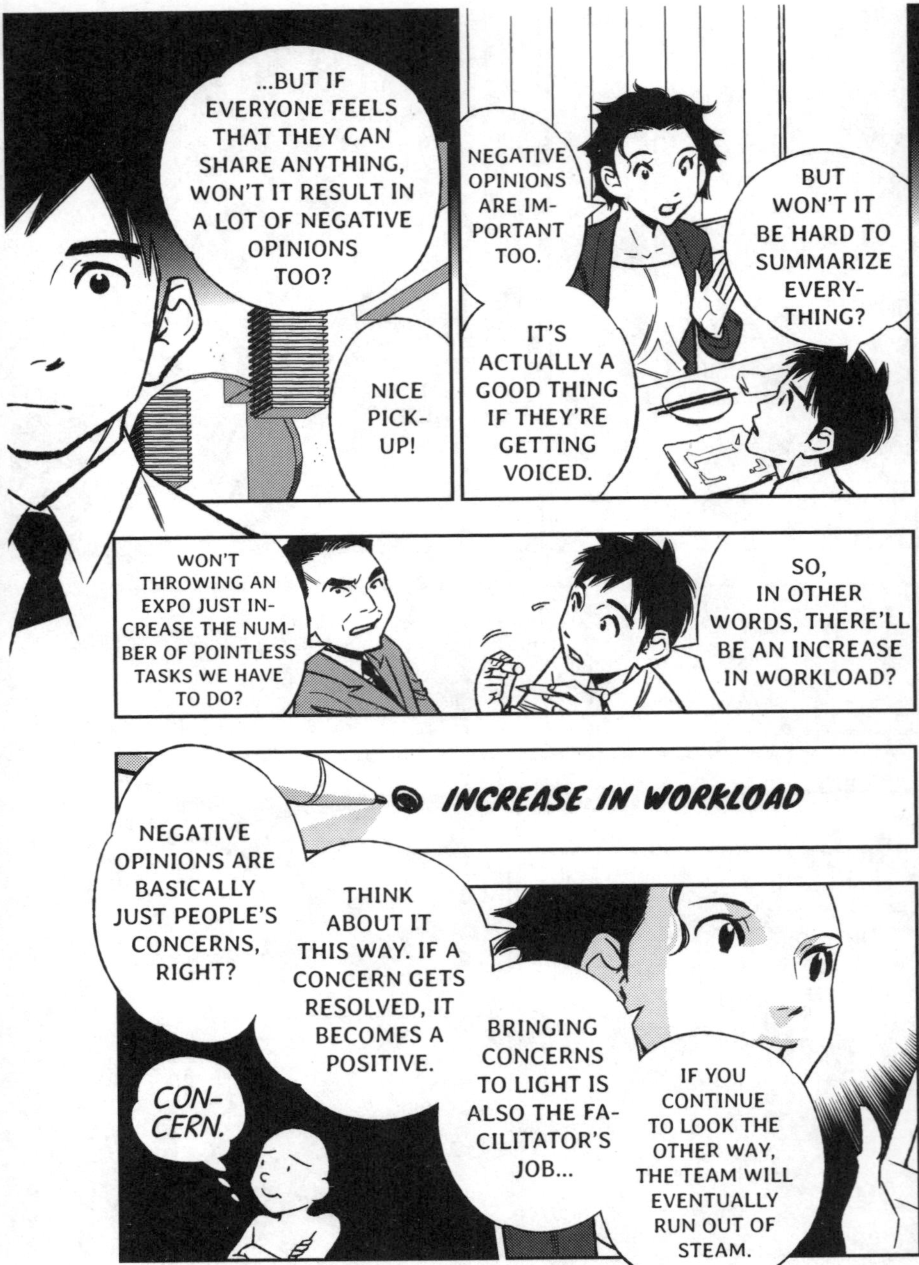

...BUT IF EVERYONE FEELS THAT THEY CAN SHARE ANYTHING, WON'T IT RESULT IN A LOT OF NEGATIVE OPINIONS TOO?
NICE PICK-UP!
NEGATIVE OPINIONS ARE IMPORTANT TOO.
IT'S ACTUALLY A GOOD THING IF THEY'RE GETTING VOICED.
BUT WON'T IT BE HARD TO SUMMARIZE EVERYTHING?
WON'T THROWING AN EXPO JUST INCREASE THE NUMBER OF POINTLESS TASKS WE HAVE TO DO?
SO, IN OTHER WORDS, THERE'LL BE AN INCREASE IN WORKLOAD?
INCREASE IN WORKLOAD
NEGATIVE OPINIONS ARE BASICALLY JUST PEOPLE'S CONCERNS, RIGHT?
THINK ABOUT IT THIS WAY. IF A CONCERN GETS RESOLVED, IT BECOMES A POSITIVE.
CON-CERN.
BRINGING CONCERNS TO LIGHT IS ALSO THE FACILITATOR'S JOB...
IF YOU CONTINUE TO LOOK THE OTHER WAY, THE TEAM WILL EVENTUALLY RUN OUT OF STEAM.

WE'D ALSO NEED TO COLLABORATE WITH THE CONSTRUCTION COMPANY...

...WHICH WILL JUST REQUIRE MORE MEETINGS, ET CETERA.

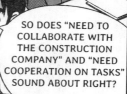

SO DOES "NEED TO COLLABORATE WITH THE CONSTRUCTION COMPANY" AND "NEED COOPERATION ON TASKS" SOUND ABOUT RIGHT?

HOWEVER, THERE ARE INDEED TIMES WHEN A LINE OF DISCUSSION GETS HELD UP IF THERE ARE ONLY NEGATIVE OPINIONS.

IF THAT'S THE CASE, IT'S A GOOD IDEA TO DRAW UP BOTH THE NEGATIVES AND THE POSITIVES.

NEGATIVES

POSITIVES

WOULD THERE BE ANY BENEFITS IF WE'RE ABLE TO MAKE THIS HAPPEN?

WELL... I GUESS, IF IT GOES WELL.

THERE'S NO QUESTION THAT THE BUILDING MATERIALS WE DEAL WITH ARE OF HIGHER QUALITY.

THE CONSTRUCTION COMPANY WANTS TO DO PROMOTIONS, TOO.

THEY'RE GOOD AT GIVING US DETAILED RESPONSES, SO THEY'RE EASY TO WORK WITH, AND WE WON'T BE DOING FLASHY DISPLAYS LIKE THE MAJOR HOUSING COMPANIES, SO IT SHOULDN'T COST TOO MUCH.

I KNOW THAT, BUT...

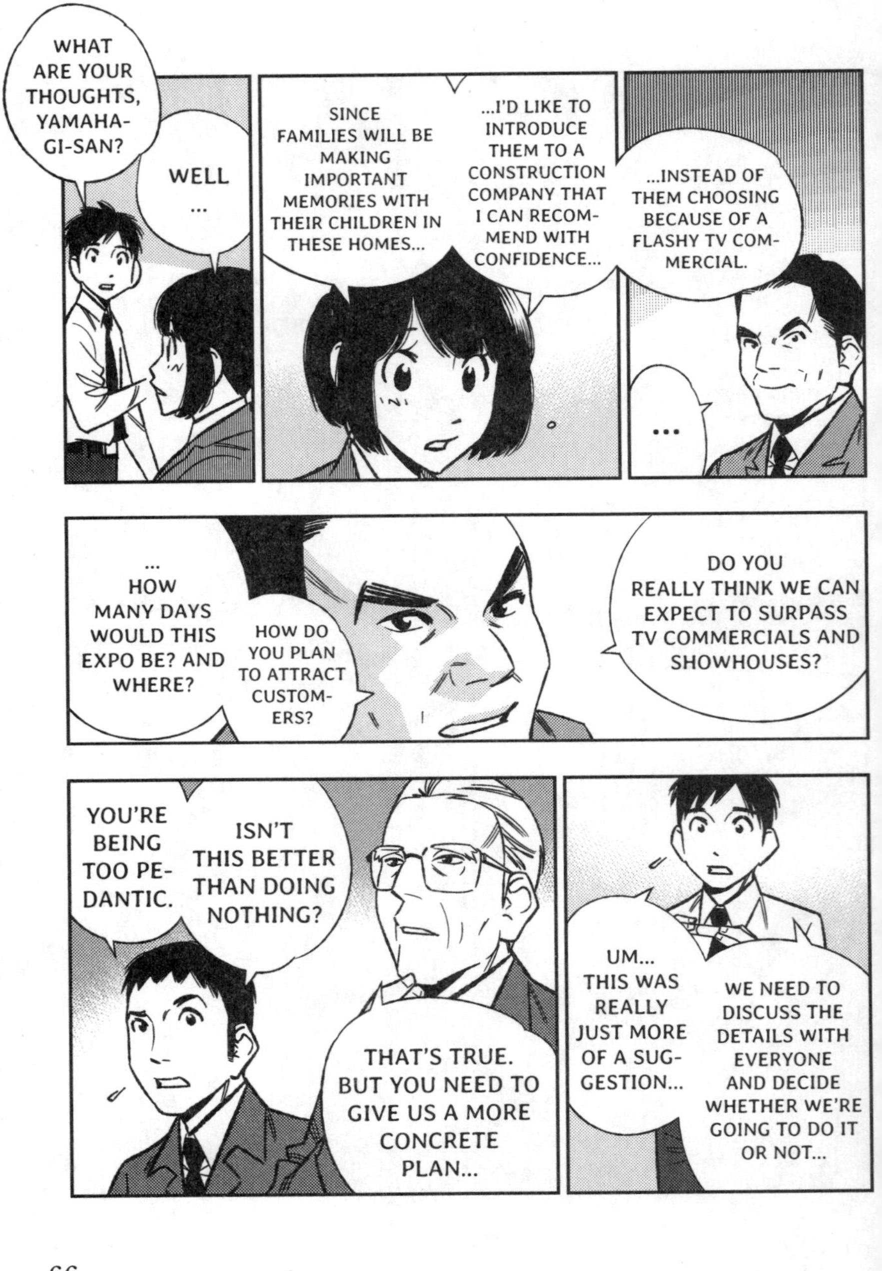
WHAT ARE YOUR THOUGHTS, YAMAHA-GI-SAN?
WELL ...
SINCE FAMILIES WILL BE MAKING IMPORTANT MEMORIES WITH THEIR CHILDREN IN THESE HOMES...
...I'D LIKE TO INTRODUCE THEM TO A CONSTRUCTION COMPANY THAT I CAN RECOM-MEND WITH CONFIDENCE...
...INSTEAD OF THEM CHOOSING BECAUSE OF A FLASHY TV COM-MERCIAL.
...
DO YOU REALLY THINK WE CAN EXPECT TO SURPASS TV COMMERCIALS AND SHOWHOUSES?
HOW DO YOU PLAN TO ATTRACT CUSTOM-ERS?
... HOW MANY DAYS WOULD THIS EXPO BE? AND WHERE?
ISN'T THIS BETTER THAN DOING NOTHING?
YOU'RE BEING TOO PE-DANTIC.
THAT'S TRUE. BUT YOU NEED TO GIVE US A MORE CONCRETE PLAN...
WE NEED TO DISCUSS THE DETAILS WITH EVERYONE AND DECIDE WHETHER WE'RE GOING TO DO IT OR NOT...
UM... THIS WAS REALLY JUST MORE OF A SUG-GESTION...

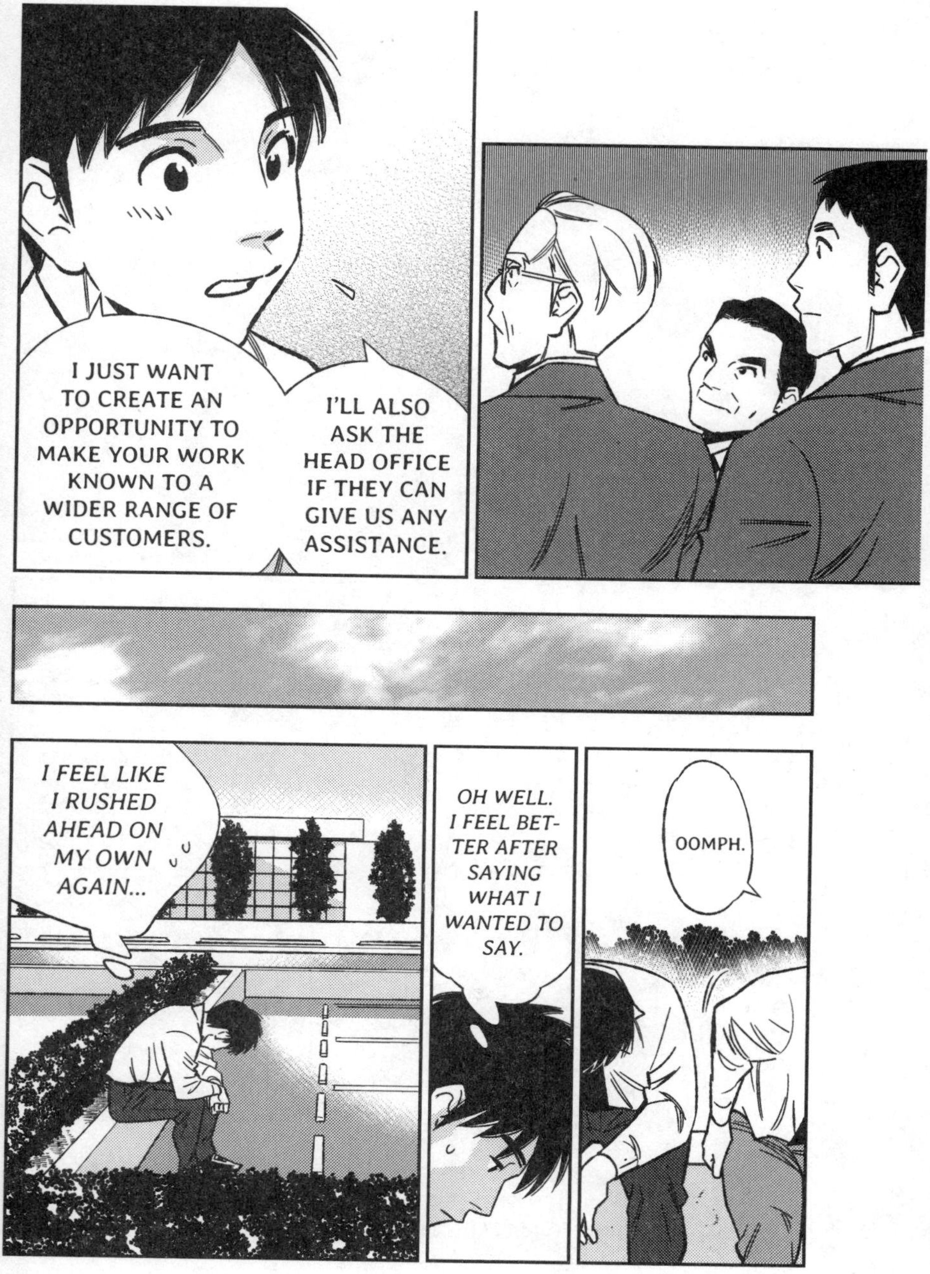
I JUST WANT TO CREATE AN OPPORTUNITY TO MAKE YOUR WORK KNOWN TO A WIDER RANGE OF CUSTOMERS.
I'LL ALSO ASK THE HEAD OFFICE IF THEY CAN GIVE US ANY ASSISTANCE.
I FEEL LIKE I RUSHED AHEAD ON MY OWN AGAIN...
OH WELL. I FEEL BET-TER AFTER SAYING WHAT I WANTED TO SAY.
OOMPH.

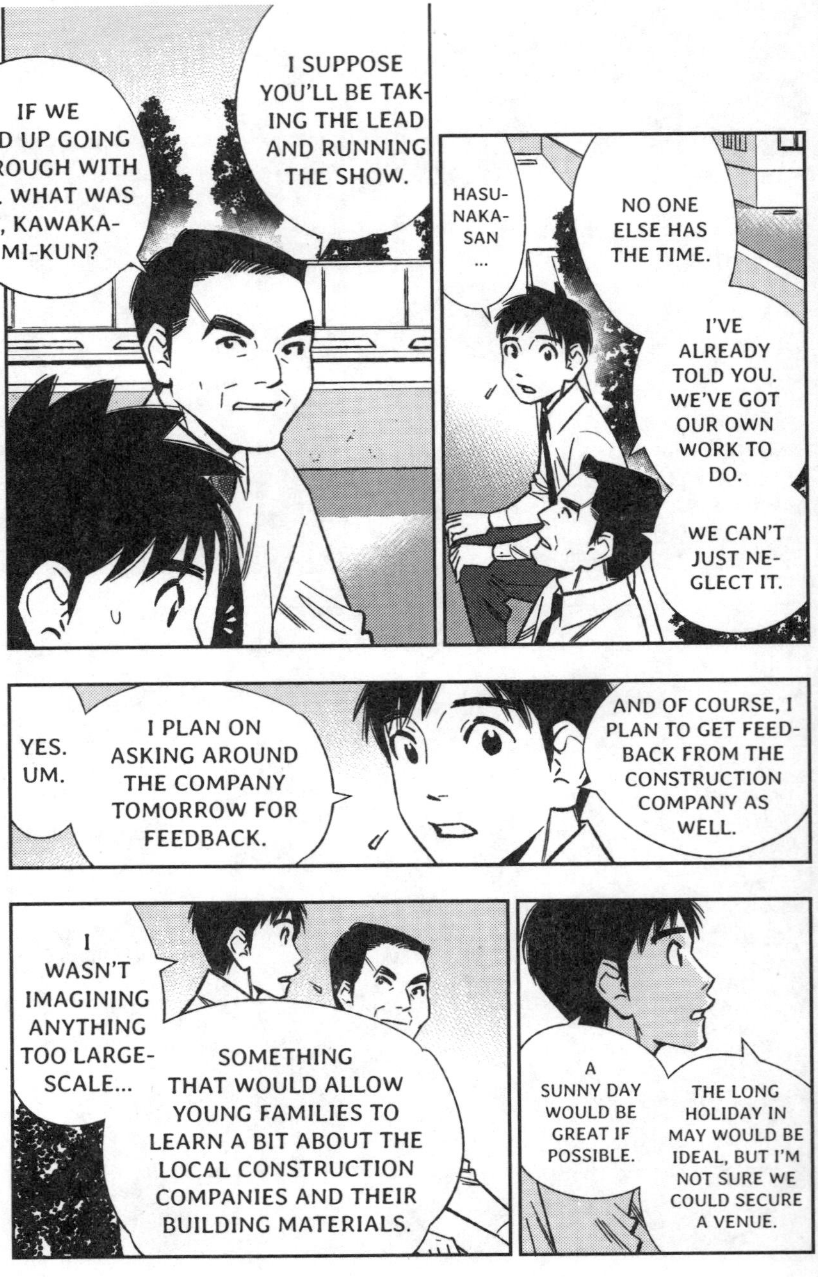
I SUPPOSE YOU'LL BE TAKING THE LEAD AND RUNNING THE SHOW.
IF WE END UP GOING THROUGH WITH IT... WHAT WAS IT, KAWAKAMI-KUN?
NO ONE ELSE HAS THE TIME.
I'VE ALREADY TOLD YOU. WE'VE GOT OUR OWN WORK TO DO.
WE CAN'T JUST NEGLECT IT.
HASUNAKA-SAN ...
AND OF COURSE, I PLAN TO GET FEEDBACK FROM THE CONSTRUCTION COMPANY AS WELL.
I PLAN ON ASKING AROUND THE COMPANY TOMORROW FOR FEEDBACK.
YES. UM.
THE LONG HOLIDAY IN MAY WOULD BE IDEAL, BUT I'M NOT SURE WE COULD SECURE A VENUE.
A SUNNY DAY WOULD BE GREAT IF POSSIBLE.
I WASN'T IMAGINING ANYTHING TOO LARGE-SCALE...
SOMETHING THAT WOULD ALLOW YOUNG FAMILIES TO LEARN A BIT ABOUT THE LOCAL CONSTRUCTION COMPANIES AND THEIR BUILDING MATERIALS.

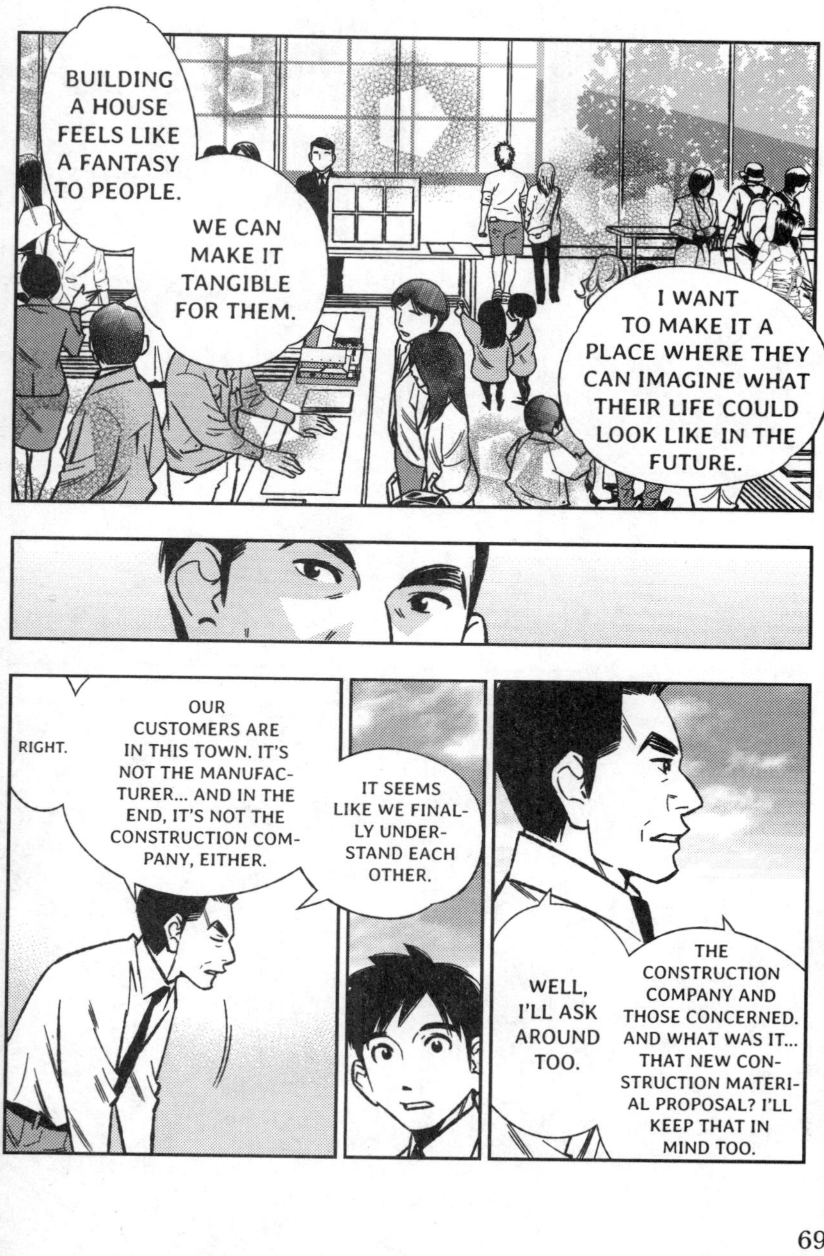
BUILDING A HOUSE FEELS LIKE A FANTASY TO PEOPLE.
WE CAN MAKE IT TANGIBLE FOR THEM.
I WANT TO MAKE IT A PLACE WHERE THEY CAN IMAGINE WHAT THEIR LIFE COULD LOOK LIKE IN THE FUTURE.
RIGHT.
OUR CUSTOMERS ARE IN THIS TOWN. IT'S NOT THE MANUFACTURER... AND IN THE END, IT'S NOT THE CONSTRUCTION COMPANY, EITHER.
IT SEEMS LIKE WE FINALLY UNDERSTAND EACH OTHER.
WELL, I'LL ASK AROUND TOO.
THE CONSTRUCTION COMPANY AND THOSE CONCERNED. AND WHAT WAS IT... THAT NEW CONSTRUCTION MATERIAL PROPOSAL? I'LL KEEP THAT IN MIND TOO.

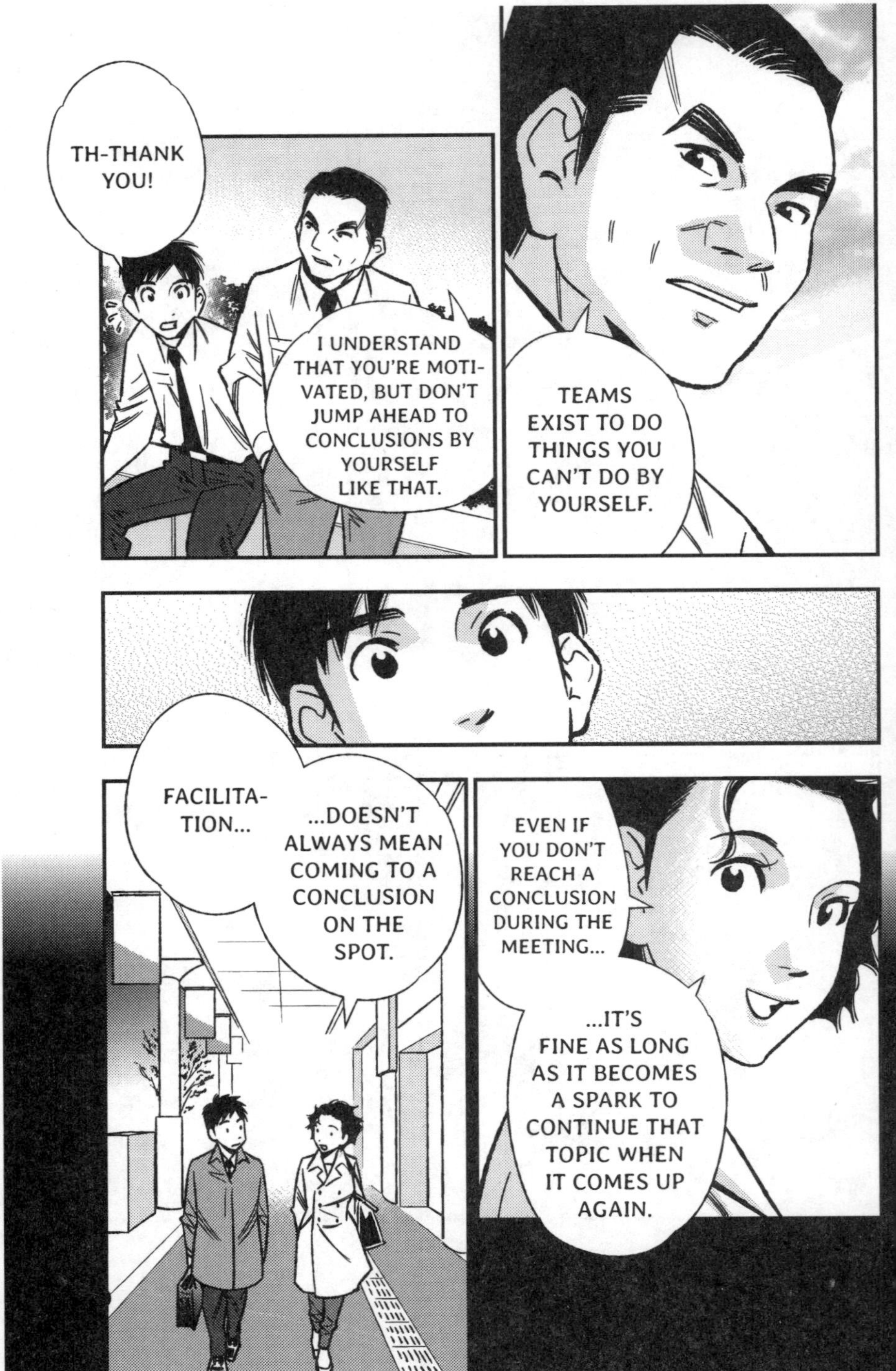
TEAMS EXIST TO DO THINGS YOU CAN'T DO BY YOURSELF.
I UNDERSTAND THAT YOU'RE MOTIVATED, BUT DON'T JUMP AHEAD TO CONCLUSIONS BY YOURSELF LIKE THAT.
TH-THANK YOU!
EVEN IF YOU DON'T REACH A CONCLUSION DURING THE MEETING...
...IT'S FINE AS LONG AS IT BECOMES A SPARK TO CONTINUE THAT TOPIC WHEN IT COMES UP AGAIN.
FACILITATION...
...DOESN'T ALWAYS MEAN COMING TO A CONCLUSION ON THE SPOT.

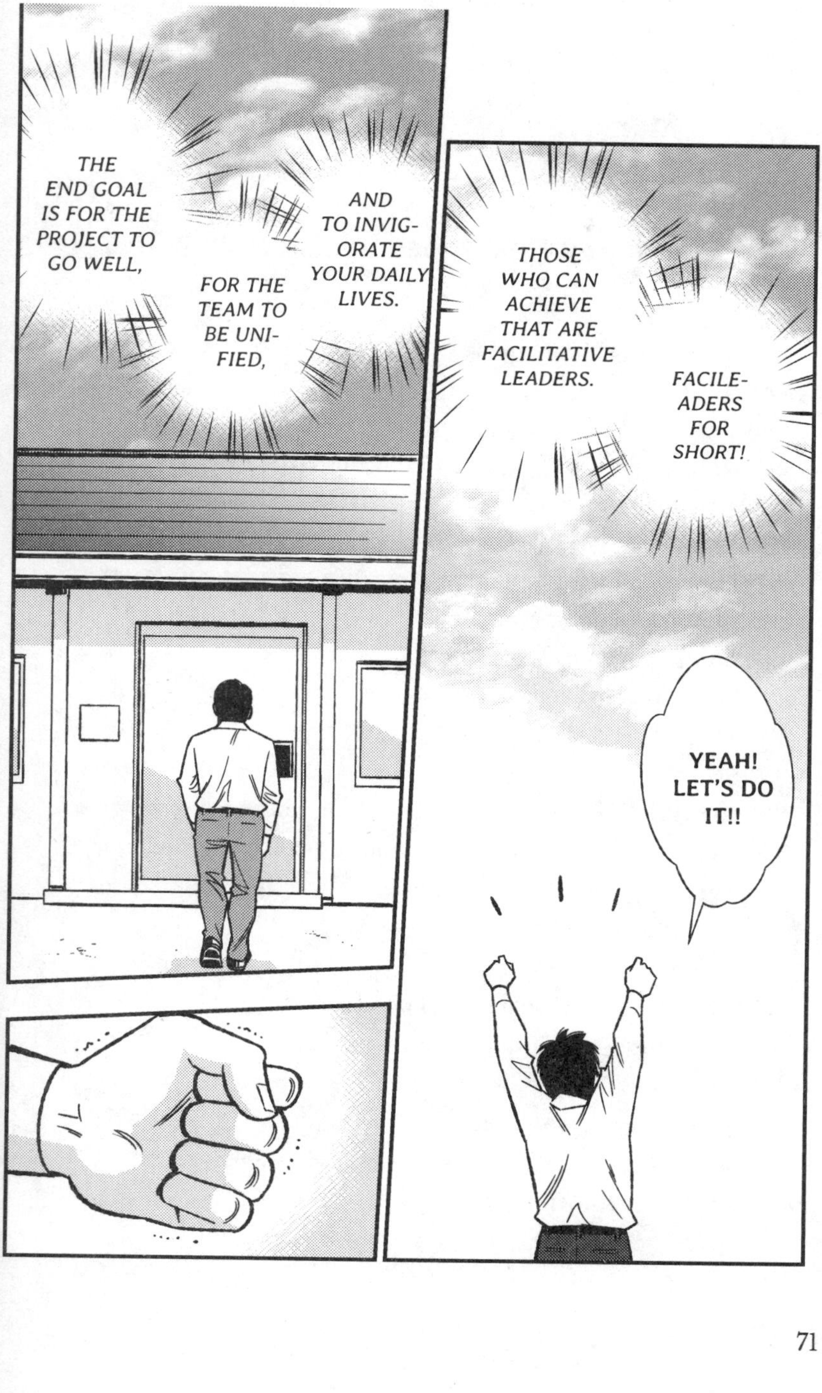
THE END GOAL IS FOR THE PROJECT TO GO WELL,
FOR THE TEAM TO BE UNI-FIED,
AND TO INVIG-ORATE YOUR DAILY LIVES.
THOSE WHO CAN ACHIEVE THAT ARE FACILITATIVE LEADERS.
FACILE-ADERS FOR SHORT!
YEAH! LET'S DO IT!!

3 Even If You Hate Meetings, Start with This

"Meetings? I don't like them."

Many people say that meetings are useless, pointless, or that they don't want to take part. Regardless of the industry, meetings are disliked by many.

We asked around some workplaces for reasons, and these were the three most common answers.
- They're too long.
- Opinions aren't voiced.
- We don't reach a conclusion.

With so many people putting aside so much time to get together, this is certainly a waste. I, for one, would certainly prefer to hold meetings that, when participants leave, they do so with the sense, "Wow, I'm glad I went!"
- ☐ They end on time.
- ☐ Everyone actively shares their opinion.
- ☐ Some sort of conclusion is always reached.

To have your meetings be like this, a useful tool to use is the whiteboard. Let's learn how to use it well and turn these large discussions into something meaningful.

Here are a few things you should write up on the whiteboard first.

O   The meeting's title;

O   Today's theme;

O   Names of the participants;

O   Today's agenda and the desired outputs;

O   Date and time (start time and expected end time).

Just by having these written down, you should be able to reduce the incidence of problems such as getting off-topic or not reaching a conclusion. It also encourages members to look up at the board, and in so doing, talk to one another directly.

If you plan on using the contents of the previous discussion as a base, it would be effective to set some time aside at the start of the meeting to go over what was discussed last time.

•   The results so far;

•   What to do next;

•   What should be achieved today.

Please be sure to share these three points.

By clarifying the goals for the day at the beginning, you can be sure that everyone's on the right page and lay the groundwork needed for gathering everyone's opinions.

In the past when I've asked businesspeople, many say they've never used a whiteboard before.

"It's not a part of the company culture."

Figure 1.

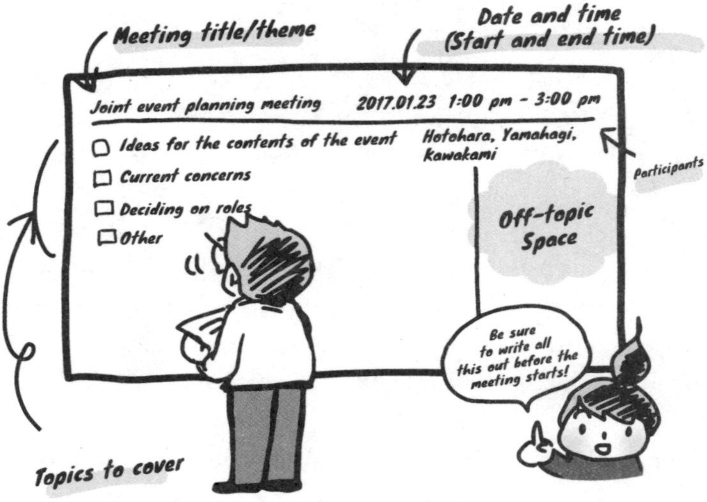
Meeting title/theme
Date and time (Start and end time)
Joint event planning meeting
2017.01.23 1:00 pm - 3:00 pm
Ideas for the contents of the event
Current concerns
Deciding on roles
Other
Hotohara, Yamahagi, Kawakami
Participants
Off-topic Space
Be sure to write all this out before the meeting starts!
Topics to cover

"I just became a leader recently. I've never been in favor of writing things down."

"Isn't that a bit over the top? Aren't memos enough of a summary?"

Regardless of the reason, standing alone in front of a whiteboard and leading the meeting while everyone else is sitting down watching you can feel a bit embarrassing. I understand that feeling well.

In that case, I recommend writing the outline out before the meeting starts. Then, take a seat close to the whiteboard during the meeting.

If possible, mark off the topics as they're discussed so that the meeting's progress can be visualized and so participants can easily check what the current topic is.

Additionally, be sure to inform participants of any meeting rules you'd like everyone to follow.
"Open for any and all opinions!"
"Please provide your reasoning with any opposing opinions."
"No personal attacks."
Write your rules up like this, and display them in a way that's easy for everyone to see.

By having them on display, it'll naturally catch everyone's eyes, and it'll be easier for everyone to keep them in mind. Don't just simply display them, take the time at the start of the meeting to briefly go over the rules with everyone, and make sure they understand them. By doing so, the meeting will run even more smoothly.

4 Take Notes on the Board During Meetings

Once you've gotten used to using a whiteboard to track the meeting's agenda and progress, your next challenge is to take notes down on the whiteboard.

For example, when participants are having a discussion, do they write notes in their own notebooks or on their own handouts? If they do, this is actually a big problem. We all tend to interpret whatever we hear as we see fit, and write it down in our own words. I'm sure you've left a meeting and later gone to exchange opinions with a coworker, only to find yourself thinking, "Did we even talk about that?" for a lot of the things they bring up.

If you want to bring out opinions from your team members and then consolidate them into the opinion of the team as a whole, here's what you need to do. Tell your members to stop taking individual notes, and urge everyone to take shared notes on the whiteboard, where they can all see them. Everyone will naturally look up, and have a discussion while looking at the board. By double-checking everyone's opinions and writing them down, those opinions will naturally be summarized in one location. It'll also stimulate more people to share their opinions, and prevent any overlaps.

The trick to writing points on the board is to **simultaneously continue the dialogue with both the speaker and the rest of the meeting participants** while doing so. Having your opinion written out differently from your intention leaves a bad taste. Each time you write up a point, make sure to ask the speaker if everything looks okay. By getting confirmation, you create a sense of security in your meetings, and show that they're a place where opinions are treated politely and with care. Being able to erase things when you make a mistake is the good part about a whiteboard. Make sure to try it out when you get a chance.

Also, there are people who will derail the discussion often during meetings. They'll repeat arguments, and they'll stagnate the discussion. Even if that happens, don't worry. On the right side of the whiteboard, draw a line and set some space aside. Whenever you feel like the conversation is straying from the current topic, **make note of it in that space**. Say something along the lines of "That's a great point, but it's a bit off-topic, so let's make a note of it here." Write it down in that space, and go back to the original topic.

By doing this, you're preventing the conversation from straying off-topic again in the same way, as well as making the speaker feel heard.

Figure 1.

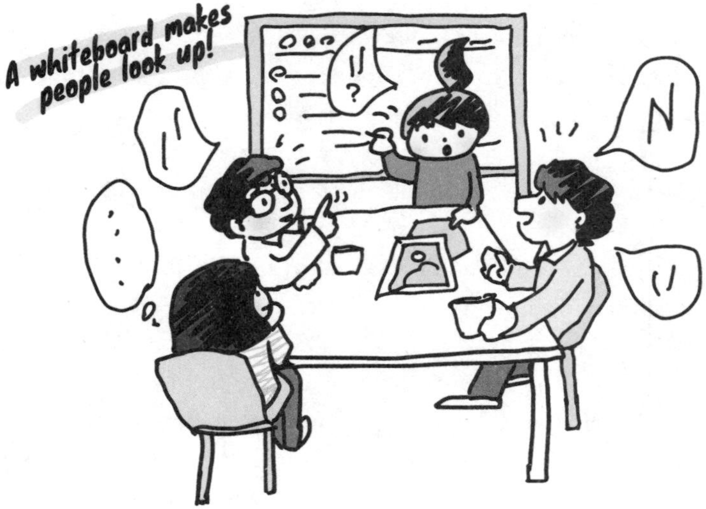
A whiteboard makes people look up!

Learn to use the whiteboard well, and skillfully organize everything said.

"I was writing notes and consolidating everyone's views on the whiteboard, but I ran out of space..."

Even in situations like this, **please don't erase the notes on the whiteboard**, and carry on with the discussion. The whiteboard acts as a summary of proceedings, an important tool for bringing out opinions, and by the end of the meeting, it becomes the shared work of all the meeting participants. It's very difficult to figure out on the spot what you can erase and what you might need later, so I can't recommend erasing any of it. If you are forced to erase something, erase the agenda. Even in that case, try to take a picture, or find another way to preserve what was written.

If there aren't enough whiteboards in the meeting space, you can substitute it by sticking a **sheet of bulletin board paper** up, or use an extra large sticky note, or even a sheet of whiteboard-like material affixed to a wall. Keep at least one of these options in storage, so that you can easily use them during meetings. Just the act of handing out something like bulletin board paper tends to encourage people to write things down and to gather their thoughts into one area, so I recommend using this strategy for small groups.

If you aren't good at taking notes while listening to someone talk, consider using **sticky notes**. Hand each participant a large sticky note, give them the time to think about the topic, and have them write their opinions down. If you do this, it's important to set some rules such as "use a thick marker" and "one opinion per sticky note," just for the sake of when they're shared. By having them write their opinions out on sticky notes and sticking them up, it becomes easier to visualize everything, as well as consolidate it all later. By grouping similar ideas and giving them headings, you can also create an affinity diagram out of the sticky notes.

In a brainstorming meeting, if you want your team members to each come up with a set number of ideas, you can distribute that number of notes to each member. They'll get a sense of achievement upon using up all their notes. They can also be useful in situations such as briefings, where you expect there to be a lot of questions. Instead of asking and answering each and every question vocally, you can ask everyone to write their questions on sticky notes, and then organize your answers much better and more efficiently.

However, if you just suddenly hand sticky notes out like Kawakami-kun, the protagonist of the manga, you might receive some adverse reactions from your team members. Be thorough in explaining what you are doing and how you wish to proceed.

With the help of whiteboards as well as these other useful and flexible tools I've mentioned, you can have a more productive meeting! Let's change meetings into an effective, useful time for the team.

5 Tips for Questions to Draw Out Everyone's Thoughts

Once you've got the basics of using a whiteboard down, let's work on your ability to ask questions that can draw out the opinions of your team. Let me introduce you to three tips for leaders to master asking these sorts of questions.

① Use positive wording

The way questions or statements are framed has a great influence on the way we think about them. If you want your audience to think positively, it's important to phrase your questions positively. For example, "What do you think we should do to make this a success?" encourages a much more positive line of thinking than, "Why aren't things going well?" Let's make sure we draw out positive thoughts from our team members by tweaking the way in which we ask our questions.

② Ask questions for your team.

The types of questions you can ask to draw out your team's opinions aren't just limited to asking them the things you wish to know directly. You can also ask questions in their stead. Questions that encourage them to think, or that broaden their perspectives, or that lead them to new realizations and courses of action that they didn't notice before. In order to improve the quality of our questions, let's start by categorizing the types of questions we can ask.

- ○ **Level 1: Yes/No Questions**
  Questions that can be answered with a yes or no. These are used to confirm things, such as information or intentions.

- ○ **Level 2: Multiple Choice Questions (Which)**
  Questions in which you present some options and encourage listeners to choose among them. You would use a question like this when the conditions of the decision have already been set, at least to some extent.

- ○ **Level 3: Closed Questions (Who / Where / When)**
  Questions that impose some limits on the scope of potential answers. These questions are used when you want people to think in a limited range, such as when, where, and who.

- ○ **Level 4: Open Questions (What / How)**
  The type of question that gives the person you're asking free reign to answer as they please. You would use these questions when you want to encourage listeners to broaden their thinking, with no limitations.

The questions in level 4 allow for total freedom. The answer is completely dependent on the person being asked. Depending on that person's maturity, it may actually provide them with too much freedom to provide a good answer. However, by pondering these questions and realizing that they are unable to give an answer, it still can become an opportunity for growth. Even if you don't get an answer, this sort of question can still have a significant impact. Please try to use these level 4 questions on a regular basis.

③ Keep questions simple

When we're asked multiple questions at once, we're unable to process them all straightaway. In order to give your team quality time to think, be conscientious of only asking simple questions, and always only one at a time. In particular, I would like you to have these two simple questions in your standard repertoire.

Number 1: Specifically?
This urges members who are a bit vague about the current situation or goals to think about things in more concrete terms. If you include the term "specifically" in your question, their thoughts will naturally drift toward facts and events. They may come to realize that they didn't have any particular basis for their opinion. By asking this regularly, you can get your team members to think deeper and start to draw out some valid, well-reasoned opinions from them.

Number 2: What else?
If you only get one answer after asking a question, try to expand on it by asking, "What else?" Try to draw out as many answers as you can first, and then sort them in order of precedence later. We tend to be satisfied when we get one answer without even realizing it, but the first answers to a given question tend to be rather basic. By asking them for more, you can further expand the scope of your team's thinking.

Using these kinds of questions to make your team members think deeply and broadly on a regular basis will undoubtedly increase the critical thinking skills of the whole team. Questions are triggers for thoughts. Keep these three points in mind, and you'll be drawing out your team's every last opinion in no time.

6 Who Do You Need in a Team? Separating the Ideal from Reality

"We don't have anyone good..."

When you ask a leader in the midst of grumbling something like that, what kind of person they do need, you will often get rather vague answers such as "someone outstanding" or "someone who can do their job." If you want to better organize your team, it's important to properly analyze and understand each of your team members.

What kind of person would be ideal for your team?
What kind of people are currently on your team?

In order to sort out your current situation and form a picture of what you'd ideally like in the future, think in terms of these three steps.

1) **Consider the work you need to do.**
   What role is your team expected to play, and what tasks are required of it? Regardless of whether it has already been done or not, or whether it's required now or in the future, list everything you can think of.

2) **Consider your current team members.**
   Once you've gotten all of those tasks written down, let's

analyze the individual members of your team. Which tasks are they good at? What do they struggle with?

3) **Consider how you'd ideally like your team members to be.** After analyzing the current situation, think about how you'd like them to be in the future. What kind of work do you want them to be able to do? Effective training and team formation are only possible once both the current and the ideal situation have been clarified.

I also recommend analyzing your team from the perspective of what an ideal working member of society looks like.

For example, since 2006, the Ministry of Economy, Trade and Industry in Japan has been advocating the "fundamental skills for business." According to them, these skills consist of three main traits: the ability to progress, the ability to think things through, and the ability to work as a team. These consist of 12 component abilities, as summarized in the figure on the next page.

In addition to this, let's organize our team members in relation to various categories such as basic academic skills related to reading and writing, individual job-specific expertise, personality, and character.

"But how can we objectively know what kind of people we have in our team?"

Figure 1.

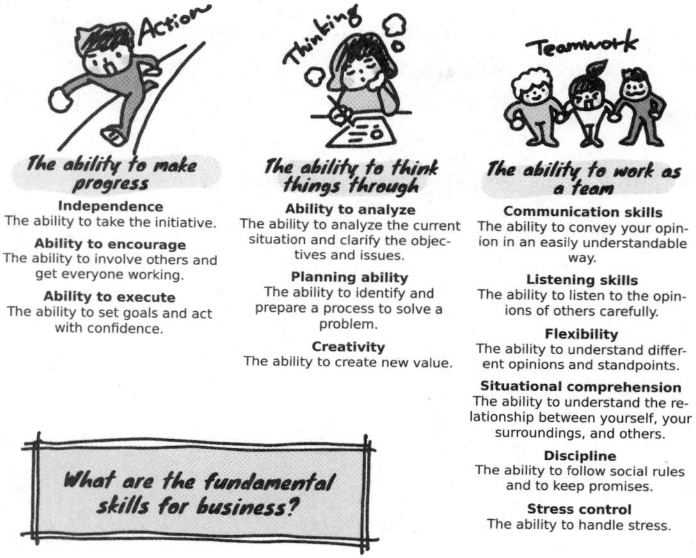

Action
Thinking
Teamwork
The ability to make progress
Independence
The ability to take the initiative.
Ability to encourage
The ability to involve others and get everyone working.
Ability to execute
The ability to set goals and act with confidence.
The ability to think things through
Ability to analyze
The ability to analyze the current situation and clarify the objectives and issues.
Planning ability
The ability to identify and prepare a process to solve a problem.
Creativity
The ability to create new value.
The ability to work as a team
Communication skills
The ability to convey your opinion in an easily understandable way.
Listening skills
The ability to listen to the opinions of others carefully.
Flexibility
The ability to understand different opinions and standpoints.
Situational comprehension
The ability to understand the relationship between yourself, your surroundings, and others.
Discipline
The ability to follow social rules and to keep promises.
Stress control
The ability to handle stress.
What are the fundamental skills for business?

If that crossed your mind, I suggest utilizing commonly used diagnostic tests. They come in various forms, from paper-based to web-based, both free and paid versions. There are many to choose from, so please research what would best suit your team's needs.

For team members who do not know their own strengths and characteristics and are having trouble envisioning their future, having the chance to learn more about themselves could be a great opportunity.

Identify the barriers to your team members' growth, and level up your team as a whole.

PART 2

Putting Facilitation to Practice

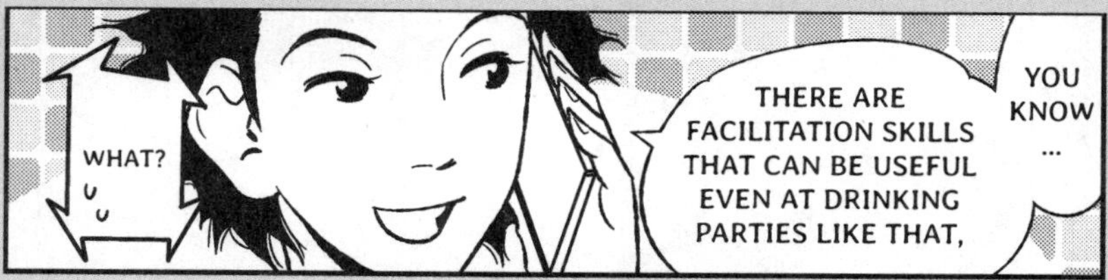
YOU KNOW ...
THERE ARE FACILITATION SKILLS THAT CAN BE USEFUL EVEN AT DRINKING PARTIES LIKE THAT,
WHAT?

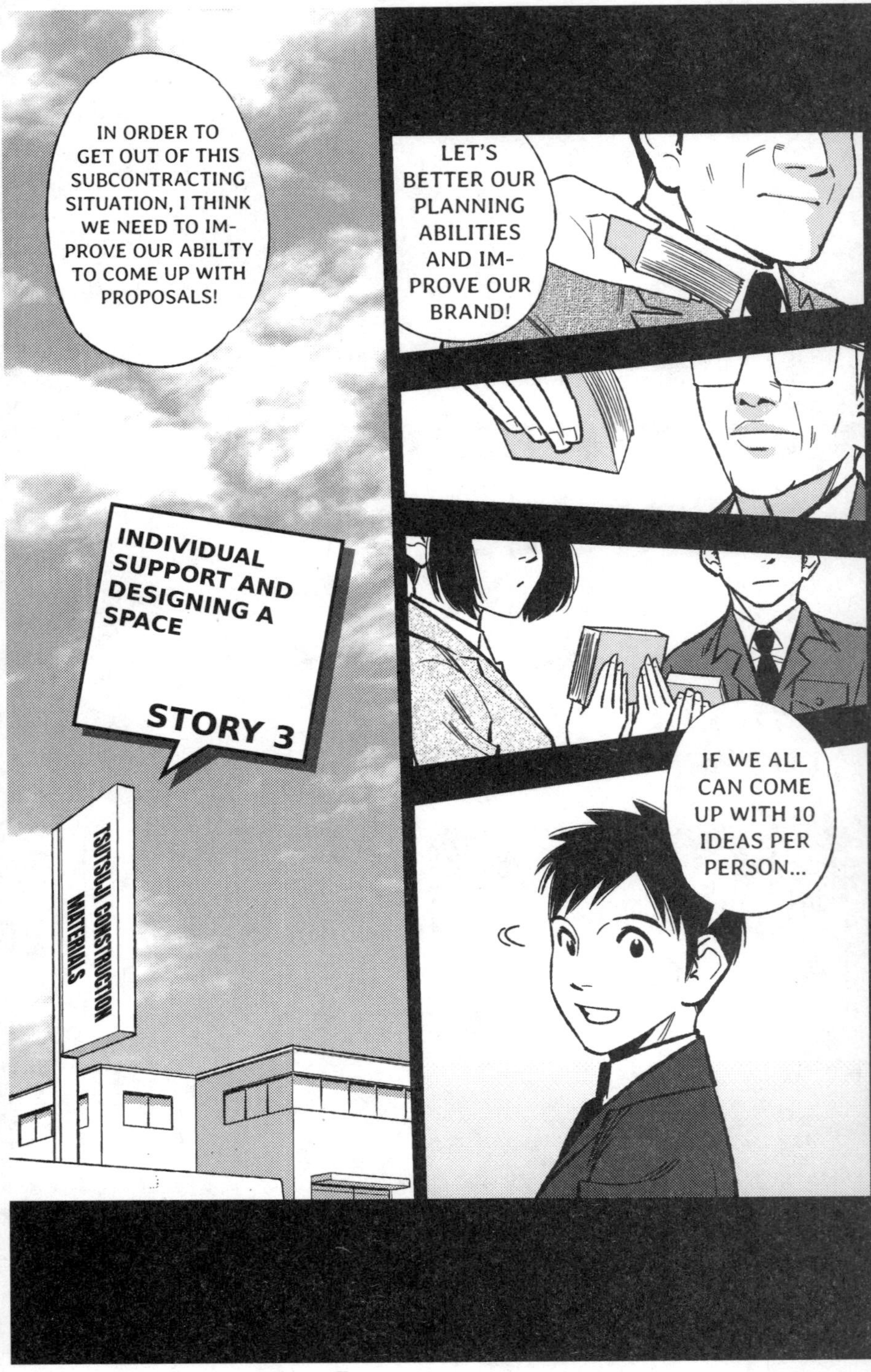
INDIVIDUAL SUPPORT AND DESIGNING A SPACE
STORY 3
TSUTSUJI CONSTRUCTION MATERIALS
IN ORDER TO GET OUT OF THIS SUBCONTRACTING SITUATION, I THINK WE NEED TO IM- PROVE OUR ABILITY TO COME UP WITH PROPOSALS!
LET'S BETTER OUR PLANNING ABILITIES AND IM- PROVE OUR BRAND!
IF WE ALL CAN COME UP WITH 10 IDEAS PER PERSON...

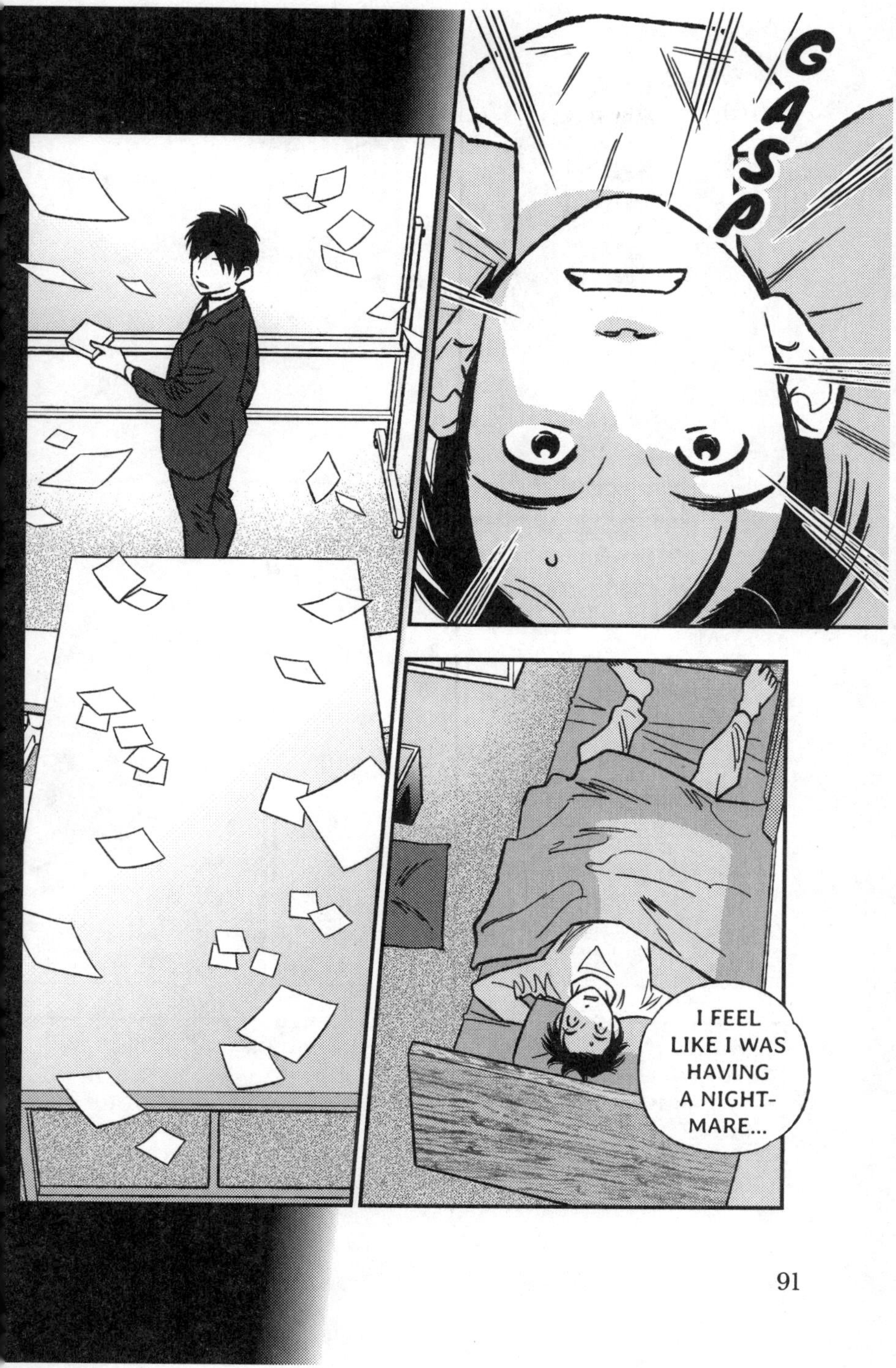
GASP
I FEEL LIKE I WAS HAVING A NIGHT-MARE...

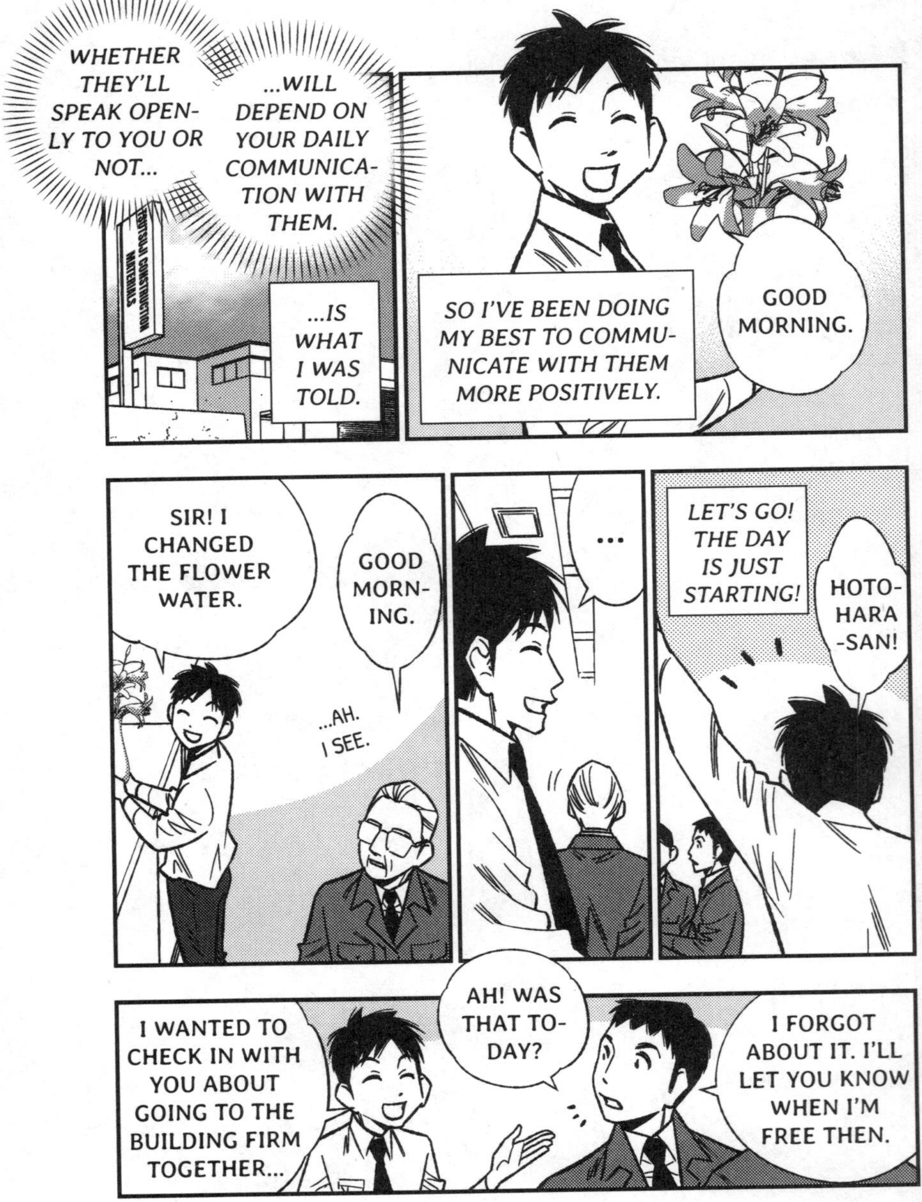
WHETHER THEY'LL SPEAK OPEN-LY TO YOU OR NOT...
...WILL DEPEND ON YOUR DAILY COMMUNICA-TION WITH THEM.
...IS WHAT I WAS TOLD.
SO I'VE BEEN DOING MY BEST TO COMMU-NICATE WITH THEM MORE POSITIVELY.
GOOD MORNING.
SIR! I CHANGED THE FLOWER WATER.
GOOD MORN-ING.
...AH. I SEE.
...
LET'S GO! THE DAY IS JUST STARTING!
HOTO-HARA -SAN!
I WANTED TO CHECK IN WITH YOU ABOUT GOING TO THE BUILDING FIRM TOGETHER...
AH! WAS THAT TO-DAY?
I FORGOT ABOUT IT. I'LL LET YOU KNOW WHEN I'M FREE THEN.

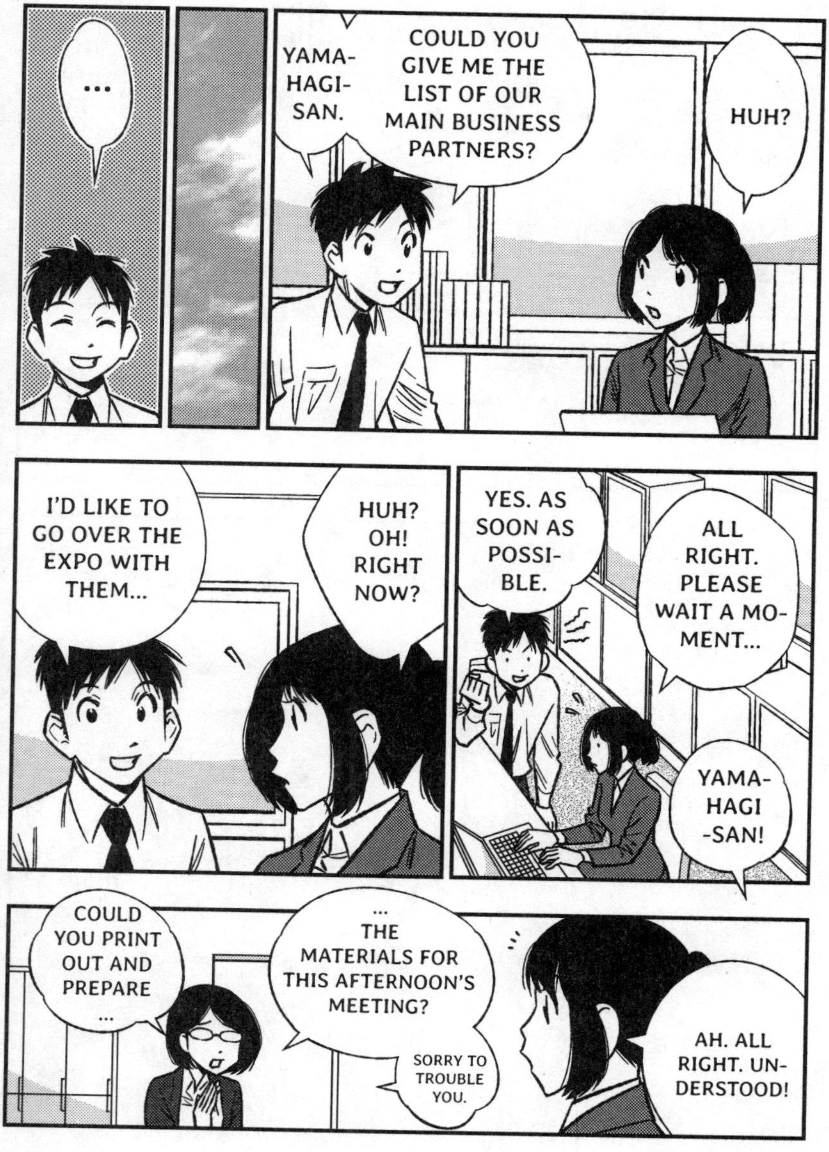
...
YAMA-HAGI-SAN.
COULD YOU GIVE ME THE LIST OF OUR MAIN BUSINESS PARTNERS?
HUH?
I'D LIKE TO GO OVER THE EXPO WITH THEM...
HUH? OH! RIGHT NOW?
YES. AS SOON AS POSSI-BLE.
ALL RIGHT. PLEASE WAIT A MO-MENT...
YAMA-HAGI -SAN!
COULD YOU PRINT OUT AND PREPARE ...
... THE MATERIALS FOR THIS AFTERNOON'S MEETING?
SORRY TO TROUBLE YOU.
AH. ALL RIGHT. UN-DERSTOOD!

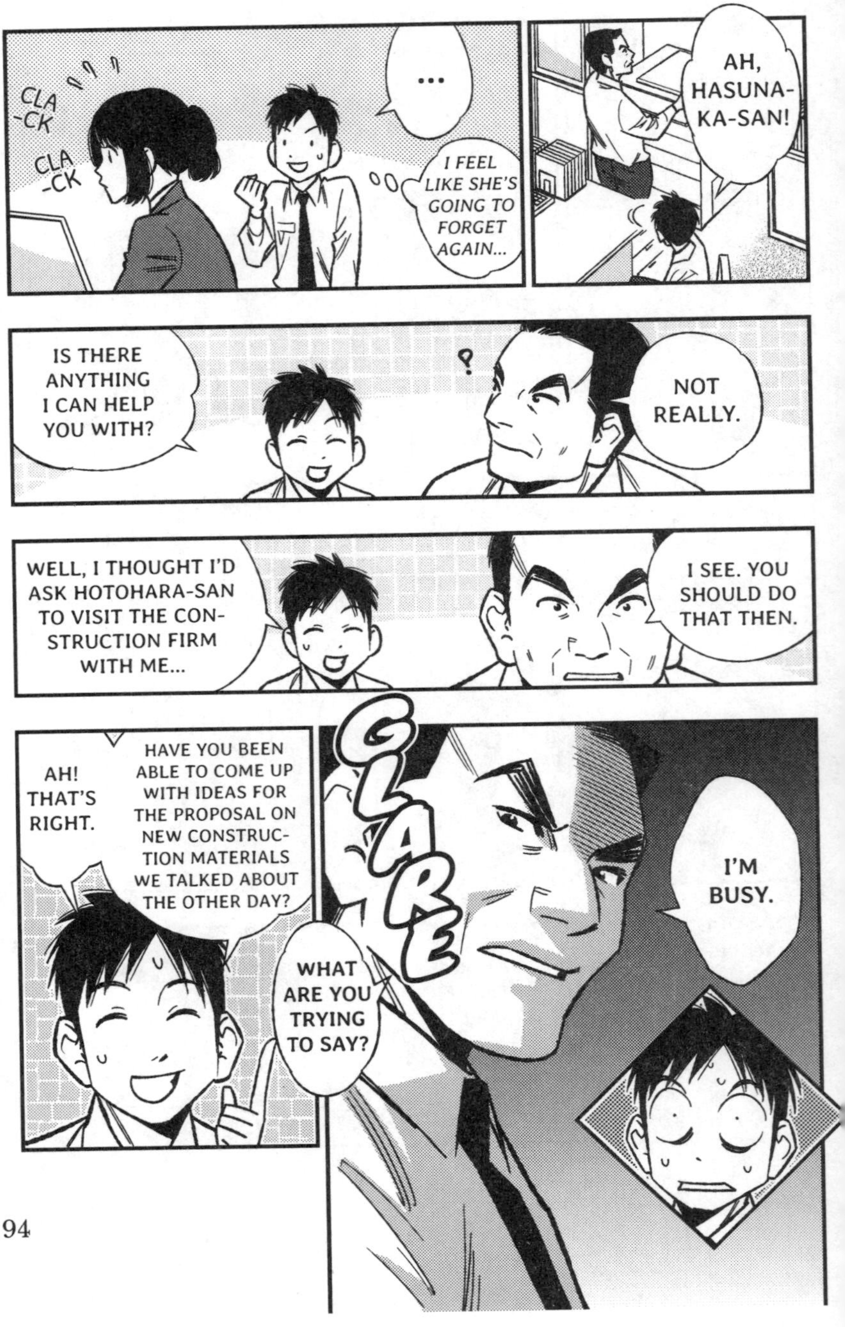
CLA-CK
CLA-CK
...
I FEEL LIKE SHE'S GOING TO FORGET AGAIN...
AH, HASUNAKA-SAN!
IS THERE ANYTHING I CAN HELP YOU WITH?
?
NOT REALLY.
WELL, I THOUGHT I'D ASK HOTOHARA-SAN TO VISIT THE CONSTRUCTION FIRM WITH ME...
I SEE. YOU SHOULD DO THAT THEN.
AH! THAT'S RIGHT.
HAVE YOU BEEN ABLE TO COME UP WITH IDEAS FOR THE PROPOSAL ON NEW CONSTRUCTION MATERIALS WE TALKED ABOUT THE OTHER DAY?
GLARE
I'M BUSY.
WHAT ARE YOU TRYING TO SAY?

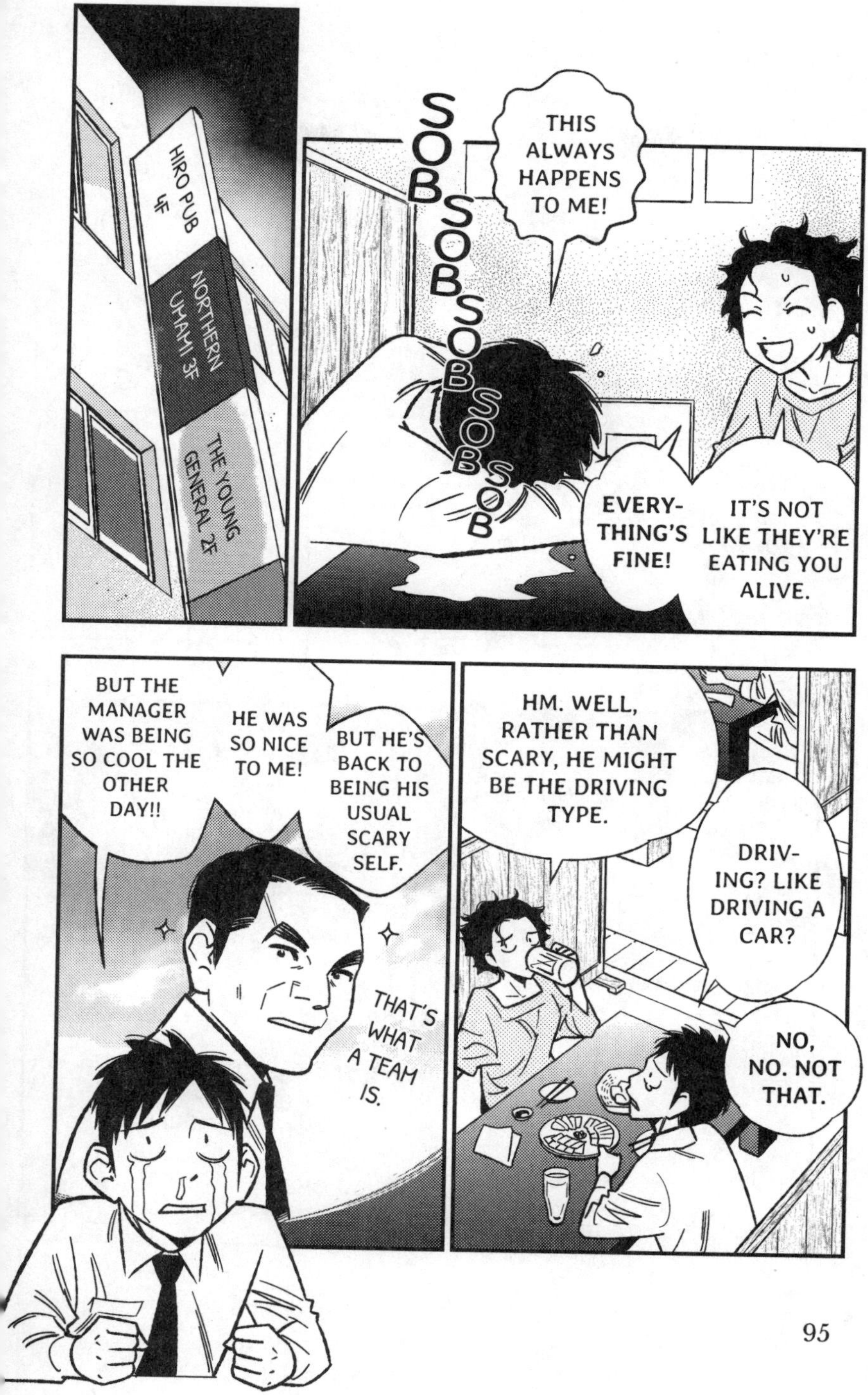

HIRO PUB 4F
NORTHERN UMAMI 3F
THE YOUNG GENERAL 2F
SOB SOB SOB SOB SOB
THIS ALWAYS HAPPENS TO ME!
IT'S NOT LIKE THEY'RE EATING YOU ALIVE.
EVERY-THING'S FINE!
BUT THE MANAGER WAS BEING SO COOL THE OTHER DAY!!
HE WAS SO NICE TO ME!
BUT HE'S BACK TO BEING HIS USUAL SCARY SELF.
THAT'S WHAT A TEAM IS.
HM. WELL, RATHER THAN SCARY, HE MIGHT BE THE DRIVING TYPE.
DRIV-ING? LIKE DRIVING A CAR?
NO, NO. NOT THAT.

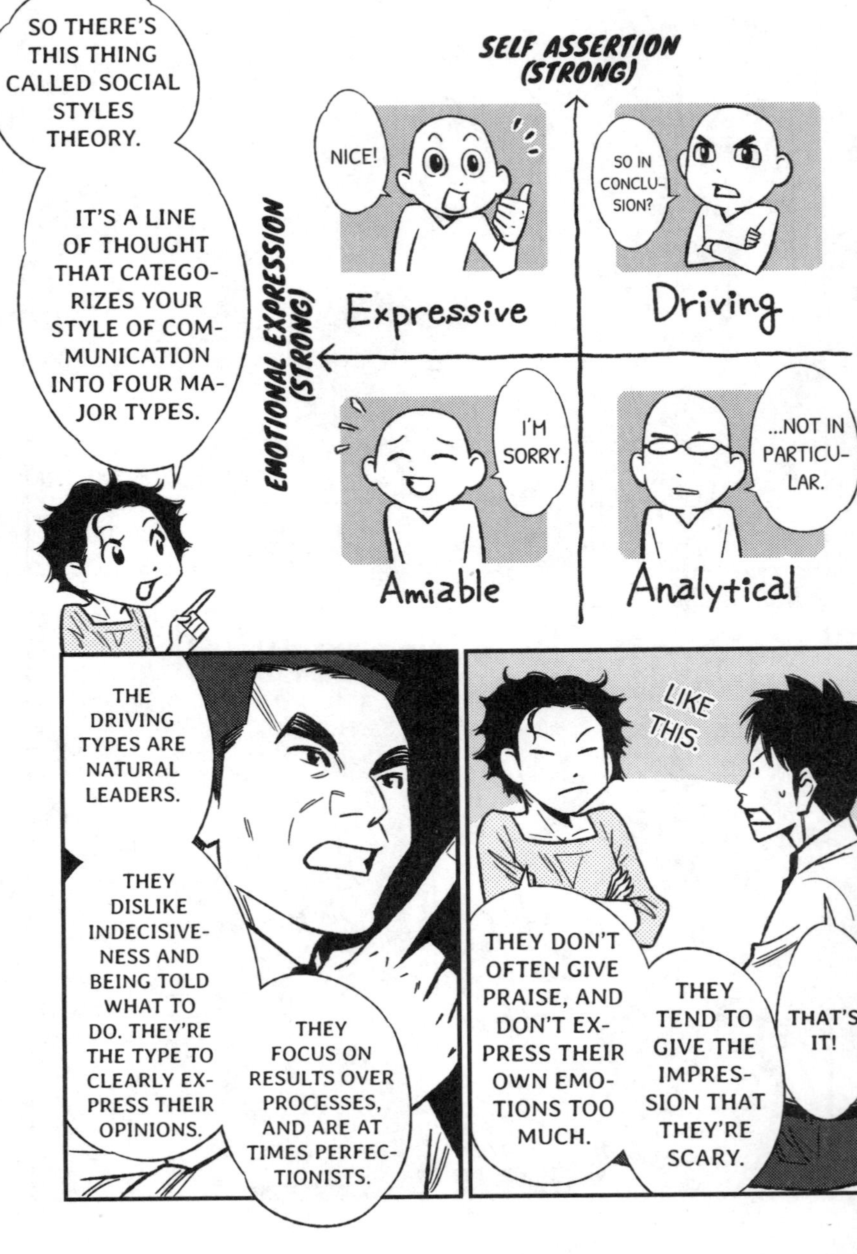
SO THERE'S THIS THING CALLED SOCIAL STYLES THEORY.
IT'S A LINE OF THOUGHT THAT CATEGO-RIZES YOUR STYLE OF COM-MUNICATION INTO FOUR MA-JOR TYPES.
SELF ASSERTION (STRONG)
EMOTIONAL EXPRESSION (STRONG)
NICE!
Expressive
SO IN CONCLU-SION?
Driving
I'M SORRY.
Amiable
...NOT IN PARTICU-LAR.
Analytical
THE DRIVING TYPES ARE NATURAL LEADERS.
THEY DISLIKE INDECISIVE-NESS AND BEING TOLD WHAT TO DO. THEY'RE THE TYPE TO CLEARLY EX-PRESS THEIR OPINIONS.
THEY FOCUS ON RESULTS OVER PROCESSES, AND ARE AT TIMES PERFEC-TIONISTS.
LIKE THIS.
THEY DON'T OFTEN GIVE PRAISE, AND DON'T EX-PRESS THEIR OWN EMO-TIONS TOO MUCH.
THEY TEND TO GIVE THE IMPRES-SION THAT THEY'RE SCARY.
THAT'S IT!

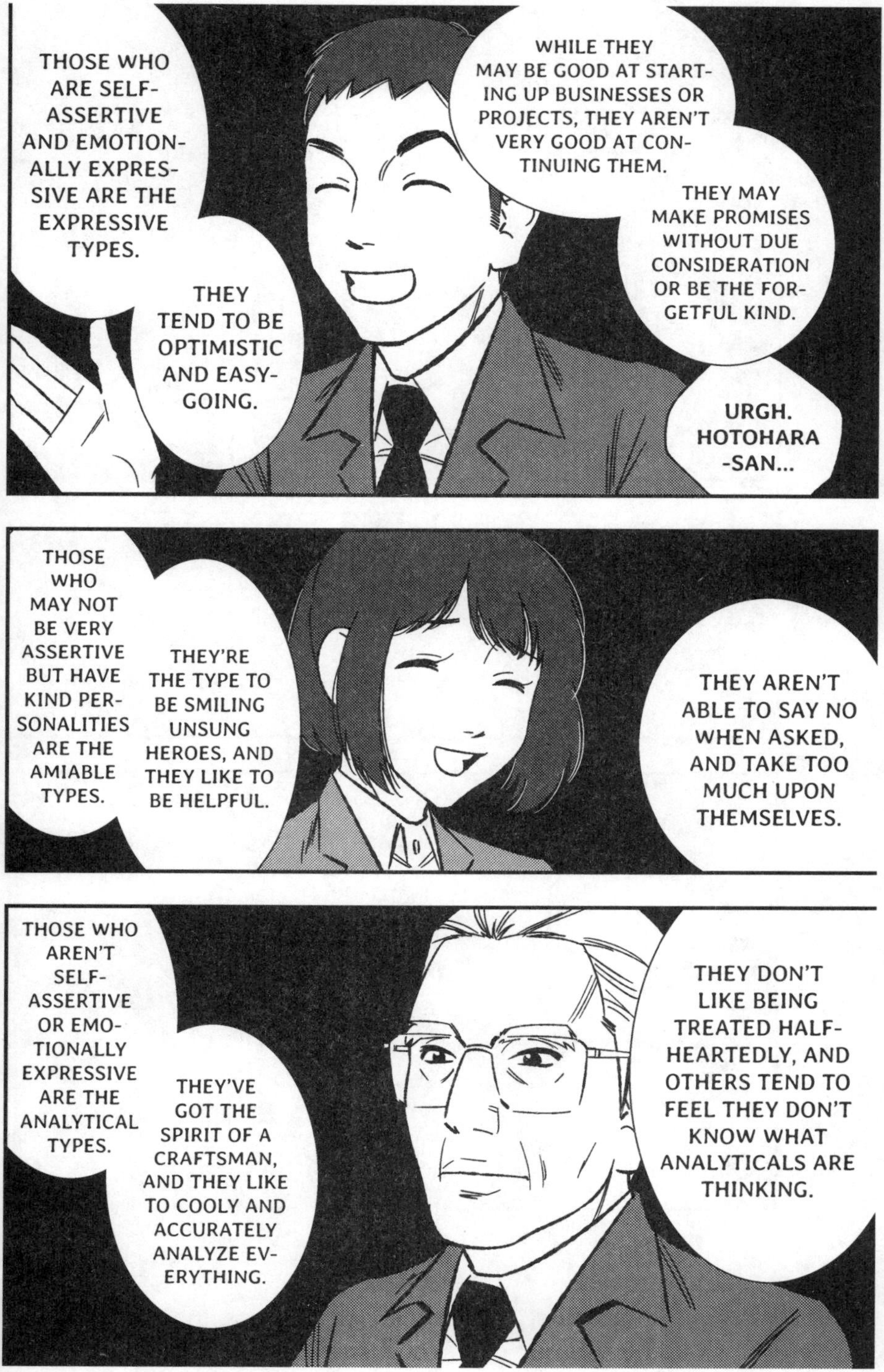
THOSE WHO ARE SELF-ASSERTIVE AND EMOTIONALLY EXPRESSIVE ARE THE EXPRESSIVE TYPES.
THEY TEND TO BE OPTIMISTIC AND EASY-GOING.
WHILE THEY MAY BE GOOD AT STARTING UP BUSINESSES OR PROJECTS, THEY AREN'T VERY GOOD AT CONTINUING THEM.
THEY MAY MAKE PROMISES WITHOUT DUE CONSIDERATION OR BE THE FORGETFUL KIND.
URGH. HOTOHARA-SAN...
THOSE WHO MAY NOT BE VERY ASSERTIVE BUT HAVE KIND PERSONALITIES ARE THE AMIABLE TYPES.
THEY'RE THE TYPE TO BE SMILING UNSUNG HEROES, AND THEY LIKE TO BE HELPFUL.
THEY AREN'T ABLE TO SAY NO WHEN ASKED, AND TAKE TOO MUCH UPON THEMSELVES.
THOSE WHO AREN'T SELF-ASSERTIVE OR EMOTIONALLY EXPRESSIVE ARE THE ANALYTICAL TYPES.
THEY'VE GOT THE SPIRIT OF A CRAFTSMAN, AND THEY LIKE TO COOLY AND ACCURATELY ANALYZE EVERYTHING.
THEY DON'T LIKE BEING TREATED HALF-HEARTEDLY, AND OTHERS TEND TO FEEL THEY DON'T KNOW WHAT ANALYTICALS ARE THINKING.

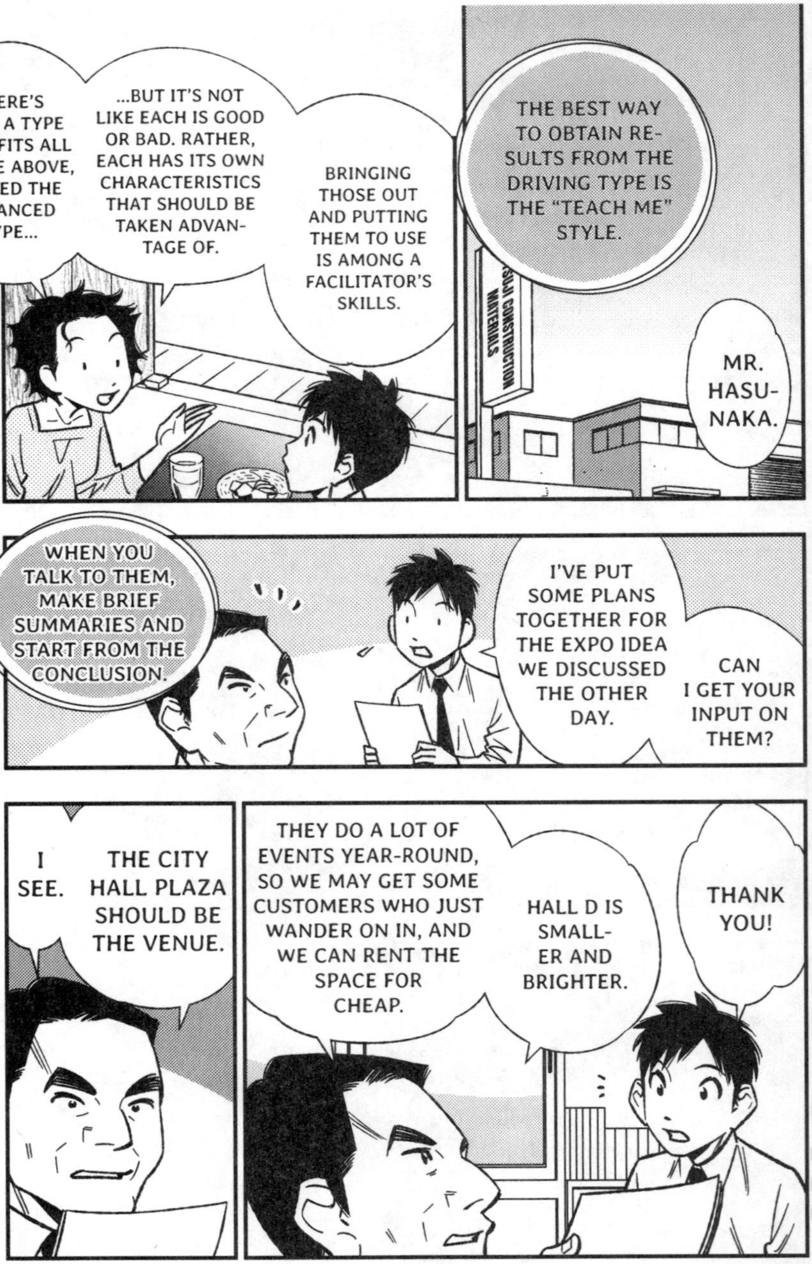
THERE'S ALSO A TYPE THAT FITS ALL OF THE ABOVE, CALLED THE BALANCED TYPE...
...BUT IT'S NOT LIKE EACH IS GOOD OR BAD. RATHER, EACH HAS ITS OWN CHARACTERISTICS THAT SHOULD BE TAKEN ADVANTAGE OF.
BRINGING THOSE OUT AND PUTTING THEM TO USE IS AMONG A FACILITATOR'S SKILLS.
THE BEST WAY TO OBTAIN RESULTS FROM THE DRIVING TYPE IS THE "TEACH ME" STYLE.
MR. HASUNAKA.
WHEN YOU TALK TO THEM, MAKE BRIEF SUMMARIES AND START FROM THE CONCLUSION.
I'VE PUT SOME PLANS TOGETHER FOR THE EXPO IDEA WE DISCUSSED THE OTHER DAY.
CAN I GET YOUR INPUT ON THEM?
I SEE.
THE CITY HALL PLAZA SHOULD BE THE VENUE.
THEY DO A LOT OF EVENTS YEAR-ROUND, SO WE MAY GET SOME CUSTOMERS WHO JUST WANDER ON IN, AND WE CAN RENT THE SPACE FOR CHEAP.
HALL D IS SMALLER AND BRIGHTER.
THANK YOU!

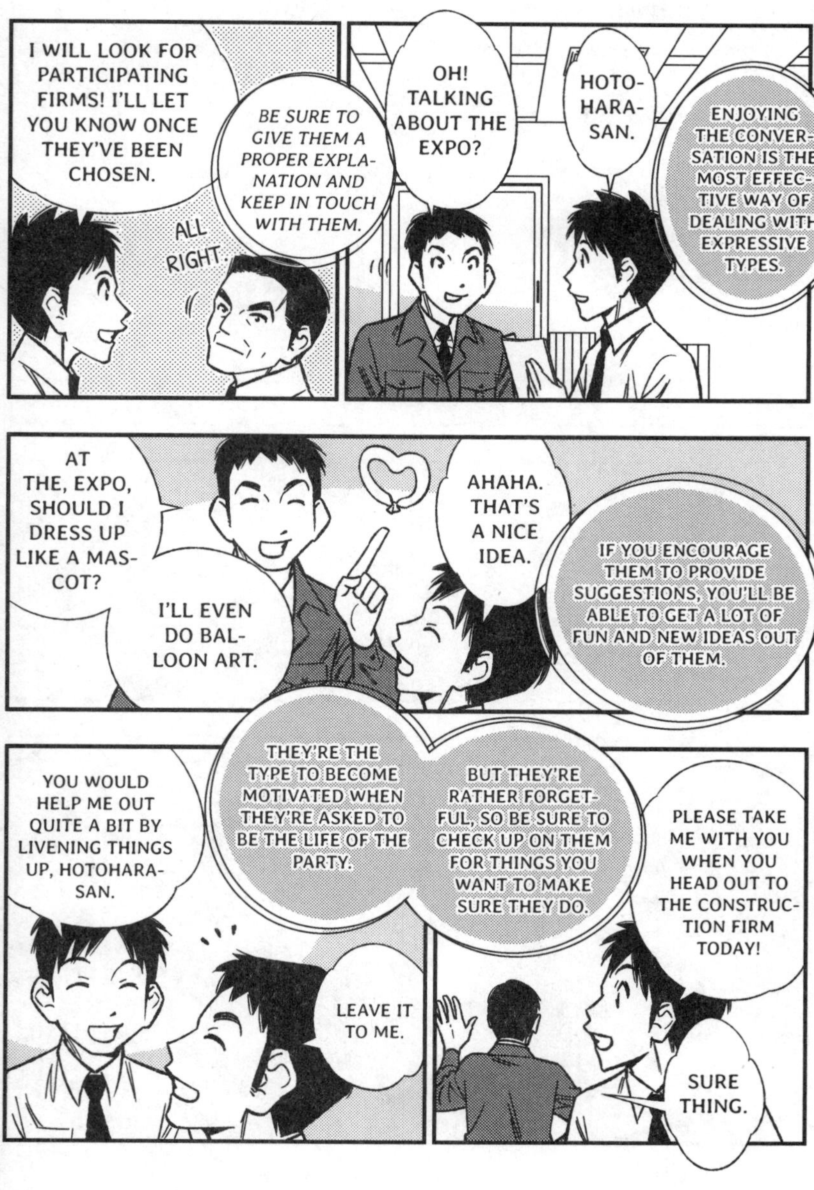
I WILL LOOK FOR PARTICIPATING FIRMS! I'LL LET YOU KNOW ONCE THEY'VE BEEN CHOSEN.
BE SURE TO GIVE THEM A PROPER EXPLANATION AND KEEP IN TOUCH WITH THEM.
ALL RIGHT.
HOTO-HARA-SAN.
OH! TALKING ABOUT THE EXPO?
ENJOYING THE CONVERSATION IS THE MOST EFFECTIVE WAY OF DEALING WITH EXPRESSIVE TYPES.
AT THE, EXPO, SHOULD I DRESS UP LIKE A MASCOT?
I'LL EVEN DO BALLOON ART.
AHAHA. THAT'S A NICE IDEA.
IF YOU ENCOURAGE THEM TO PROVIDE SUGGESTIONS, YOU'LL BE ABLE TO GET A LOT OF FUN AND NEW IDEAS OUT OF THEM.
YOU WOULD HELP ME OUT QUITE A BIT BY LIVENING THINGS UP, HOTOHARA-SAN.
THEY'RE THE TYPE TO BECOME MOTIVATED WHEN THEY'RE ASKED TO BE THE LIFE OF THE PARTY.
LEAVE IT TO ME.
BUT THEY'RE RATHER FORGETFUL, SO BE SURE TO CHECK UP ON THEM FOR THINGS YOU WANT TO MAKE SURE THEY DO.
PLEASE TAKE ME WITH YOU WHEN YOU HEAD OUT TO THE CONSTRUCTION FIRM TODAY!
SURE THING.

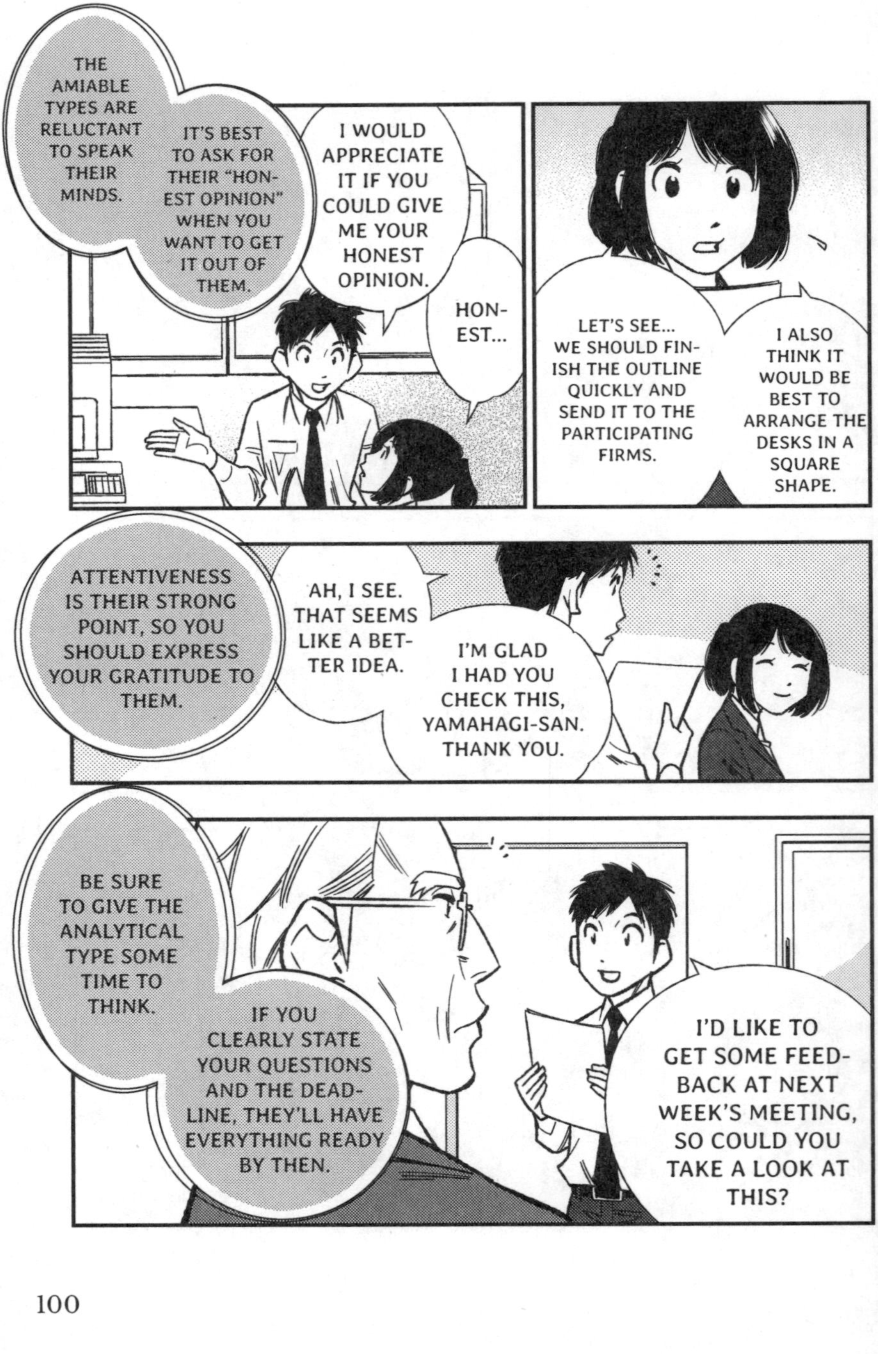
THE AMIABLE TYPES ARE RELUCTANT TO SPEAK THEIR MINDS.
IT'S BEST TO ASK FOR THEIR "HONEST OPINION" WHEN YOU WANT TO GET IT OUT OF THEM.
I WOULD APPRECIATE IT IF YOU COULD GIVE ME YOUR HONEST OPINION.
HON-EST...
LET'S SEE... WE SHOULD FINISH THE OUTLINE QUICKLY AND SEND IT TO THE PARTICIPATING FIRMS.
I ALSO THINK IT WOULD BE BEST TO ARRANGE THE DESKS IN A SQUARE SHAPE.
ATTENTIVENESS IS THEIR STRONG POINT, SO YOU SHOULD EXPRESS YOUR GRATITUDE TO THEM.
AH, I SEE. THAT SEEMS LIKE A BETTER IDEA.
I'M GLAD I HAD YOU CHECK THIS, YAMAHAGI-SAN. THANK YOU.
BE SURE TO GIVE THE ANALYTICAL TYPE SOME TIME TO THINK.
IF YOU CLEARLY STATE YOUR QUESTIONS AND THE DEADLINE, THEY'LL HAVE EVERYTHING READY BY THEN.
I'D LIKE TO GET SOME FEEDBACK AT NEXT WEEK'S MEETING, SO COULD YOU TAKE A LOOK AT THIS?

THIS IS THE TURNOUT FOR WEEKENDS AT THIS VENUE.
SO WE SHOULD PREPARE THIS MANY PAM-PHLETS...
MAKING REPORTS BASED ON DETAILED DATA...
...AND COMMUNI-CATING YOUR IDEAS PROPER-LY WILL GAIN YOU THEIR TRUST.
I SEE. THIS IS PRETTY REALISTIC.
THIS SEEMS LIKE IT'LL BE TIME CON-SUMING, BUT IT LOOKS LIKE WE CAN WORK WITH A SMALL BUDGET.
GO AHEAD WITH IT.
THANK YOU!
HUM ♫ HUM ♫.
THANKS TO YOU, MY LIFE HAS GOTTEN MUCH EASIER.

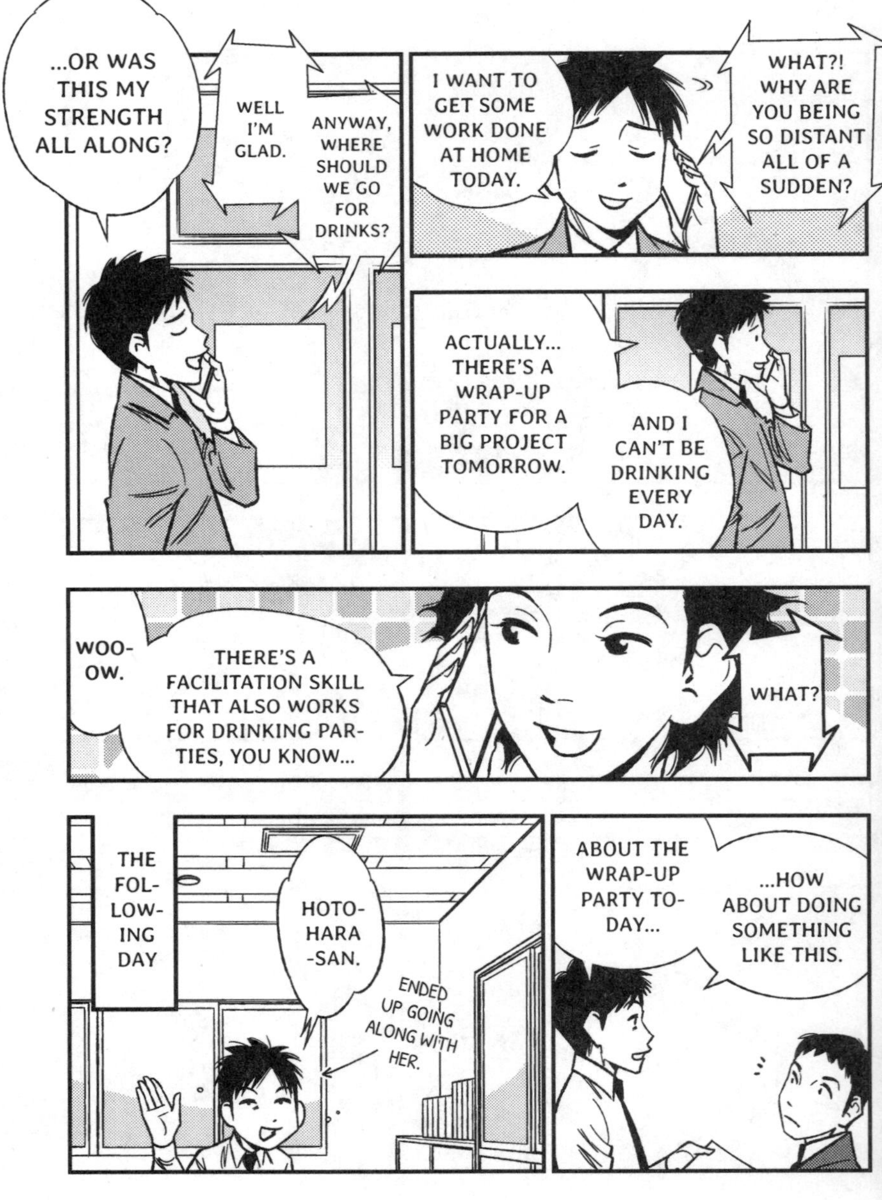

I WANT TO GET SOME WORK DONE AT HOME TODAY.
WHAT?! WHY ARE YOU BEING SO DISTANT ALL OF A SUDDEN?
...OR WAS THIS MY STRENGTH ALL ALONG?
WELL I'M GLAD.
ANYWAY, WHERE SHOULD WE GO FOR DRINKS?
ACTUALLY... THERE'S A WRAP-UP PARTY FOR A BIG PROJECT TOMORROW.
AND I CAN'T BE DRINKING EVERY DAY.
WOO-OW.
THERE'S A FACILITATION SKILL THAT ALSO WORKS FOR DRINKING PAR-TIES, YOU KNOW...
WHAT?
THE FOL-LOW-ING DAY
HOTO-HARA -SAN.
ENDED UP GOING ALONG WITH HER.
ABOUT THE WRAP-UP PARTY TO-DAY...
...HOW ABOUT DOING SOMETHING LIKE THIS.

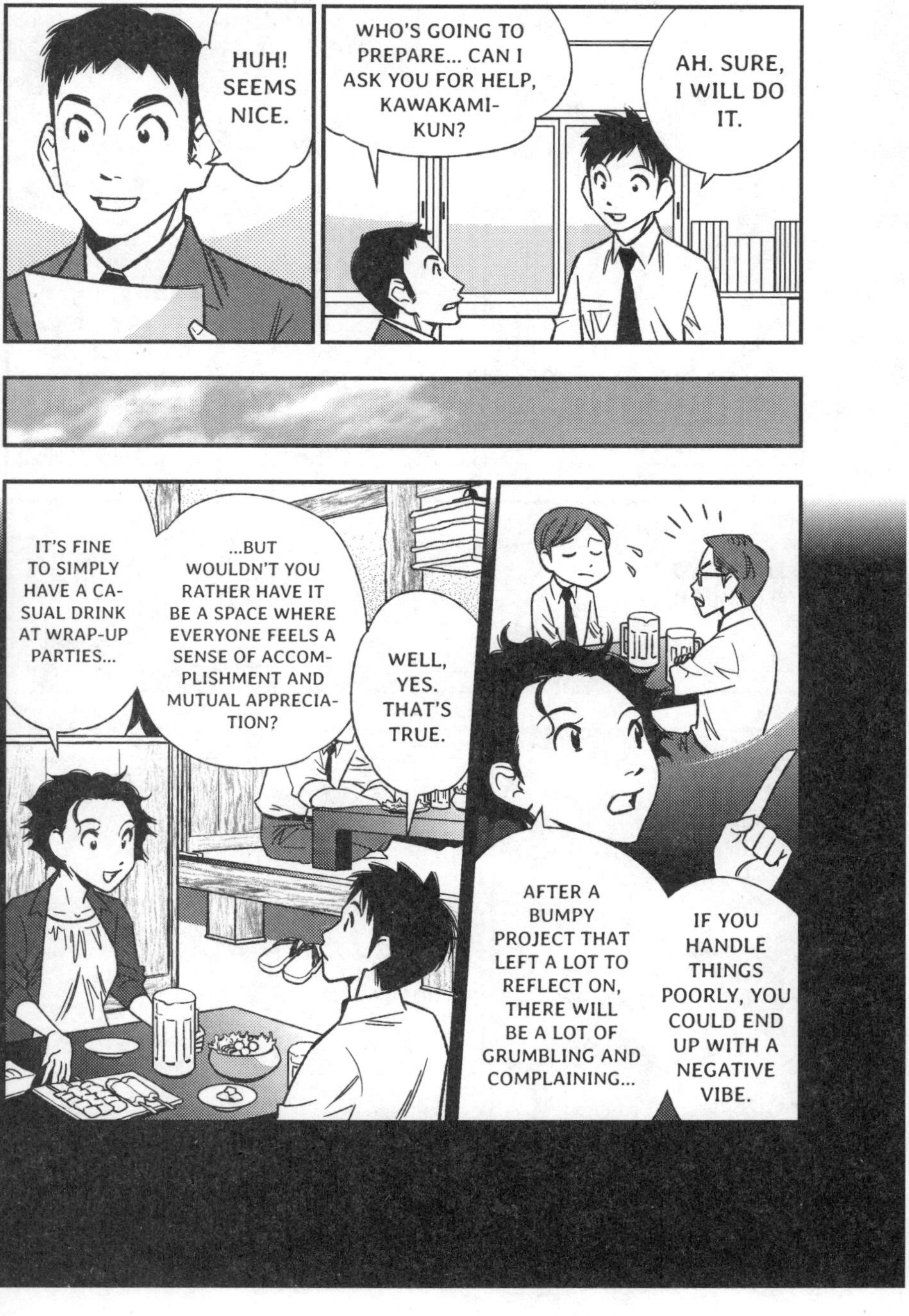
HUH! SEEMS NICE.
WHO'S GOING TO PREPARE... CAN I ASK YOU FOR HELP, KAWAKAMI-KUN?
AH. SURE, I WILL DO IT.
IT'S FINE TO SIMPLY HAVE A CASUAL DRINK AT WRAP-UP PARTIES...
...BUT WOULDN'T YOU RATHER HAVE IT BE A SPACE WHERE EVERYONE FEELS A SENSE OF ACCOMPLISHMENT AND MUTUAL APPRECIATION?
WELL, YES. THAT'S TRUE.
AFTER A BUMPY PROJECT THAT LEFT A LOT TO REFLECT ON, THERE WILL BE A LOT OF GRUMBLING AND COMPLAINING...
IF YOU HANDLE THINGS POORLY, YOU COULD END UP WITH A NEGATIVE VIBE.

A WAY TO PREVENT THAT FROM HAPPENING...

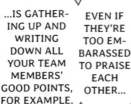

...IS GATHERING UP AND WRITING DOWN ALL YOUR TEAM MEMBERS' GOOD POINTS, FOR EXAMPLE.

EVEN IF THEY'RE TOO EMBARASSED TO PRAISE EACH OTHER...

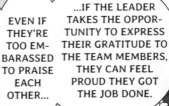

...IF THE LEADER TAKES THE OPPORTUNITY TO EXPRESS THEIR GRATITUDE TO THE TEAM MEMBERS, THEY CAN FEEL PROUD THEY GOT THE JOB DONE.

...AND SO THANKS TO EVERYONE, WE WERE ABLE TO OVERCOME THIS HUGE HURDLE.

THANK YOU SO MUCH!

YAY! HOTOHARA!

AND WE'VE EVEN GOT A MESSAGE FROM A SPECIAL SOMEONE!

HUH? WHO?

UH... I'M HASUNAKA FROM SALES.

I WASN'T ABLE TO JOIN YOU ALL TODAY, BUT...

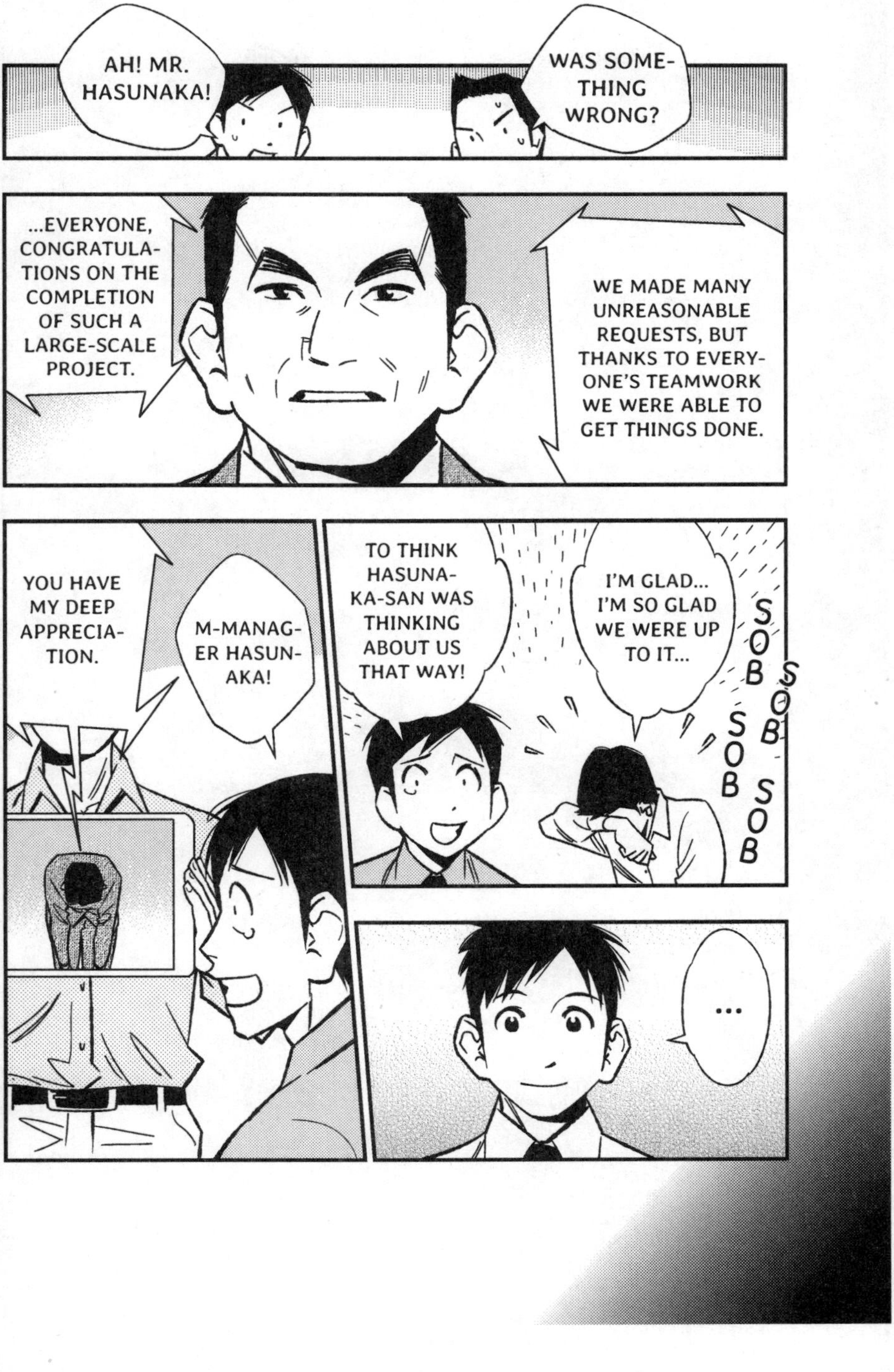
AH! MR. HASUNAKA!
WAS SOME-THING WRONG?
...EVERYONE, CONGRATULA-TIONS ON THE COMPLETION OF SUCH A LARGE-SCALE PROJECT.
WE MADE MANY UNREASONABLE REQUESTS, BUT THANKS TO EVERY-ONE'S TEAMWORK WE WERE ABLE TO GET THINGS DONE.
YOU HAVE MY DEEP APPRECIA-TION.
M-MANAG-ER HASUN-AKA!
TO THINK HASUNA-KA-SAN WAS THINKING ABOUT US THAT WAY!
I'M GLAD... I'M SO GLAD WE WERE UP TO IT...
SOB SOB SOB SOB
...

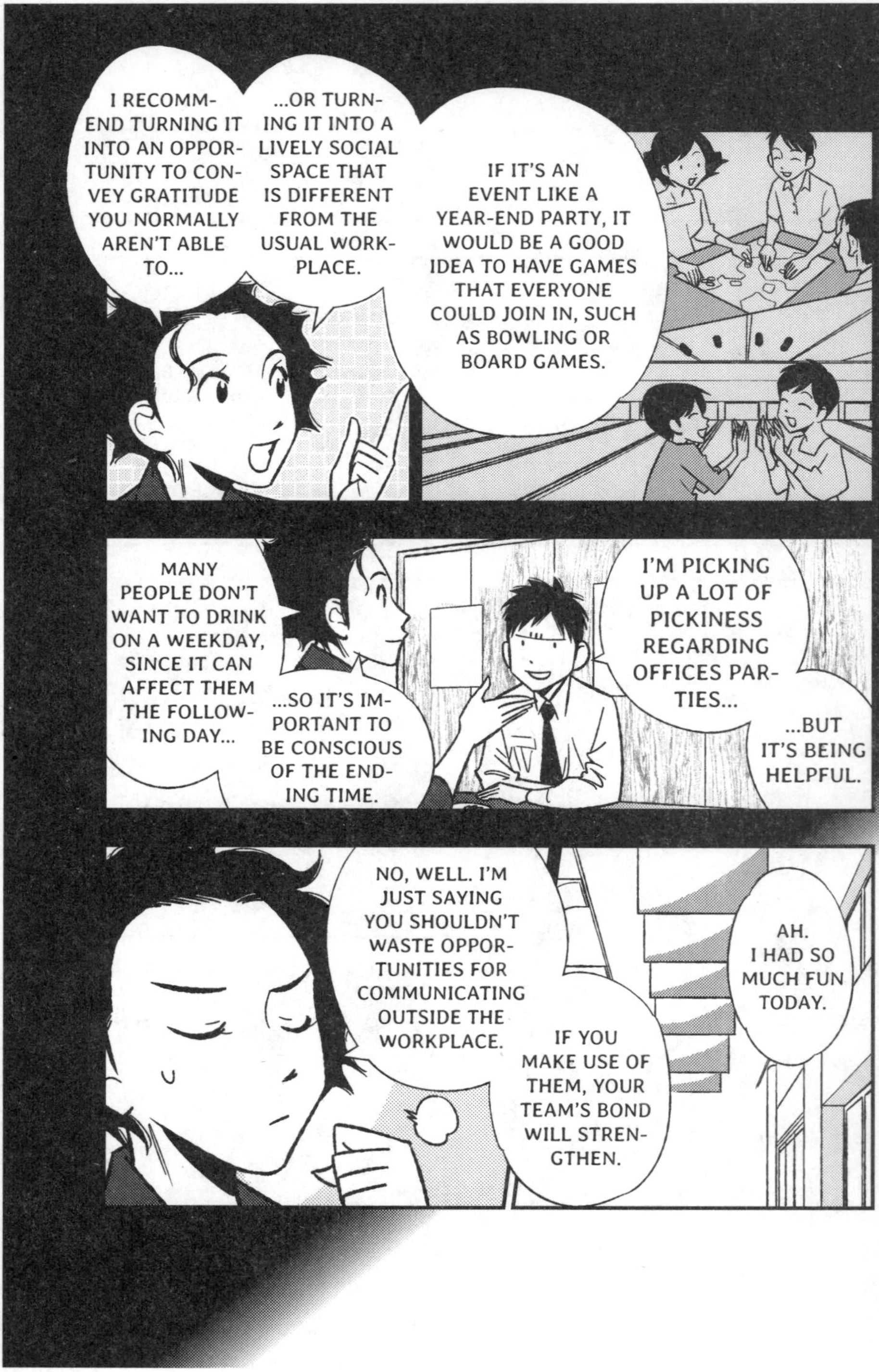
I RECOMMEND TURNING IT INTO AN OPPORTUNITY TO CONVEY GRATITUDE YOU NORMALLY AREN'T ABLE TO...
...OR TURNING IT INTO A LIVELY SOCIAL SPACE THAT IS DIFFERENT FROM THE USUAL WORKPLACE.
IF IT'S AN EVENT LIKE A YEAR-END PARTY, IT WOULD BE A GOOD IDEA TO HAVE GAMES THAT EVERYONE COULD JOIN IN, SUCH AS BOWLING OR BOARD GAMES.
MANY PEOPLE DON'T WANT TO DRINK ON A WEEKDAY, SINCE IT CAN AFFECT THEM THE FOLLOWING DAY...
...SO IT'S IMPORTANT TO BE CONSCIOUS OF THE ENDING TIME.
I'M PICKING UP A LOT OF PICKINESS REGARDING OFFICES PARTIES...
...BUT IT'S BEING HELPFUL.
NO, WELL. I'M JUST SAYING YOU SHOULDN'T WASTE OPPORTUNITIES FOR COMMUNICATING OUTSIDE THE WORKPLACE.
IF YOU MAKE USE OF THEM, YOUR TEAM'S BOND WILL STRENGTHEN.
AH. I HAD SO MUCH FUN TODAY.

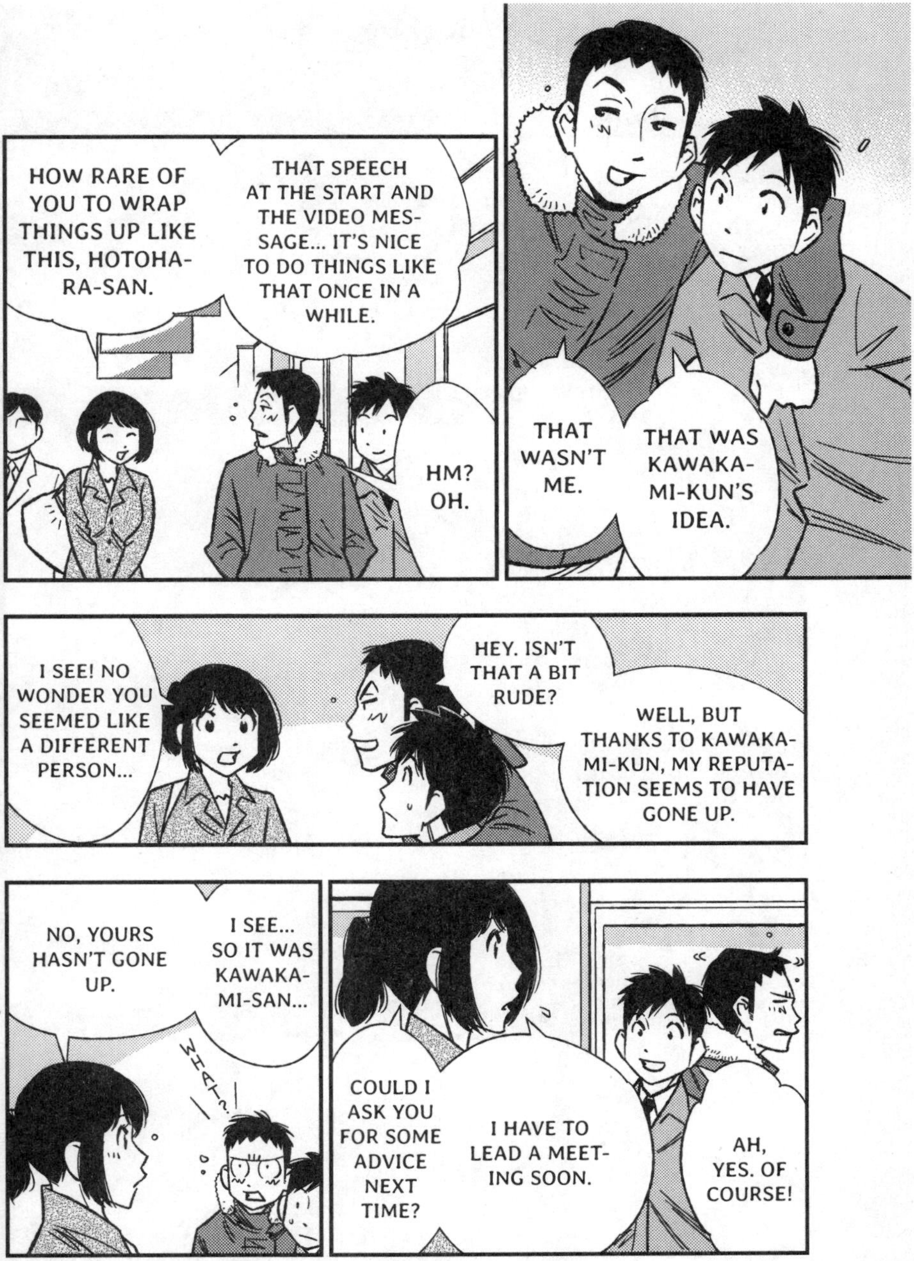

HOW RARE OF YOU TO WRAP THINGS UP LIKE THIS, HOTOHA-RA-SAN.
THAT SPEECH AT THE START AND THE VIDEO MES-SAGE... IT'S NICE TO DO THINGS LIKE THAT ONCE IN A WHILE.
HM? OH.
THAT WASN'T ME.
THAT WAS KAWAKA-MI-KUN'S IDEA.
I SEE! NO WONDER YOU SEEMED LIKE A DIFFERENT PERSON...
HEY. ISN'T THAT A BIT RUDE?
WELL, BUT THANKS TO KAWAKA-MI-KUN, MY REPUTA-TION SEEMS TO HAVE GONE UP.
NO, YOURS HASN'T GONE UP.
I SEE... SO IT WAS KAWAKA-MI-SAN...
WHAT?!
I HAVE TO LEAD A MEET-ING SOON.
COULD I ASK YOU FOR SOME ADVICE NEXT TIME?
AH, YES. OF COURSE!

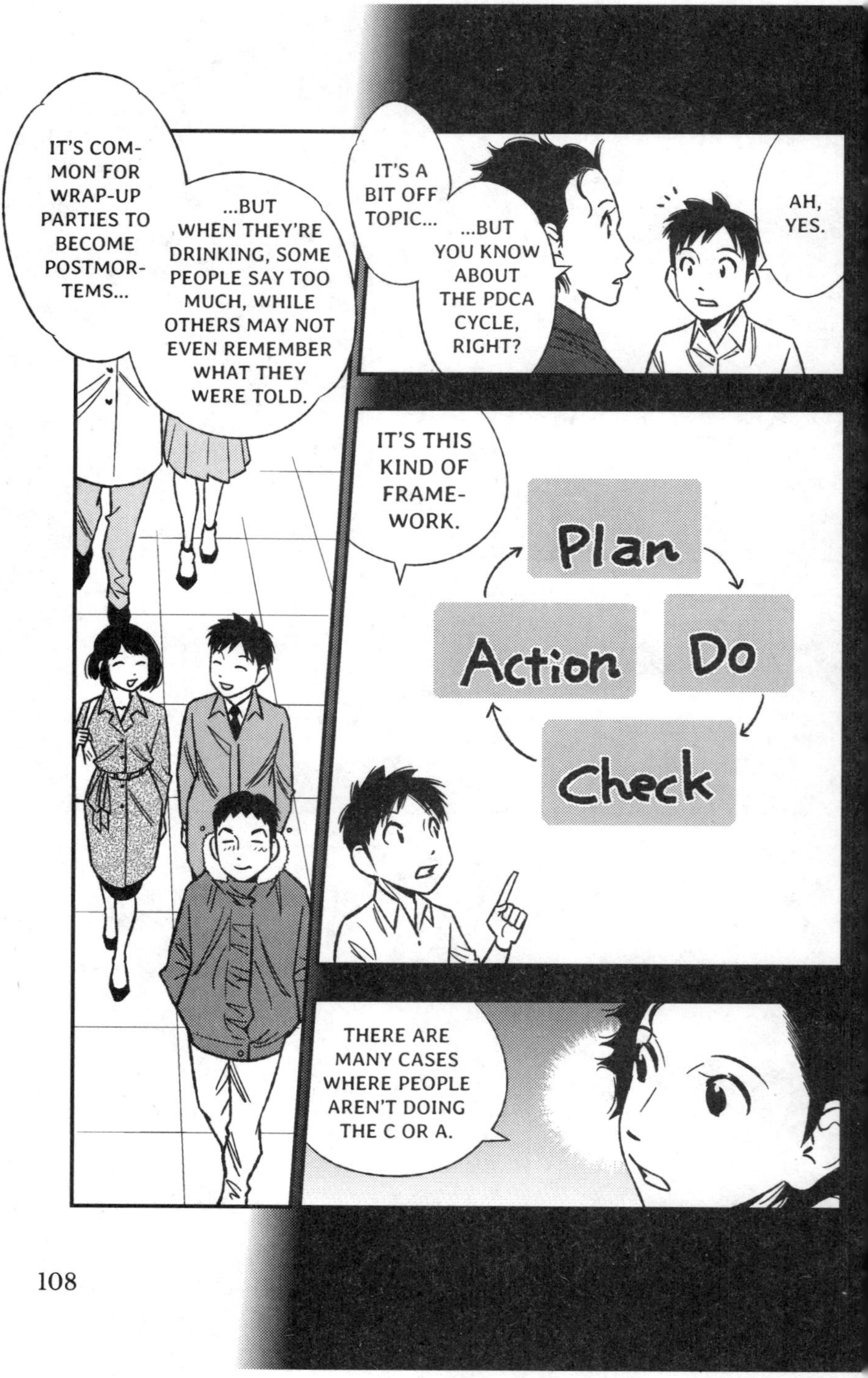

IT'S COMMON FOR WRAP-UP PARTIES TO BECOME POSTMORTEMS...
...BUT WHEN THEY'RE DRINKING, SOME PEOPLE SAY TOO MUCH, WHILE OTHERS MAY NOT EVEN REMEMBER WHAT THEY WERE TOLD.
IT'S A BIT OFF TOPIC...
...BUT YOU KNOW ABOUT THE PDCA CYCLE, RIGHT?
AH, YES.
IT'S THIS KIND OF FRAMEWORK.
Plan
Do
Check
Action
THERE ARE MANY CASES WHERE PEOPLE AREN'T DOING THE C OR A.

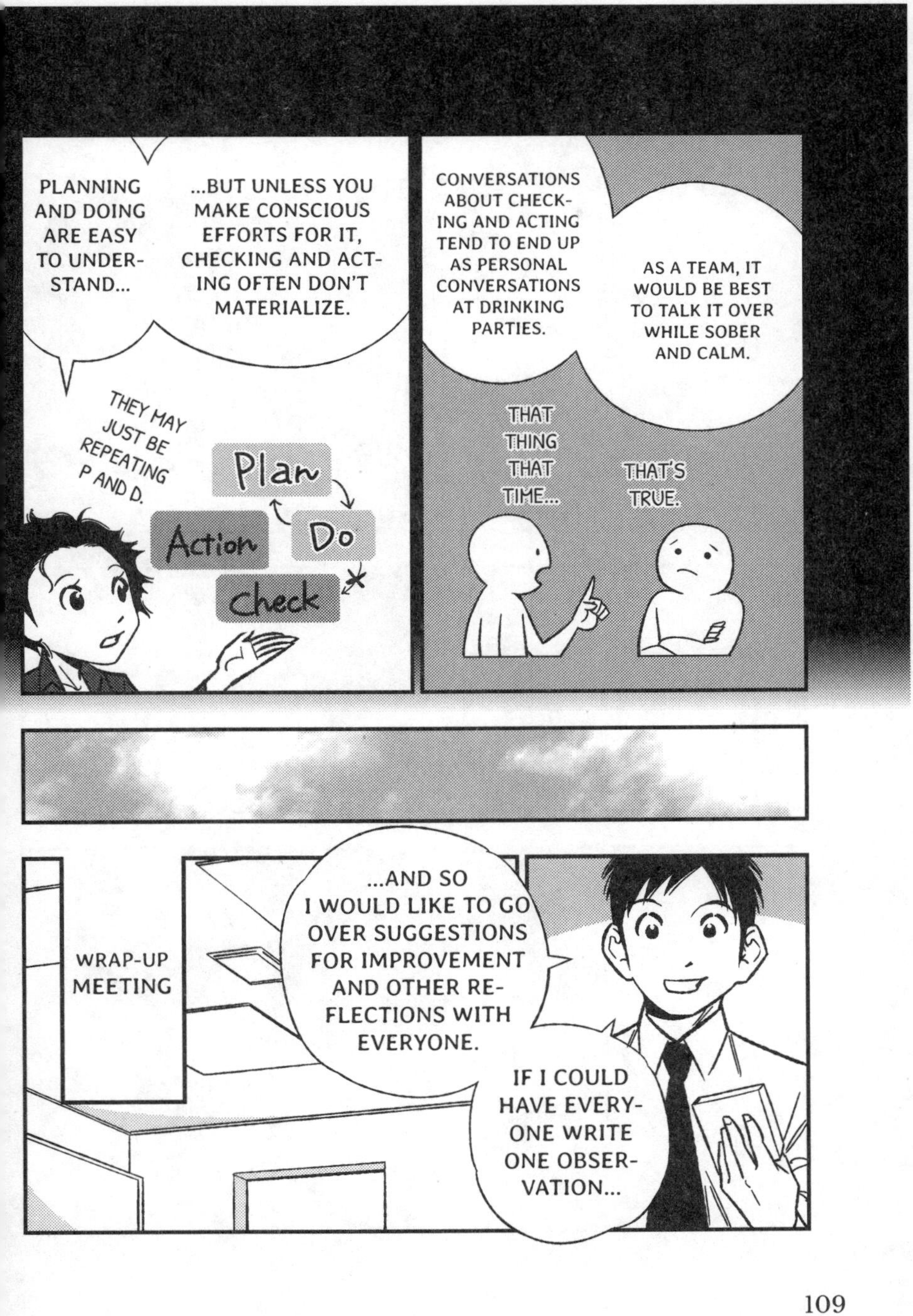
PLANNING AND DOING ARE EASY TO UNDER-STAND...
...BUT UNLESS YOU MAKE CONSCIOUS EFFORTS FOR IT, CHECKING AND ACT-ING OFTEN DON'T MATERIALIZE.
THEY MAY JUST BE REPEATING P AND D.
Plan
Do
Check
Action
CONVERSATIONS ABOUT CHECK-ING AND ACTING TEND TO END UP AS PERSONAL CONVERSATIONS AT DRINKING PARTIES.
AS A TEAM, IT WOULD BE BEST TO TALK IT OVER WHILE SOBER AND CALM.
THAT THING THAT TIME...
THAT'S TRUE.
WRAP-UP MEETING
...AND SO I WOULD LIKE TO GO OVER SUGGESTIONS FOR IMPROVEMENT AND OTHER RE-FLECTIONS WITH EVERYONE.
IF I COULD HAVE EVERY-ONE WRITE ONE OBSER-VATION...

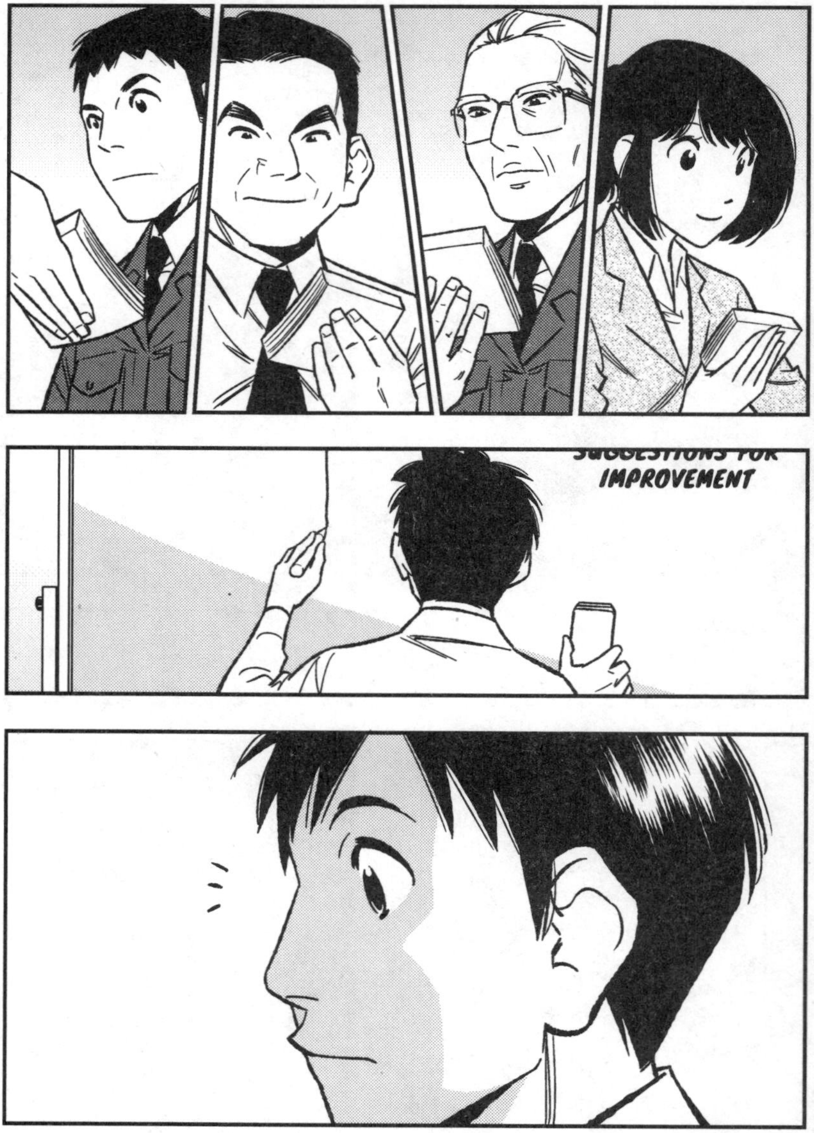
SUGGESTIONS FOR
IMPROVEMENT

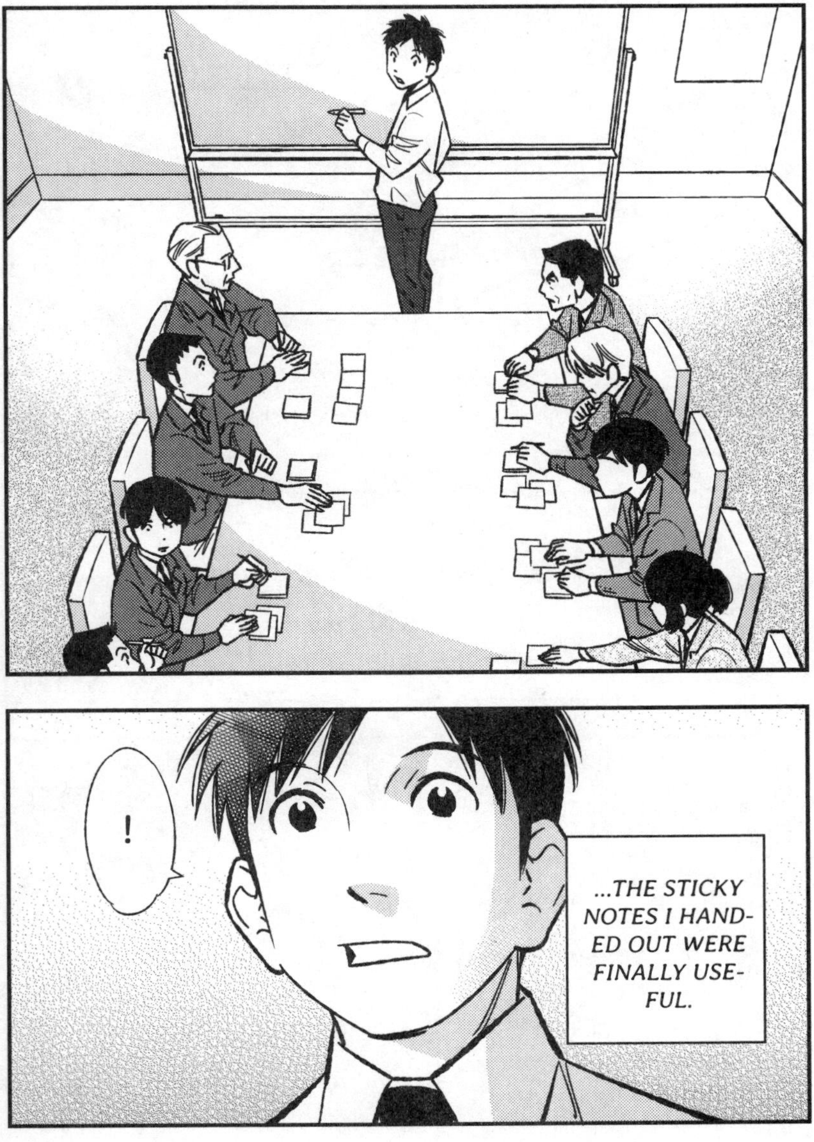
!
...THE STICKY NOTES I HANDED OUT WERE FINALLY USEFUL.

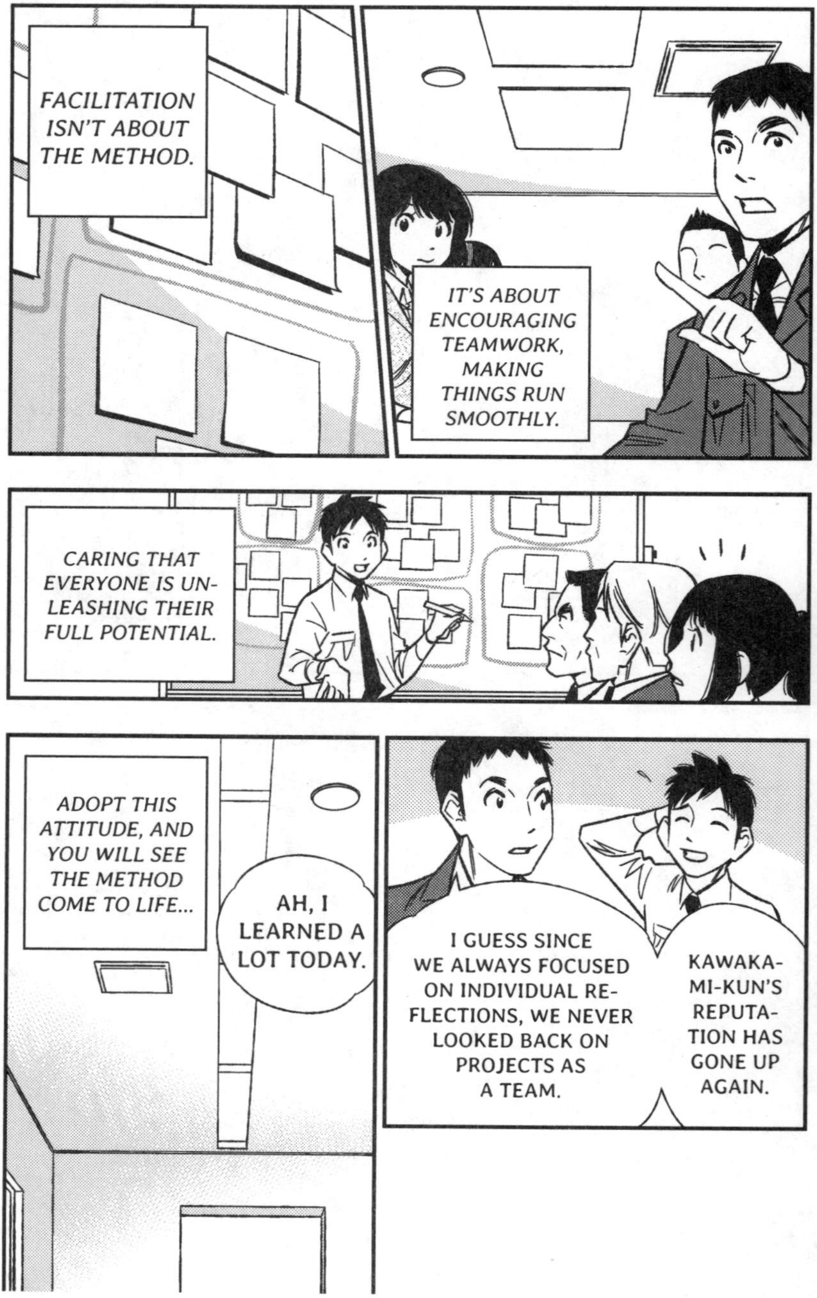
FACILITATION ISN'T ABOUT THE METHOD.
IT'S ABOUT ENCOURAGING TEAMWORK, MAKING THINGS RUN SMOOTHLY.
CARING THAT EVERYONE IS UN-LEASHING THEIR FULL POTENTIAL.
ADOPT THIS ATTITUDE, AND YOU WILL SEE THE METHOD COME TO LIFE...
AH, I LEARNED A LOT TODAY.
I GUESS SINCE WE ALWAYS FOCUSED ON INDIVIDUAL RE-FLECTIONS, WE NEVER LOOKED BACK ON PROJECTS AS A TEAM.
KAWAKA-MI-KUN'S REPUTA-TION HAS GONE UP AGAIN.

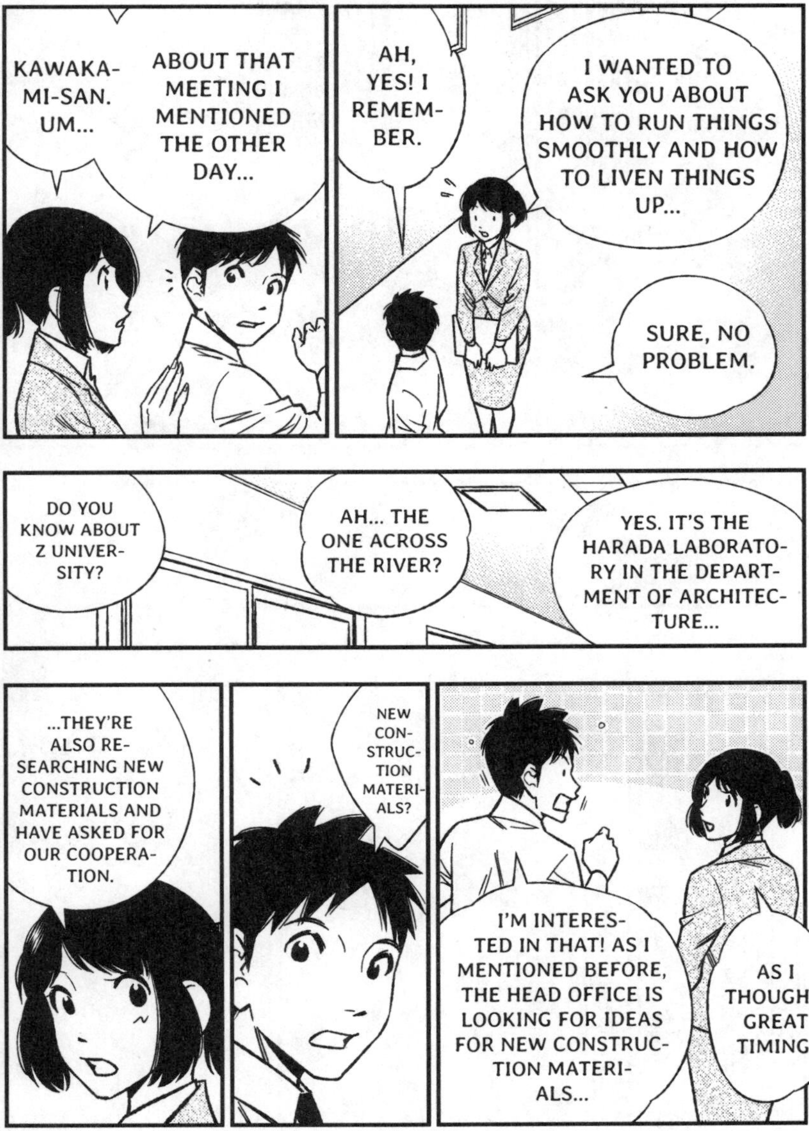
KAWAKA-MI-SAN. UM...
ABOUT THAT MEETING I MENTIONED THE OTHER DAY...
AH, YES! I REMEMBER.
I WANTED TO ASK YOU ABOUT HOW TO RUN THINGS SMOOTHLY AND HOW TO LIVEN THINGS UP...
SURE, NO PROBLEM.
DO YOU KNOW ABOUT Z UNIVERSITY?
AH... THE ONE ACROSS THE RIVER?
YES. IT'S THE HARADA LABORATORY IN THE DEPARTMENT OF ARCHITECTURE...
...THEY'RE ALSO RESEARCHING NEW CONSTRUCTION MATERIALS AND HAVE ASKED FOR OUR COOPERATION.
NEW CONSTRUCTION MATERIALS?
I'M INTERESTED IN THAT! AS I MENTIONED BEFORE, THE HEAD OFFICE IS LOOKING FOR IDEAS FOR NEW CONSTRUCTION MATERIALS...
AS I THOUGHT. GREAT TIMING.

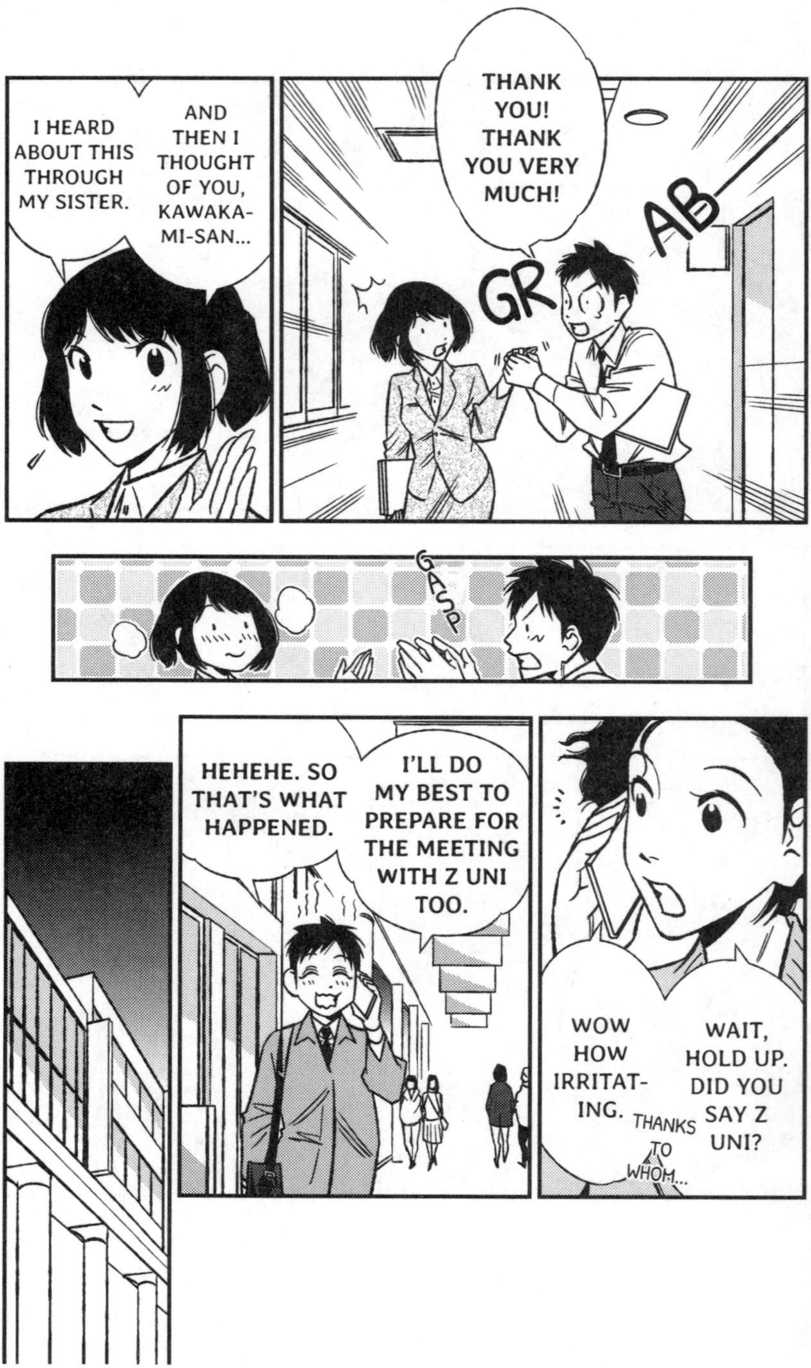
I HEARD ABOUT THIS THROUGH MY SISTER.
AND THEN I THOUGHT OF YOU, KAWAKA-MI-SAN...
THANK YOU! THANK YOU VERY MUCH!
GRAB
GASP
HEHEHE. SO THAT'S WHAT HAPPENED.
I'LL DO MY BEST TO PREPARE FOR THE MEETING WITH Z UNI TOO.
WAIT, HOLD UP. DID YOU SAY Z UNI?
WOW HOW IRRITAT-ING.
THANKS TO WHOM...

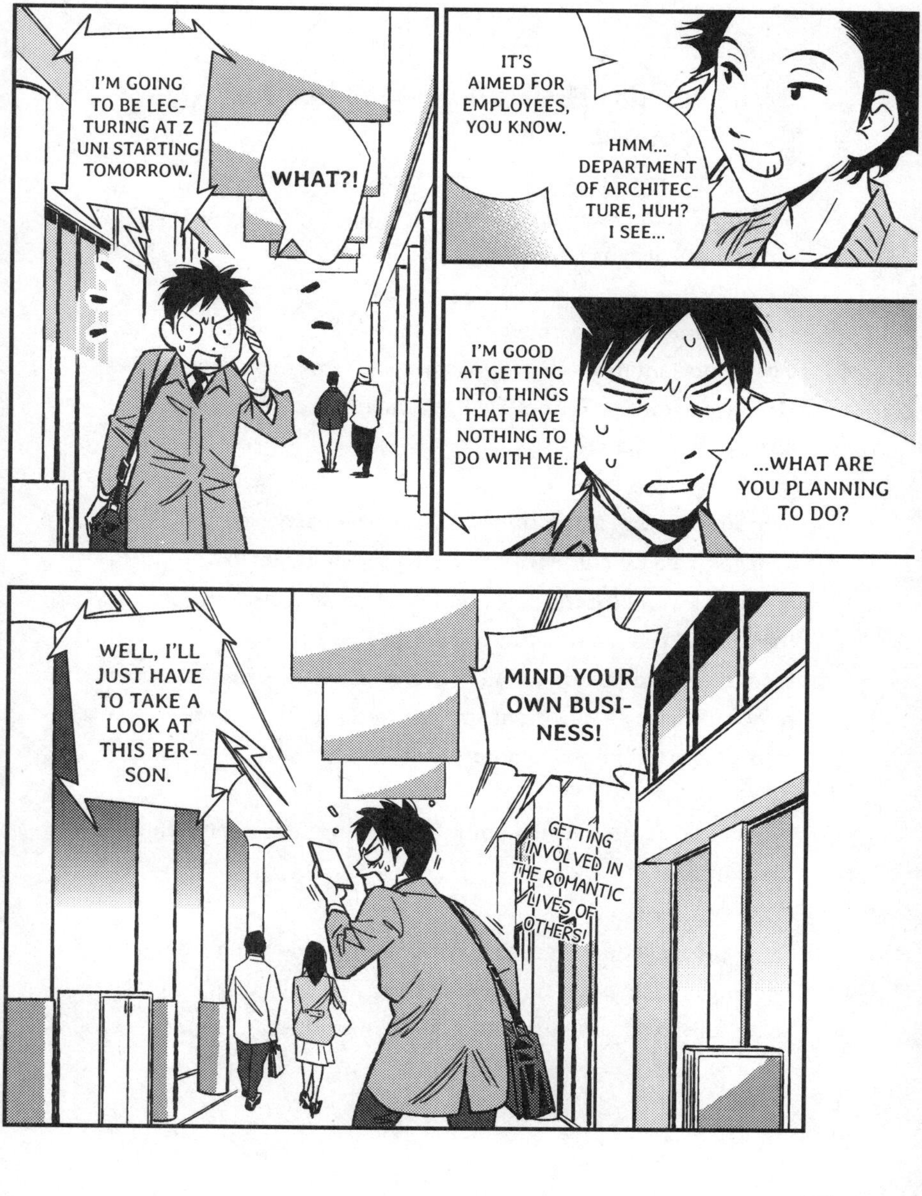
I'M GOING TO BE LECTURING AT Z UNI STARTING TOMORROW.
WHAT?!
IT'S AIMED FOR EMPLOYEES, YOU KNOW.
HMM... DEPARTMENT OF ARCHITECTURE, HUH? I SEE...
I'M GOOD AT GETTING INTO THINGS THAT HAVE NOTHING TO DO WITH ME.
...WHAT ARE YOU PLANNING TO DO?
WELL, I'LL JUST HAVE TO TAKE A LOOK AT THIS PERSON.
MIND YOUR OWN BUSINESS!
GETTING INVOLVED IN THE ROMANTIC LIVES OF OTHERS!

7 Everyday Facilitation—Not Just for Meetings

As shown in the manga, facilitation skills are great for meetings, but you can also use them in other contexts.

For example, even work functions can be an avenue for facilitation! The important thing is that your preparations match the scene. Here are a few tips for practicing facilitation at some different types of work functions.

Work Function Facilitation ①: Welcome Party
The goal of a welcome party is for everyone to get to know the new employees, and for the new employees to get more familiar with their coworkers, so the important thing here is self-introductions from both sides. Everyone feels more than a little nervous when they're entering a new environment, and a lot of that nervousness stems from not knowing others well.

Introductions should start with the current staff rather than the newcomers.

Once the newcomers get to know the team to some extent, it becomes much easier for them to relax and talk about themselves, so be sure to take the time to properly introduce everyone.

Work Function Facilitation ②: End-of-Year Party

I recommend setting up an activity that everyone can participate in and that doesn't put people on the defensive. Creating opportunities for team members to interact with each other in new ways, without letting them get stuck in a rut, is important for a successful team. If you can get everyone to work together on something that encourages them to show different sides of themselves, they can start to discover new things about each other.

Work Function Facilitation ③: Wrap-Up Party

Of course, at these parties you always need a celebratory toast, but it's also a great opportunity to praise each team member individually for their contribution and hard work. If you feel too embarrassed to say it out loud, I recommend writing small letters to them.

Save the criticisms and points for improvement for a work meeting, when everyone is sober.

Work Function Facilitation ④: A Regular Drinking Party

The standard "let's go out for a drink." For these, it's best to set an ending time and wrap it up straightaway when that time comes. Just like when you eat, drink in moderation. If cutting it off makes you feel like you haven't quite talked enough yet, it's probably the perfect timing.

Drinking parties, when used well, can become a good opportunity to bring the team together. Let's get the team going with good facilitation.

Pointer Lesson 3

The PDCA Facilitation Cycle

PDCA was originally proposed as a method of quality control and production management. The cycle is made up of four stages: Plan, Do, Check, and Act. The more you cycle through it, the better the result should become. However, teams often find themselves not able to complete this cycle smoothly, with many getting stuck in a cycle between the "Plan" and "Do" stages.

"In my team, I think a lot of projects are left unfinished, just like in the manga."

I think that's the case with many teams. Speaking in terms of the PDCA cycle, everyone comes together for the "Plan" stage, but teams will rarely do their "Check." For example, you'll find that most teams do not have project review meetings. Most meetings are concerned with a single stage: "Plan." They are meetings to decide on what needs to be done, or how to proceed. That, or meetings to discuss the progress of a project, but most teams rarely hold meetings to discuss the project after it has been completed.

Since teams aren't taking a step back and asking, "So how did that go?" the "Act," or improvement step, varies greatly from person to person. It's not a problem for team members who are already conscientious of making improvements as they work, but the workplace is full of inexperienced workers who don't realize that there are improvements to be made in the first place.

I used to work in sales in the construction and IT industries, and I really regret the fact that we never held review meetings after a big sale. There must have been opportunities for learning, studying, and improving after each project, but we never created opportunities needed to capitalize on them.

"So the parts of the project before the sale tended to be prioritized?"

That's right. That's why I think that if there's no one there to say, "Let's do this because it's necessary," and if no one puts the system in place, review meetings will simply not happen. What points do we need to reflect on? What adjustments should we make in the future? You need to make a time and place to answer these questions.

It may be tough to make the time solely for this reason, but it should be possible to hold a review meeting at least once a quarter.

In the research for meeting improvement, participants were asked to hold a meeting with the theme "meeting challenges and remedies," and the prevailing opinion of team members in these meetings was, "What our company is doing now is sufficient." The truth is that most people are fed up with regular meetings and would rather not take part if possible. These meetings take up a large amount of time for a large number of people, so they have the potential to be an enormous waste. Even though everyone feels like it's a problem, it's so ingrained in their daily life that they just soldier on without even thinking about it. If you'd like to change this, all you have to do is wait for the opportunity to hold a review with the theme of "meetings." There are quite a few people who say that this worked for them when they tried it at their workplace.

I would like you to create these opportunities to reflect and improve. Use themes appropriate to your workplace and what you think might need improvement, such as "sales issues and improvement measures," "education," or "the on-site environment."

"If it was a failed project, or if it was an issue that caused trouble for their workmates, there will be some team members who won't want to review it, right?"

Yes, that's true! They'll say something such as, "Please, don't bring it up again..." right?

In the cases where the project didn't go well, you have to take steps to make sure the review doesn't just turn into a blame game. For example, if a company's multiple sales branches gather for a meeting, there will be some that have met their sales quotas and some that haven't, all to different levels of severity. Teams that didn't make their quotas obviously won't want to bring it up. However, it's often the case that teams that did meet their quota also won't bring it up either, so as to not run the risk of looking arrogant. However, their results and success story not being shared means the offices that failed to meet their quotas aren't able to learn anything or garner any tips on how they might improve. In that case, I don't think there's any point holding a meeting in the first place. If it's going to be held regardless, we should make it a meaningful time for everyone. I think that this is the exact situation where we need a facilitator to draw out and promote a useful discussion.

8 Organizing People and Setting a Mood with Desk Layouts

You've gathered your team and started the meeting. However, nobody's really sharing their opinions.

This may be due to the desk placement.

If you want all of your participants to feel relaxed when speaking up, it is important to give them a setting that doesn't make them feel nervous. Let me provide you with a few effective meeting room layouts.

○ The Hollow Square Layout

This is a common layout used in meetings. Since everyone can see each other, anyone can become the speaker. However, if there are a large number of people, this layout has the tendency to become quite large, with people sitting a long way from each other. Additionally, since it creates a large empty space in the middle, you would require a large room.

○ The U-shape Layout

You set the desks down on three sides, as if you're drawing the letter U. Like the hollow square layout, you can see everyone's face, with the key difference being that the speaker is able to stand in front of all of the desks. They can also speak to each participant individually, so it's a nice layout that allows the speaker to easily interact with everyone.

Decide based on the objective and the number of people!

Meeting room layout

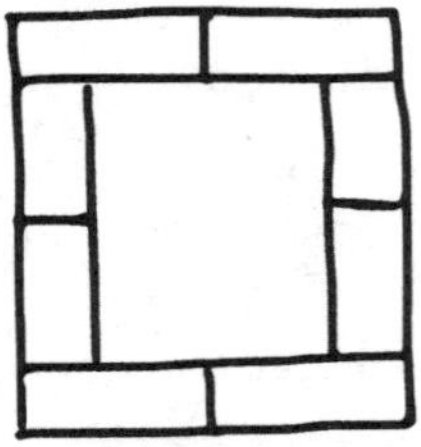

① Hollow Square Layout

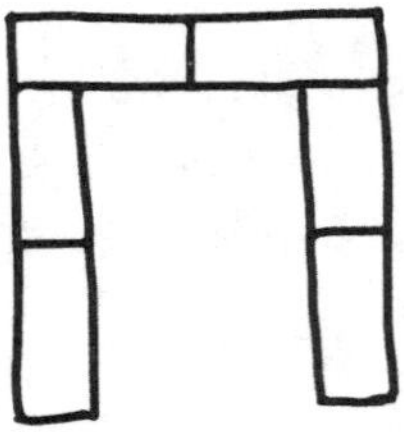

② U-Shape Layout

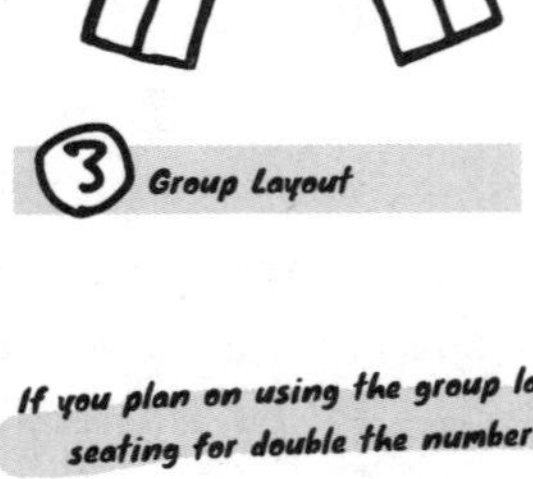

③ Group Layout

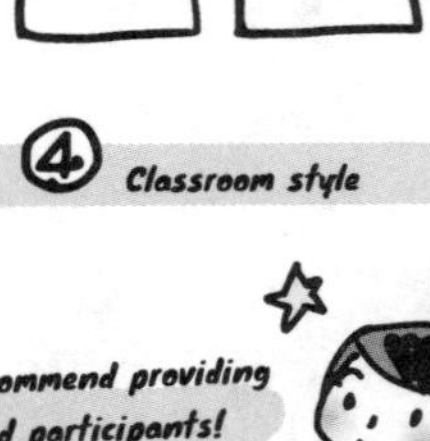

④ Classroom style

If you plan on using the group layout, I recommend providing seating for double the number of expected participants!

○ **The Group Layout**

This is a layout that creates groups of four to six people. It's great for situations where there are a lot of people, but you want participants to be able to talk face-to-face. By arranging these desks radially, with the speaker's desk at the center, it creates a sense of unity.

○ **Classroom Style**

This is the layout where everyone faces forward, like you would in a classroom. Everyone faces the same direction, so this layout is best for situations where the speaker is predominantly just sharing information. A variant of this layout is the horseshoe layout, where the desks are laid out in concentric arcs, rather than straight lines. Participants are able to see the faces of those sitting directly opposite them, so this layout also creates a sense of unity inside the venue.

If you use a layout that's different from the usual, participants will walk in and think, "Wow, today's different," which can actually give them a fresh attitude during the meeting, too. Choose an appropriate layout for both the purpose of the meeting and the number of people.

9 Understanding Differences with Social Style Theory

"You only want to talk about your own opinion."
"I want you to speak up more, though!"

You'll encounter all kinds of people in meetings. Along with the people who speak their minds concisely, there are people who are reluctant to express their opinions at all and people who easily get emotional. If you want to draw out everyone's opinions in equal measure, you need to be able to handle each type individually. You need to figure out what their communication style is and take action accordingly.

Social style theory, proposed by sociologist David Merrill in the 1970s, is a social classification system consisting of four categories. You observe the person's external attitude, and classify them based on two axes: self-assertiveness and emotional expressiveness. We tend to think of emotions in terms of happiness, sadness, anger, and pleasure, but it's more fitting to view anger toward someone as a display of self-assertiveness.

I will now introduce the four types. As you read, try to keep in mind what your own type may be, as well as that of your coworkers.

Self-Assertive
Nice
So, in conclusion?
Driving
Expressive
Emotionally Expressive
I'm sorry
Analytical
Amiable

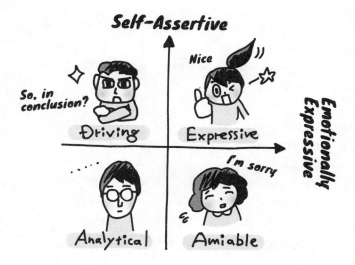

(1) Driving (High Self-Assertion / Low Emotional Expression): A realist type that likes doing things their way and dislikes being told what to do

They are born leaders, they love strategy and competition, and dislike being told what to do. They decide their own paths and don't require praise to feel motivated. The trick to getting the most out of this personality type is by **asking for their input**.

These driving types often communicate one-sidedly, such as when giving instructions. They dislike having to pay close attention to what others have to say and may unconsciously interrupt them.

They are easily irritated by indecision, and in such interactions may harshly demand that people get to their point. They take it for granted that they have to do their job well and are totally okay with not having their work be acknowledged but dislike having to file detailed reports.

In meetings they are prone to speak their minds without fear of confrontation, so they will often engage in conflict with others. They tend to think that work is work, so they like to separate personal relationships from their professional life and generally avoid sentimental topics. They also dislike being thoroughly questioned or controlled, so when aiming to extract ideas and input from them, it's best to ask for that input directly and pass them the ball.

How to Identify Them

They often speak quickly and logically. Driving types may be either talkative or speak very little, but in either case are very assertive. They are effective at creating and executing plans, but have a tendency to strongly oppose any sort of outside intervention. With a naturally stern expression, they often give off a "scary" impression and have a poker face that can be hard to read.

Keys to an Effective Interaction

It's often best to let them take the lead, asking for their opinions and input. Don't neglect to file reports with this type of boss in particular, opening them with your conclusion and keeping them as short as possible.

With these types of subordinates, if you communicate their goals clearly and fully entrust them with their work, they will become motivated. Instead of frequently checking in with them, it's more effective to agree on a deadline for reporting back on, and leave the work up to them until then. However, be sure to clearly convey their hierarchical obligations and work responsibilities, and entrust them with the work once they've clearly understood both.

Effective Questions
"What would you do in this situation?"
"I'd like to hear your opinion."
"Can you share your plans with me?"

How to Praise Them
With driving types, it's most effective to praise their results, or their subordinates and team, rather than themselves. "Thanks to your guidance, Bob did a great job." "That project came out perfect." Being entrusted with leadership roles and receiving high expectations also motivates driving types.

If you give them vague praise such as "Amazing" or "Great job!" before you've established a relationship of trust, driving types might suspect your praise to be dishonest. Constrastingly, this personality type tends to easily welcome compliments from people they respect or recognize as a superior.

(2) **Expressive (Self-Assertion: High / Emotional Expression: High):**
The type to feel like there's no point in it if it's not fun; they like to liven things up and act on instinct
Work and study have to be fun! Expressives love surprises, are very optimistic, and believe there's no point in fussing about details. They're the type to act on impulse, only stopping to consider later. The trick to getting the most out of this personality type is by **praising them.**

Expressive types love talking and dislike silence and embody the life of the party in various settings. Since they're averse to silent moments, they tend to be the first ones to speak up in meetings. They talk a lot and laugh a lot—even if they're told to quiet down, they have the ability to amicably laugh it off. They use a lot of sound effects and tend to exaggerate their stories. Since they speak on instinct, they aren't very good at explaining the basis of their opinions. They love being an influence on the people around them, so showing appreciation for their opinions tends to motivate them.

How to Identify Them
Expressives speak quickly and at a good pace. They are at ease with

public speaking, are talkative, and use a lot of sound effects in their speech. They gesticulate loudly and are also facially expressive.

However, since they have a strong desire to entertain, their tales can become rather tall. Further, though they are fun, entertaining people, when they go too far they may project a shallow personality. They're unable to suppress their facial expressions, to the extent that they may come across as kiddish at times.

Keys to an Effective Interaction

Enjoy the conversation—that's about it. Expressives enjoy over-the-top reactions such as "And? What happened then?" and "Right! Right!" or "Wow! I see!"—these types of reactions will liven up the conversation even further. Be direct when you want to end the conversation or when you want them to be quiet. They aren't the type to get hurt easily, so it may be effective to scold them on occasion. Expressives love being put in charge of projects or jobs, but they aren't at their best when being told what to do in a lot of detail.

These types of bosses tend to forget what they've heard. They also have a tendency to take commitments lightly, so be sure to properly manage risk with them. Also, rather than criticizing someone for their lack of clarity, they are happy to instead guide them through to a clear proposal.

Subordinates of this type are often fickle and forgetful (and don't feel guilty about it), so consider it necessary to check up on them regarding the work you want them to do. They feel motivated when relied upon to be the life of the party.

Effective Questions
"What do you think?"
"Do you have any opinions on this?"
"What do you want to do?"

How to Praise Them
They tend to feel happy about any sort of praise, even the ambiguous kind such as, "Amazing work," "Great effort," and "Nicely done." Compliments tend to simply motivate them, so it's good to reward them with praise. However, it's also easy for them to get carried away, so don't forget to check in on their work and point them toward any obligations they may neglect.

(3)　Amiable (Self-Assertion: Low / Emotional Expression: High): They're the type to do their best if it's for the sake of others; they want to be useful and are cooperative by nature

They don't tend to make waves in their interpersonal relationships and are calm personalities. They're the type to take notice if colleagues are struggling, to worry about what's expected of them, and to want to do their best for the sake of their peers. The trick to getting the most out of this personality type is by **showing appreciation for their assistance**. The smiling amiable types have a pleasant aura to them but struggle with saying no and, as a consequence, can get their hands pretty full. As such, amiables are fragile yet well-meaning people.

In meetings they are good listeners who nod attentively without pushing their opinion—consequently, they may find themselves taking on extra work without realizing it. They don't tend to express their own opinion, so words of encouragement such as, "It would be helpful if you shared your opinion" or "We appreciate your contributions" can be effective in getting the most out of amiables.

Amiables have a strong desire to get along with others and are unable to overlook those in need. They're the type who can't say no when asked upon, so they end up working overtime on a daily basis because of other people's work. Amiables often work jobs that revolve around interpersonal support, such as nurses, hygienists, clerical staff, or tech support, and tend to have a strong volunteering spirit. They always have a kind facial expression and are often said to have a healing spirit. Rather than expressing their own opinion, they value everyone's ideas and mutual harmony and as such don't make ideal leaders.

How to Identify Them
Amiables usually talk in a paced and soothing tone. They dislike public speaking and are anxious about how they are perceived by

others. They listen carefully to what others have to say and nod frequently in response. They don't often say no when asked to do something and are humble when praised.

Keys to an Effective Interaction

Convey your gratitude to amiables. This type is usually concerned about how they are perceived by others and whether their presence is necessary. They'll show growth through words such as, "We need you here," or "I'm glad you're here," and "Thank you for your efforts." They are averse to direct conversations, and when under pressure may not share their real opinion but rather what others expect to hear. When you want to know their real feelings, try to engage as gently and positively as possible.

At first glance, this type of boss may give the impression that they can't be relied upon, and often they themselves feel they aren't suited to be a leader. Since amiables are considerate and attentive, be sure to appreciate your boss in that regard, and politely offer them some help with managerial tasks. And of course, convey that feeling in both words and actions.

Subordinates of this type tend to feel uneasy about being entrusted with an entire job and being left to it by themselves. When you entrust a job to an amiable type, be sure to check up on them regularly and give them advice. Even then, words of appreciation are indispensable.

Examples of Effective Questions

"You're always such a big help. I'd like to ask you for your honest opinion about this matter, if it's all right with you."

"Thanks for your help the other day. I'd like to ask for some help today too, but please tell me how you feel about it."

"I'll ask for everyone's opinion, but what do you think of this?"

How to Praise Them

"Thank you for your efforts," "You're a lifesaver," "You're always such a big help," "I'm glad you're here." Frequently acknowledge their presence. Note that they usually don't express their dissatisfaction or make complaints—rather, they're the type to keep it inside. As such, if you make them work hard for a long time without any gratitude or appreciation, they may suddenly quit. Be sure to be attentive.

(4) Analytical (Self-Assertion: Low / Emotional Expression: Low):

An intellectual type that does everything exactly as planned

Analyticals always make plans and preparations beforehand. They value their own skills and try to make as few mistakes as possible. They do everything according to plan. They believe there is value in committing diligently to one's work. The trick to getting the most out of this personality type is by telling them to **"think over it by the next meeting."**

From the viewpoint of those around them, analytical types have the spirit of a craftsman. They work at their own pace, and complete their work diligently, without issue. They like thoroughly completing the work they're given, one task at a time. They don't like their work to be influenced by others, so they often choose jobs they can do by themselves. Depending on the analytical, some may not even mind working in complete silence, not talking to coworkers for days. They don't speak up much during meetings, but if they are given instructions and told what to discuss beforehand, they will prepare and participate accordingly.

How to Identify Them
They often speak slowly and don't talk too much. It may take them a lot of time to open up. A characteristic of analyticals is that they provide the most extensive answers to what's asked of them. And they will answer yes/no questions with a succinct yes or a no.

They aren't very physically expressive and don't frequently express their opinions either, so coworkers often feel they don't know what analyticals are thinking. They also don't particularly like talking about themselves.

Keys to an Effective Interaction
Take your time and be specific. When asking for their opinion, it's important to give them time to consider. If you want them to express their opinion at a meeting, let them know several

days in advance, if possible, and they will be readily prepared to participate by the meeting day. Make those questions as specific as possible. They tend to not express their opinion if they don't understand what they're being asked, what is expected of them, and for what reason. Once they start speaking, don't interrupt them and hear them out until the end.

Analytical bosses like reports based on detailed data. Be sure to convey your plans and work processes adequately. It's important that they trust you to have that down.

For these types of subordinates, be sure to give them detailed directions. They value accuracy and tend to dislike jobs that are handled half-heartedly. Also, they have a good memory of both what they were told and what they said, so they tend to dislike unnecessary interactions. They are good at managing ongoing projects and organizing information, and they'll be motivated when relied upon while simultaneously being valued.

Examples of Effective Questions

"This is the state of this project, right? Can you think of how to make it that way instead? Let me know at next week's meeting."
"What's the situation now, in regard to this month's sales goals?"
"Give me the consumer analysis results later."
"We plan on having the company head in this direction from now on, but could you give me feedback as someone who works here?"

"What do you think about X? I'll make some time for discussing this, so let me know how you feel then."

How to Praise Them
It is effective to specifically and objectively praise their results. Never give them ambiguous praise—if they won't understand why they're being praised, it won't resonate with them.
Analyticals are often proud of their own skills, so praise them for them. And even then, don't forget to be specific!

If you don't feel like you're any of these types, or if you feel like you're all of the above, you are the balanced type. You may tend to change your attitude based on the person or situation you're dealing with, regardless of your own feelings. This type of personality is very common in workplaces that handle affairs dispassionately and without displays of individuality, such as city halls, prefectural offices, and office administrations.

No type is either good or bad. By being aware of both your and your coworkers' personal tendencies and keeping in mind how to get the most out of them, you can moderate your approach. Social Styles are a convenient and easy-to-understand theory for this. For those who want to know more, I recommend deepening your understanding through books related to this topic.

HANDLING COMPLAINTS WITH GROW!

Opportunities to lead team members through problem-solving situations will present themselves at various times.

For example, if a subordinate complains or speaks up about their dissatisfaction, what you have is a chance to throw it back to them. After listening to what's bothering them, ask them about their ideal solution: **"What do you think should happen?"**

We tend to feel dissatisfaction when our ideals and reality are far apart. That is why you should make the gap between that ideal and reality clear, in order to solve the problem. At times like these, it's useful to use the **GROW model**. The GROW model is a framework that makes both the goal and the reality apparent. By analyzing the gap between them, we're able to draw out the options and affirm the will to solve the problem.

It can be helpful when tackling problems and anxieties.
It's common to start by focusing on the goal, but when it comes to problem-solving, it may be easier to start by understanding the **state of affairs**.

What's going on right now, and what do you think is the problem? Ideally speaking, what should things look like, and where should we aim for?

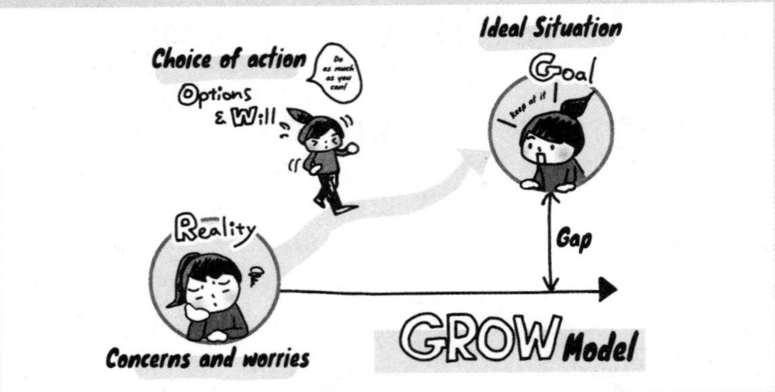
Ideal Situation
Goal
Keep at it
Choice of action
Do as much as you can!
Options
& Will
Reality
Gap
Concerns and worries
GROW Model

After clarifying the differences between those two, discuss the **options** for getting closer to your goal.

The point here is to **lay out as many options as possible.**

After drawing out a lot of ideas, the final step is to decide on specific measures and to confirm everyone's willingness to implement them. Let's summarize this part with the **effectiveness & implementation analysis**—i.e. visualize the opinions on the agenda and analyze the effectiveness and feasibility of each with A = high, B = moderate, and C = low. By doing so, you will end up with an effective problem-solving plan.

Listen to your coworkers' complaints and handle them with GROW. Be conscious of it on a daily basis, and continue to sharpen your coworkers' problem-solving ability.

PART 3

Applying Facilitation

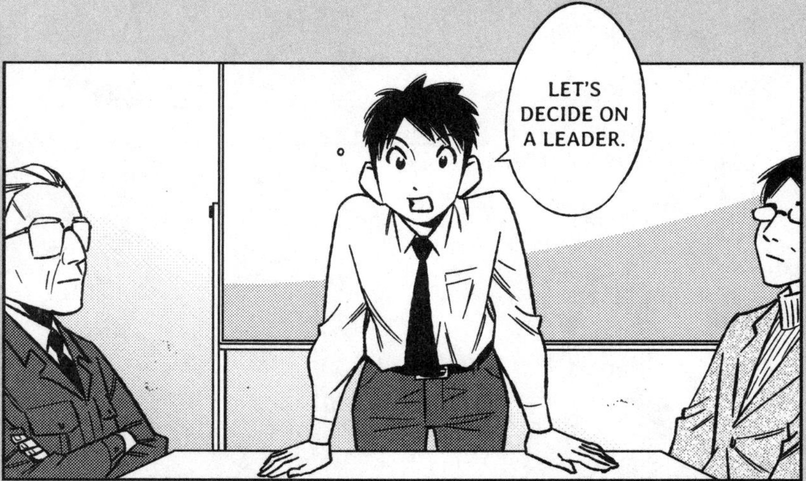
LET'S DECIDE ON A LEADER.

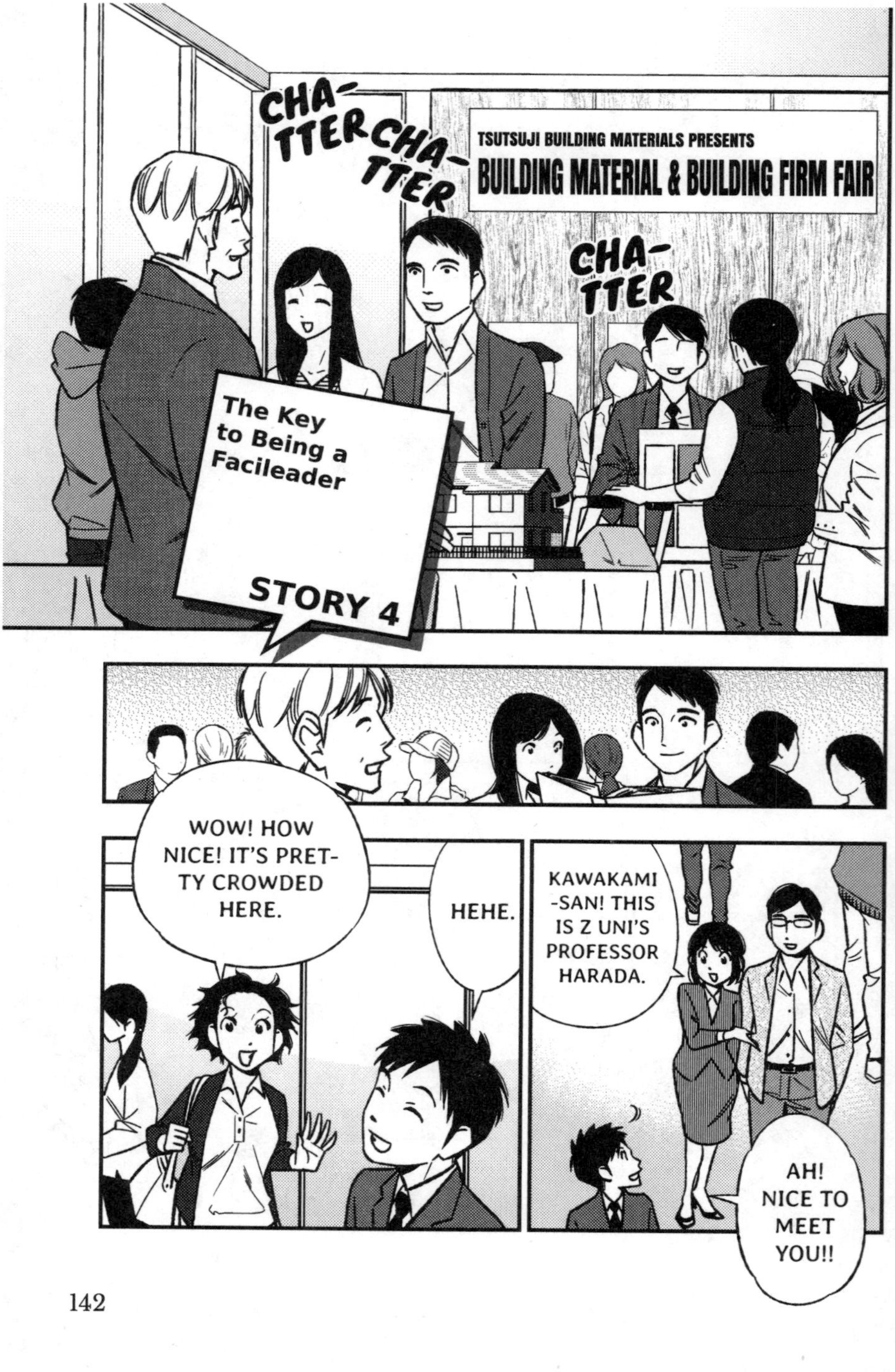
CHA-TTER CHA-TTER
TSUTSUJI BUILDING MATERIALS PRESENTS
BUILDING MATERIAL & BUILDING FIRM FAIR
CHA-TTER
The Key to Being a Facileader
STORY 4
WOW! HOW NICE! IT'S PRET-TY CROWDED HERE.
HEHE.
KAWAKAMI-SAN! THIS IS Z UNI'S PROFESSOR HARADA.
AH! NICE TO MEET YOU!!

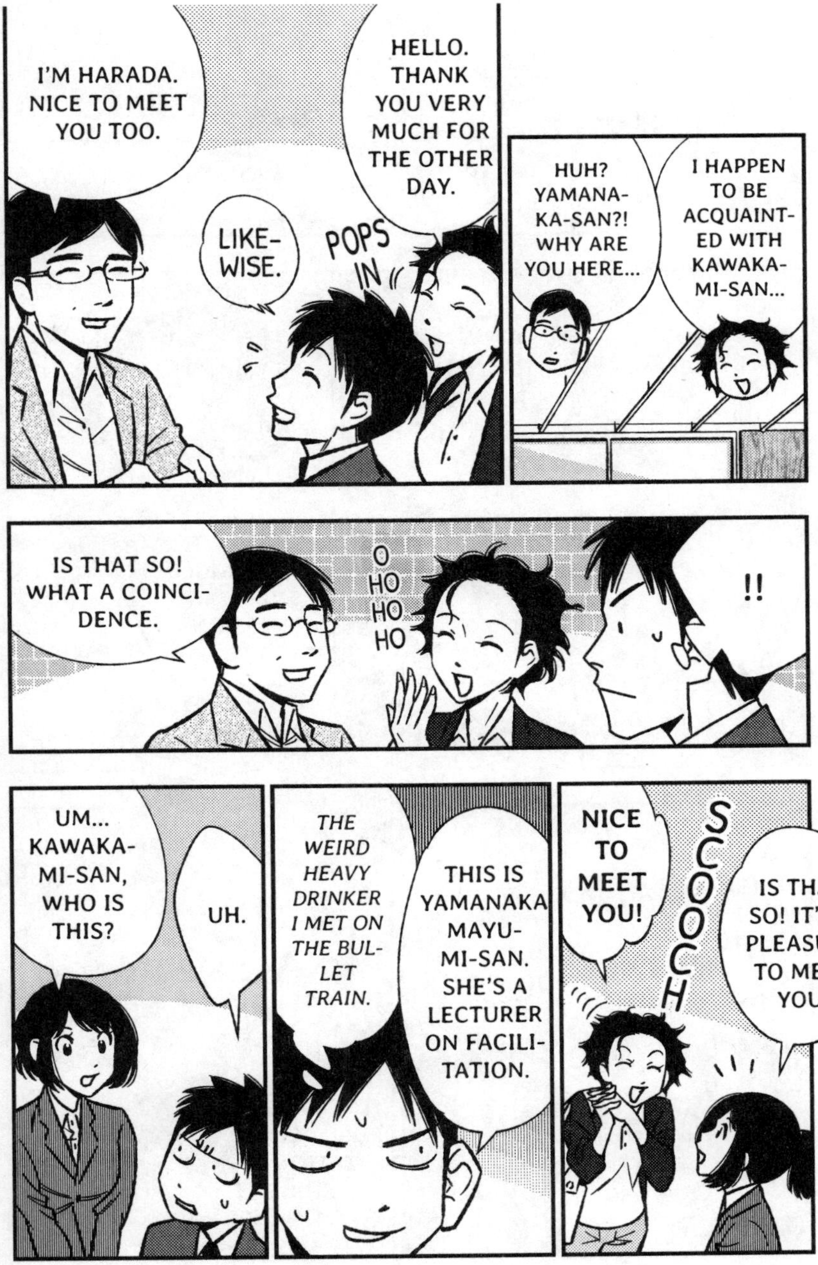
I'M HARADA. NICE TO MEET YOU TOO.
HELLO. THANK YOU VERY MUCH FOR THE OTHER DAY.
LIKE-WISE.
POPS IN
HUH? YAMANA-KA-SAN?! WHY ARE YOU HERE...
I HAPPEN TO BE ACQUAINT-ED WITH KAWAKA-MI-SAN...
IS THAT SO! WHAT A COINCI-DENCE.
O HO HO HO
!!
UM... KAWAKA-MI-SAN, WHO IS THIS?
UH.
THE WEIRD HEAVY DRINKER I MET ON THE BUL-LET TRAIN.
THIS IS YAMANAKA MAYU-MI-SAN. SHE'S A LECTURER ON FACILI-TATION.
NICE TO MEET YOU!
SCOOCH
IS THAT SO! IT'S A PLEASURE TO MEET YOU.

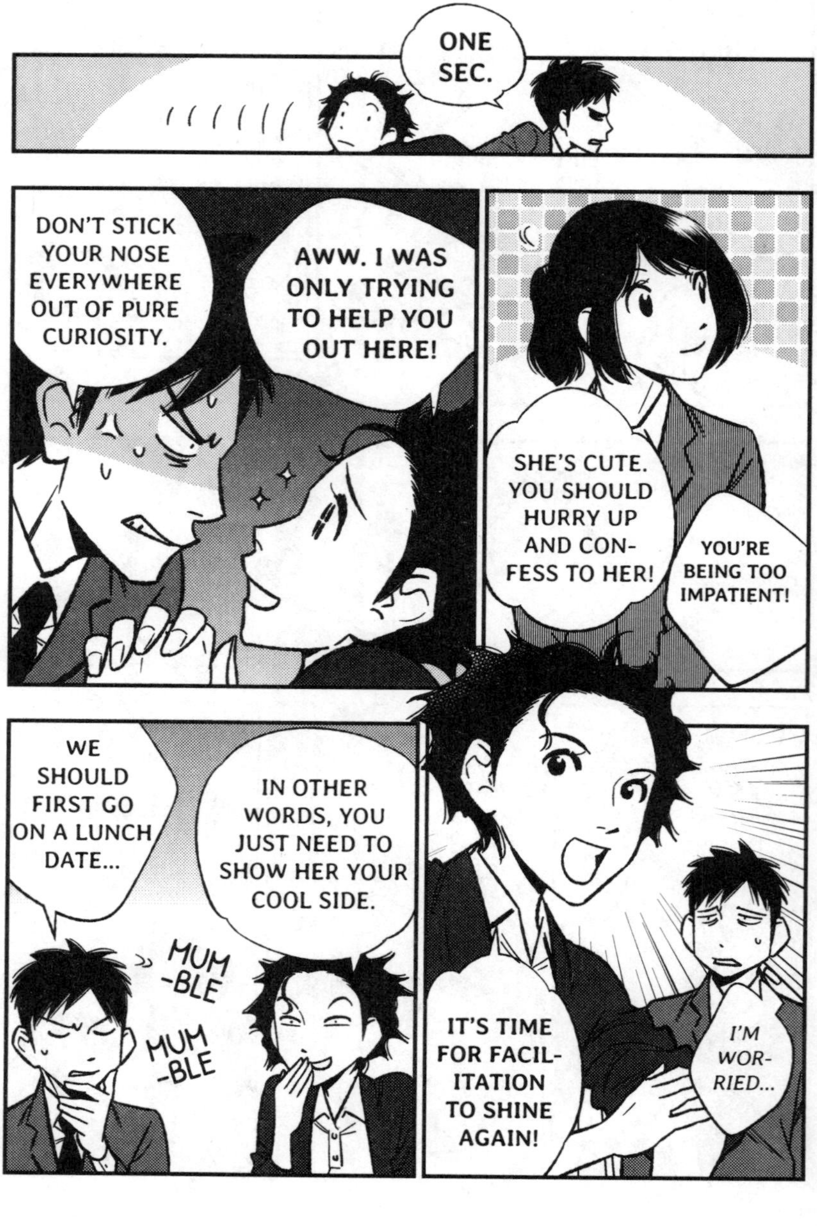
ONE SEC.
DON'T STICK YOUR NOSE EVERYWHERE OUT OF PURE CURIOSITY.
AWW. I WAS ONLY TRYING TO HELP YOU OUT HERE!
SHE'S CUTE. YOU SHOULD HURRY UP AND CON-FESS TO HER!
YOU'RE BEING TOO IMPATIENT!
WE SHOULD FIRST GO ON A LUNCH DATE...
MUM-BLE
MUM-BLE
IN OTHER WORDS, YOU JUST NEED TO SHOW HER YOUR COOL SIDE.
IT'S TIME FOR FACIL-ITATION TO SHINE AGAIN!
I'M WOR-RIED...

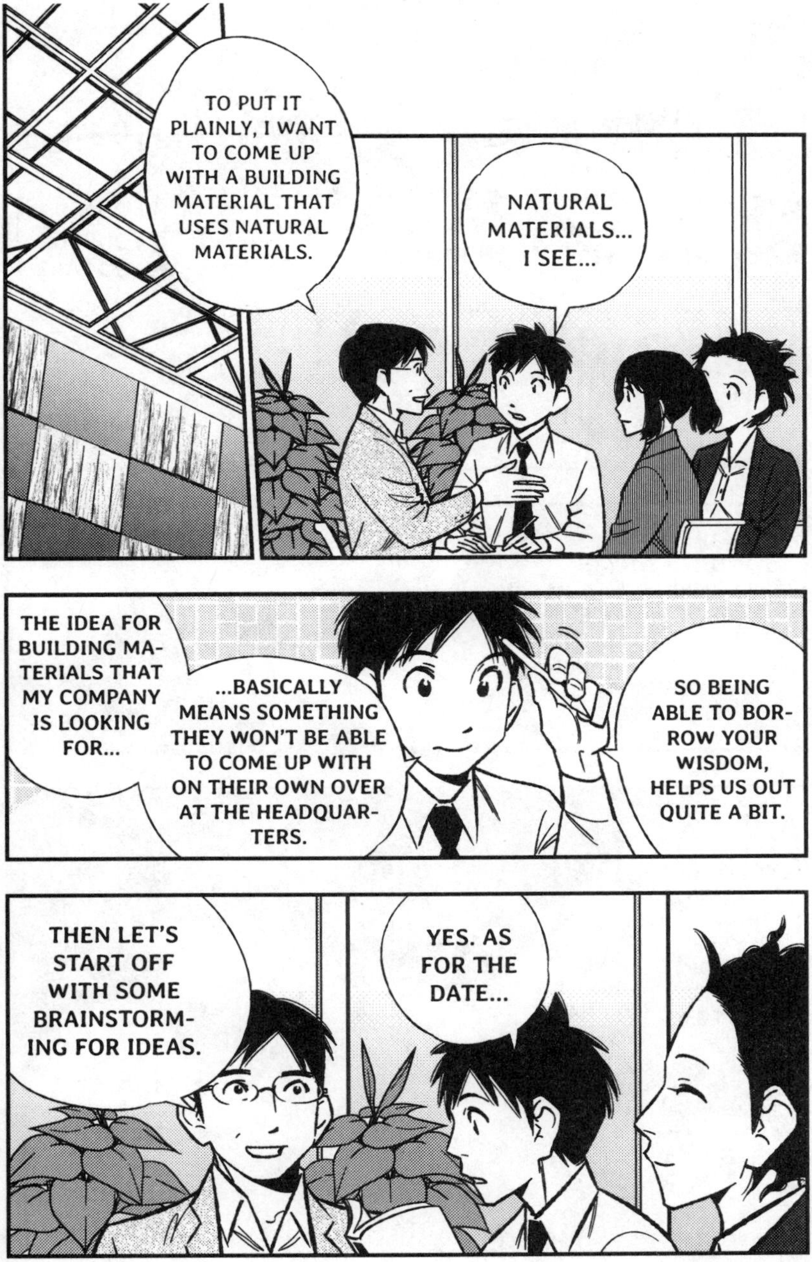
TO PUT IT PLAINLY, I WANT TO COME UP WITH A BUILDING MATERIAL THAT USES NATURAL MATERIALS.
NATURAL MATERIALS... I SEE...
THE IDEA FOR BUILDING MATERIALS THAT MY COMPANY IS LOOKING FOR...
...BASICALLY MEANS SOMETHING THEY WON'T BE ABLE TO COME UP WITH ON THEIR OWN OVER AT THE HEADQUARTERS.
SO BEING ABLE TO BORROW YOUR WISDOM, HELPS US OUT QUITE A BIT.
THEN LET'S START OFF WITH SOME BRAINSTORMING FOR IDEAS.
YES. AS FOR THE DATE...

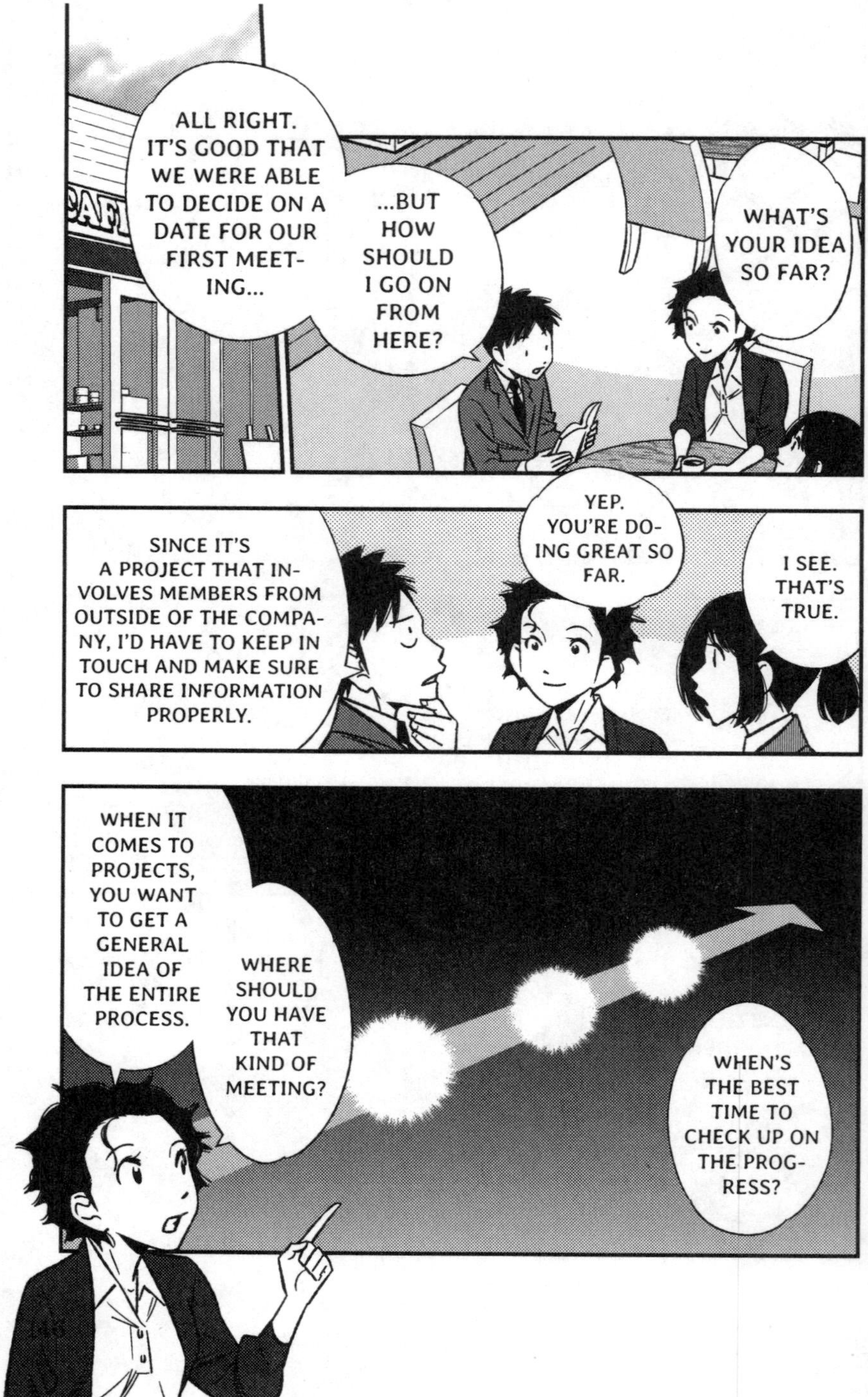
ALL RIGHT. IT'S GOOD THAT WE WERE ABLE TO DECIDE ON A DATE FOR OUR FIRST MEET-ING...
...BUT HOW SHOULD I GO ON FROM HERE?
WHAT'S YOUR IDEA SO FAR?
SINCE IT'S A PROJECT THAT IN-VOLVES MEMBERS FROM OUTSIDE OF THE COMPA-NY, I'D HAVE TO KEEP IN TOUCH AND MAKE SURE TO SHARE INFORMATION PROPERLY.
YEP. YOU'RE DO-ING GREAT SO FAR.
I SEE. THAT'S TRUE.
WHEN IT COMES TO PROJECTS, YOU WANT TO GET A GENERAL IDEA OF THE ENTIRE PROCESS.
WHERE SHOULD YOU HAVE THAT KIND OF MEETING?
WHEN'S THE BEST TIME TO CHECK UP ON THE PROG-RESS?

I SEE. SO YOU MAKE PLANS FOR NECESSARY MEETINGS BASED ON THE ENTIRETY OF IT.

YEP. IT'LL ACT AS DEADLINES FOR VARIOUS TASKS.

HM... I DO TALK BASED ON THE ENTIRETY OF MEETINGS SOMETIMES...

...BUT TO THINK I CAN DO THE SAME FOR PROJECTS.

I FEEL LIKE I'M GOING TO NEED A LOT OF IMAGINA-TION.

ENTIRE

AS EXPECT-ED OF YOU, KAWAKA-MI-KUN! YOU GET IT!

GLANCE GLANCE NICE!

THE WAY SHE'S TRYING TO PRAISE ME SEEMS SO FAKE.

THE OTHER IMPORTANT THING IS...

JUST MAKE SURE THIS DOESN'T AFFECT OUR ORIGINAL DUTY.

AND HOW LONG WILL THIS TAKE?

HUH! THIS SEEMS FUN. SHOULD I INVITE SOME-ONE?

MAYBE HIM... OR HER?

I WOULD LIKE TO DIS-CUSS THINGS UNTIL I AM SATISFIED.

147

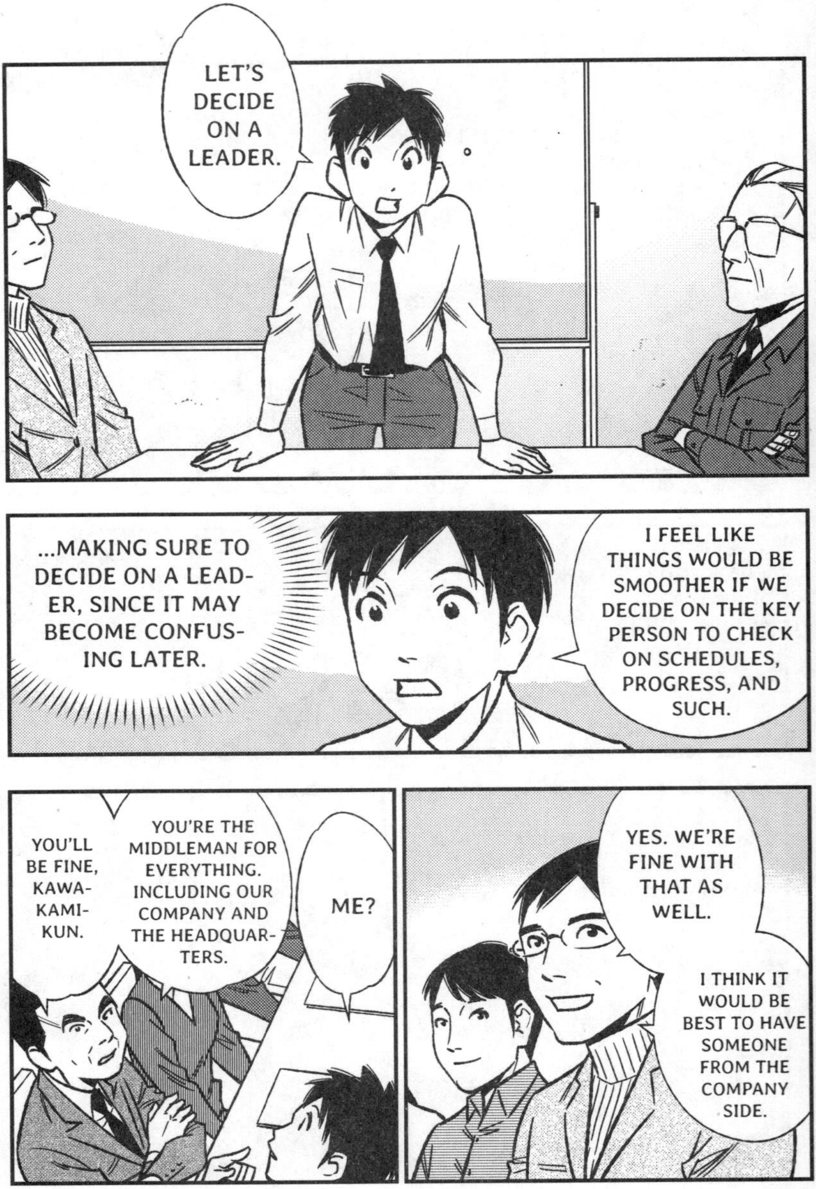

LET'S DECIDE ON A LEADER.
...MAKING SURE TO DECIDE ON A LEAD-ER, SINCE IT MAY BECOME CONFUS-ING LATER.
I FEEL LIKE THINGS WOULD BE SMOOTHER IF WE DECIDE ON THE KEY PERSON TO CHECK ON SCHEDULES, PROGRESS, AND SUCH.
YOU'RE THE MIDDLEMAN FOR EVERYTHING. INCLUDING OUR COMPANY AND THE HEADQUAR-TERS.
YOU'LL BE FINE, KAWA-KAMI-KUN.
ME?
YES. WE'RE FINE WITH THAT AS WELL.
I THINK IT WOULD BE BEST TO HAVE SOMEONE FROM THE COMPANY SIDE.

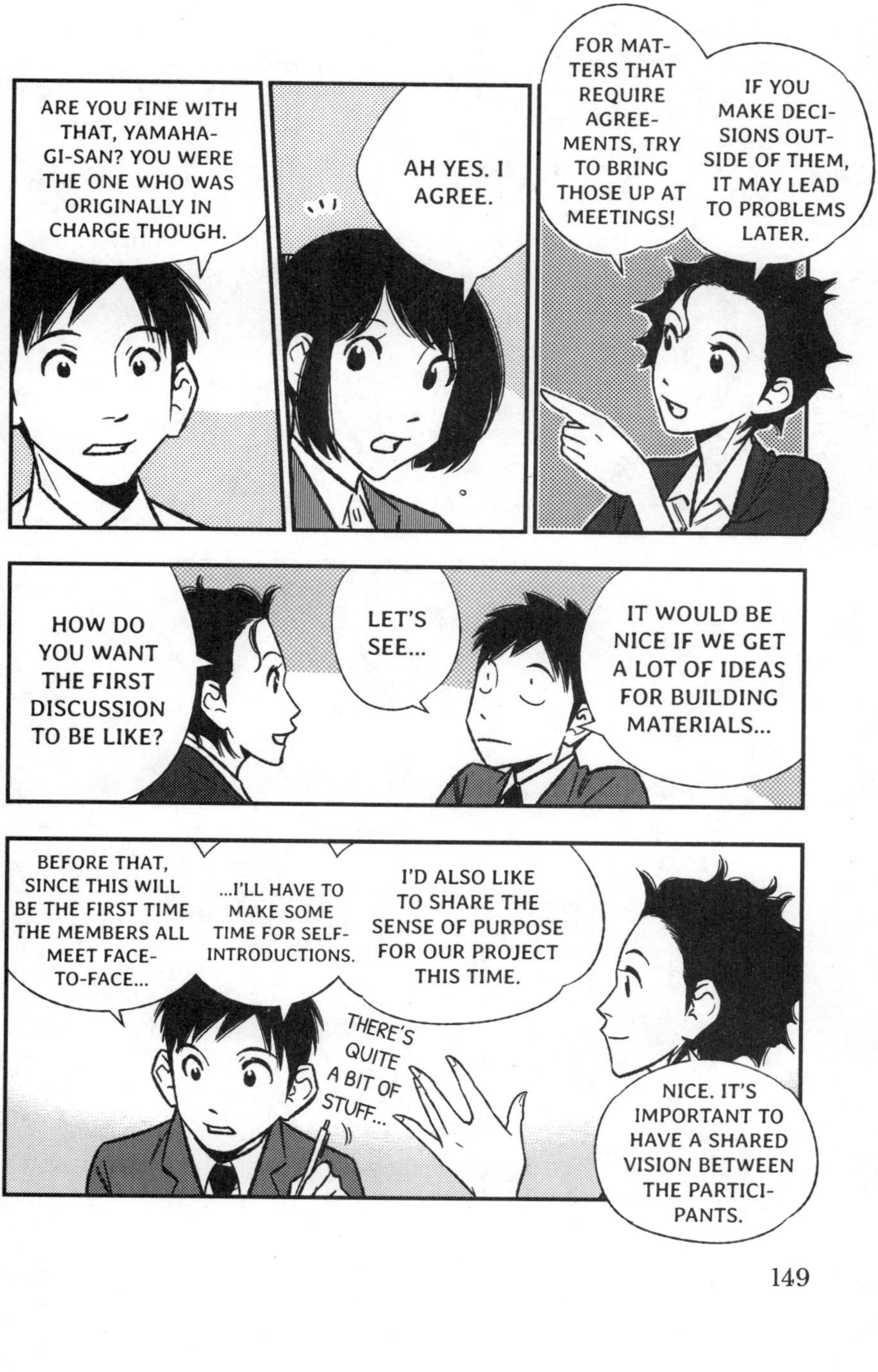
ARE YOU FINE WITH THAT, YAMAHAGI-SAN? YOU WERE THE ONE WHO WAS ORIGINALLY IN CHARGE THOUGH.
AH YES. I AGREE.
FOR MATTERS THAT REQUIRE AGREEMENTS, TRY TO BRING THOSE UP AT MEETINGS!
IF YOU MAKE DECISIONS OUTSIDE OF THEM, IT MAY LEAD TO PROBLEMS LATER.
HOW DO YOU WANT THE FIRST DISCUSSION TO BE LIKE?
LET'S SEE...
IT WOULD BE NICE IF WE GET A LOT OF IDEAS FOR BUILDING MATERIALS...
BEFORE THAT, SINCE THIS WILL BE THE FIRST TIME THE MEMBERS ALL MEET FACE-TO-FACE...
...I'LL HAVE TO MAKE SOME TIME FOR SELF-INTRODUCTIONS.
I'D ALSO LIKE TO SHARE THE SENSE OF PURPOSE FOR OUR PROJECT THIS TIME.
THERE'S QUITE A BIT OF STUFF...
NICE. IT'S IMPORTANT TO HAVE A SHARED VISION BETWEEN THE PARTICIPANTS.

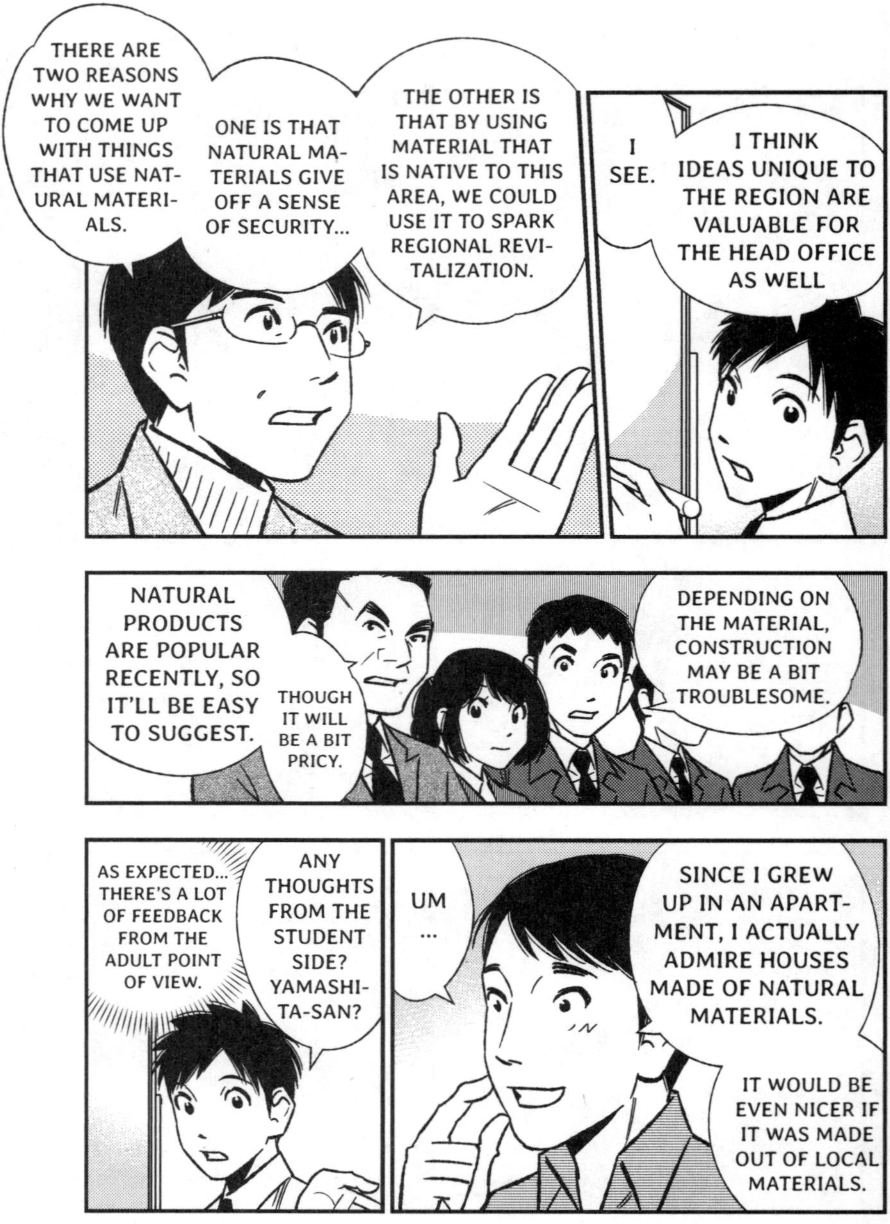
THERE ARE TWO REASONS WHY WE WANT TO COME UP WITH THINGS THAT USE NATURAL MATERIALS.
ONE IS THAT NATURAL MATERIALS GIVE OFF A SENSE OF SECURITY...
THE OTHER IS THAT BY USING MATERIAL THAT IS NATIVE TO THIS AREA, WE COULD USE IT TO SPARK REGIONAL REVITALIZATION.
I SEE.
I THINK IDEAS UNIQUE TO THE REGION ARE VALUABLE FOR THE HEAD OFFICE AS WELL
NATURAL PRODUCTS ARE POPULAR RECENTLY, SO IT'LL BE EASY TO SUGGEST.
THOUGH IT WILL BE A BIT PRICY.
DEPENDING ON THE MATERIAL, CONSTRUCTION MAY BE A BIT TROUBLESOME.
AS EXPECTED... THERE'S A LOT OF FEEDBACK FROM THE ADULT POINT OF VIEW.
ANY THOUGHTS FROM THE STUDENT SIDE? YAMASHITA-SAN?
UM ...
SINCE I GREW UP IN AN APARTMENT, I ACTUALLY ADMIRE HOUSES MADE OF NATURAL MATERIALS.
IT WOULD BE EVEN NICER IF IT WAS MADE OUT OF LOCAL MATERIALS.

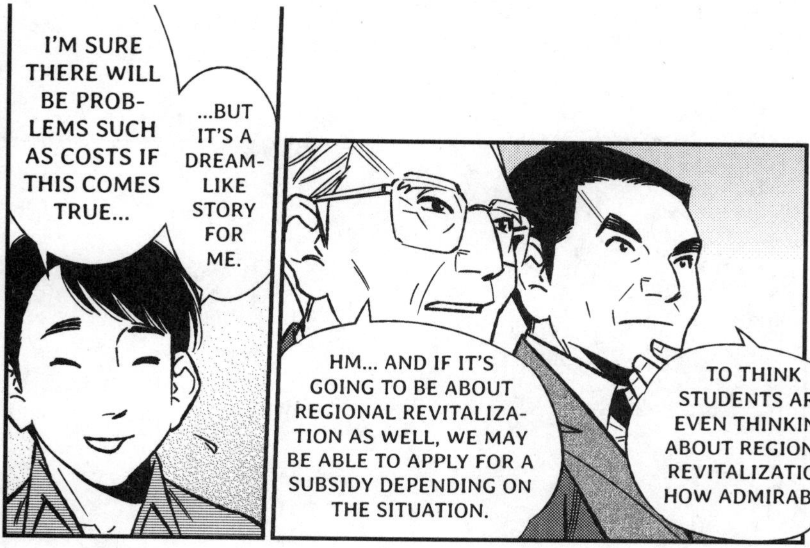
I'M SURE THERE WILL BE PROBLEMS SUCH AS COSTS IF THIS COMES TRUE...
...BUT IT'S A DREAM-LIKE STORY FOR ME.
HM... AND IF IT'S GOING TO BE ABOUT REGIONAL REVITALIZATION AS WELL, WE MAY BE ABLE TO APPLY FOR A SUBSIDY DEPENDING ON THE SITUATION.
TO THINK STUDENTS ARE EVEN THINKING ABOUT REGIONAL REVITALIZATION. HOW ADMIRABLE.

USE NATURAL MATERIALS IN ORDER TO CREATE A NEW BUILDING MATERIAL THAT CAN PROMOTE REGIONAL REVITALIZATION!

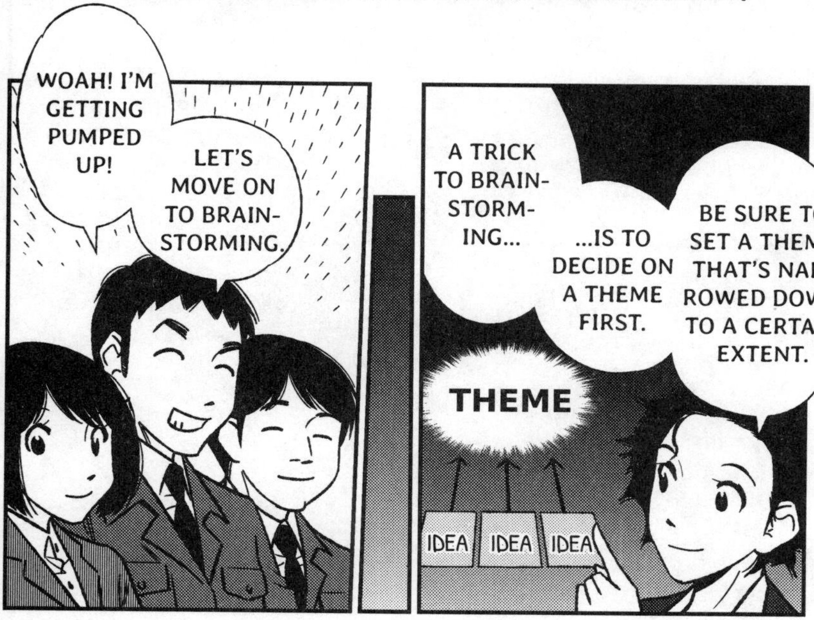
WOAH! I'M GETTING PUMPED UP!
LET'S MOVE ON TO BRAIN-STORMING.
A TRICK TO BRAIN-STORM-ING...
...IS TO DECIDE ON A THEME FIRST.
BE SURE TO SET A THEME THAT'S NARROWED DOWN TO A CERTAIN EXTENT.
THEME
IDEA
IDEA
IDEA

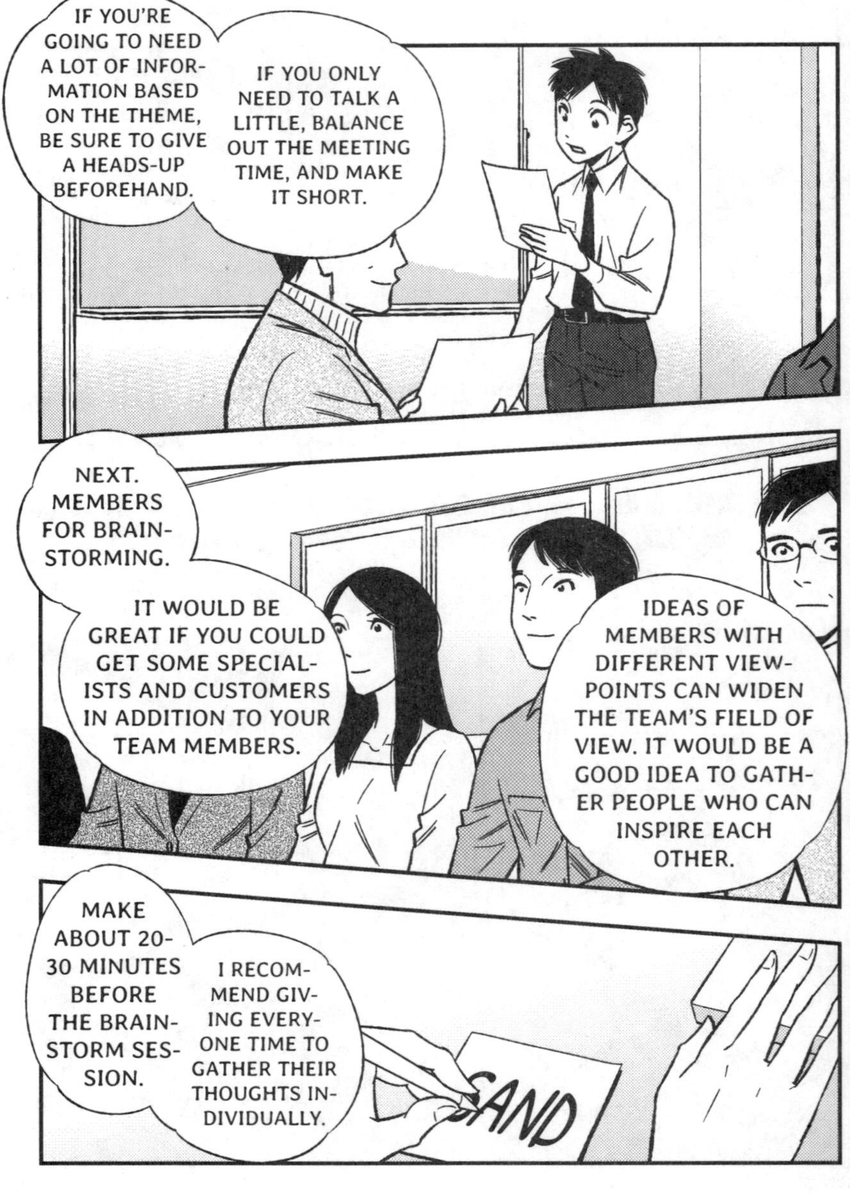
IF YOU'RE GOING TO NEED A LOT OF INFOR-MATION BASED ON THE THEME, BE SURE TO GIVE A HEADS-UP BEFOREHAND.
IF YOU ONLY NEED TO TALK A LITTLE, BALANCE OUT THE MEETING TIME, AND MAKE IT SHORT.
NEXT. MEMBERS FOR BRAIN-STORMING.
IT WOULD BE GREAT IF YOU COULD GET SOME SPECIAL-ISTS AND CUSTOMERS IN ADDITION TO YOUR TEAM MEMBERS.
IDEAS OF MEMBERS WITH DIFFERENT VIEW-POINTS CAN WIDEN THE TEAM'S FIELD OF VIEW. IT WOULD BE A GOOD IDEA TO GATH-ER PEOPLE WHO CAN INSPIRE EACH OTHER.
MAKE ABOUT 20-30 MINUTES BEFORE THE BRAIN-STORM SES-SION.
I RECOM-MEND GIV-ING EVERY-ONE TIME TO GATHER THEIR THOUGHTS IN-DIVIDUALLY.
SAND

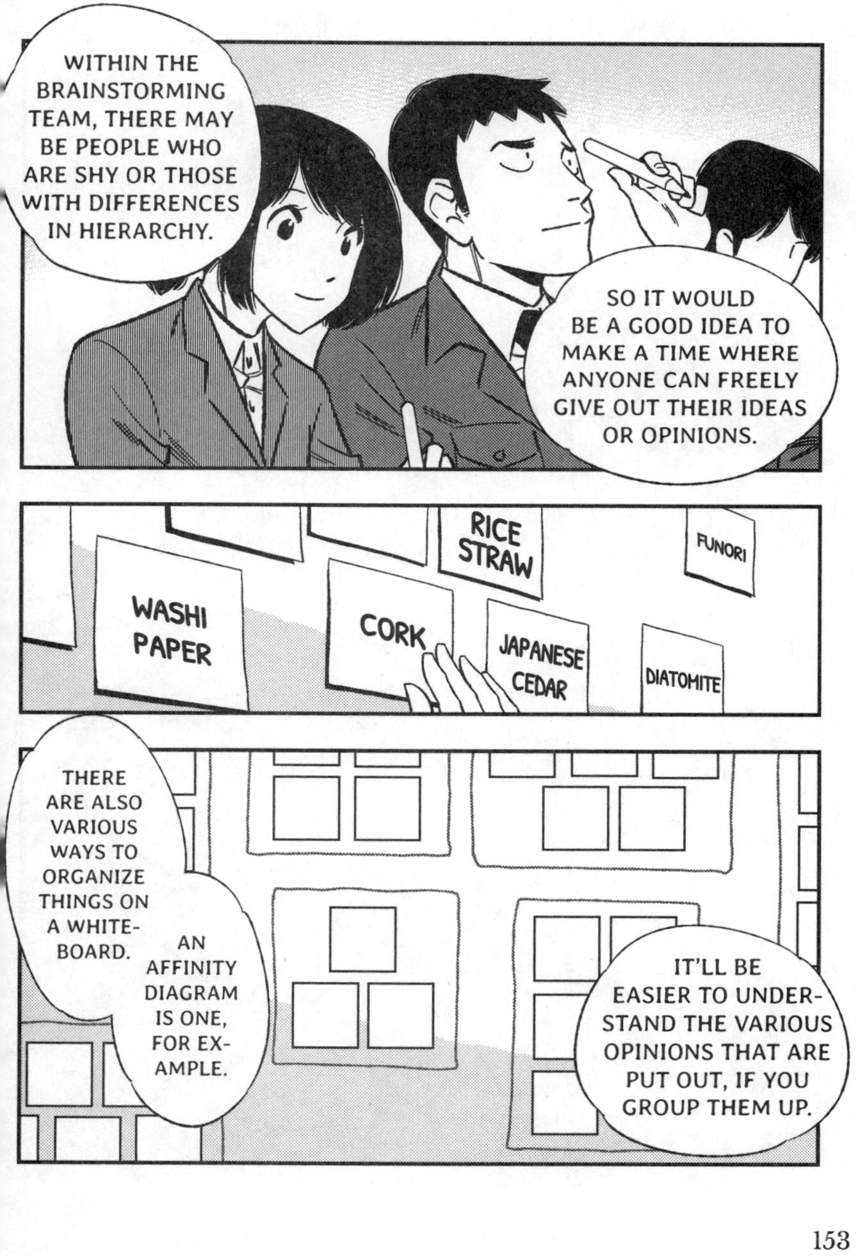
WITHIN THE BRAINSTORMING TEAM, THERE MAY BE PEOPLE WHO ARE SHY OR THOSE WITH DIFFERENCES IN HIERARCHY.
SO IT WOULD BE A GOOD IDEA TO MAKE A TIME WHERE ANYONE CAN FREELY GIVE OUT THEIR IDEAS OR OPINIONS.
RICE STRAW
FUNORI
WASHI PAPER
CORK
JAPANESE CEDAR
DIATOMITE
THERE ARE ALSO VARIOUS WAYS TO ORGANIZE THINGS ON A WHITE-BOARD.
AN AFFINITY DIAGRAM IS ONE, FOR EX-AMPLE.
IT'LL BE EASIER TO UNDER-STAND THE VARIOUS OPINIONS THAT ARE PUT OUT, IF YOU GROUP THEM UP.

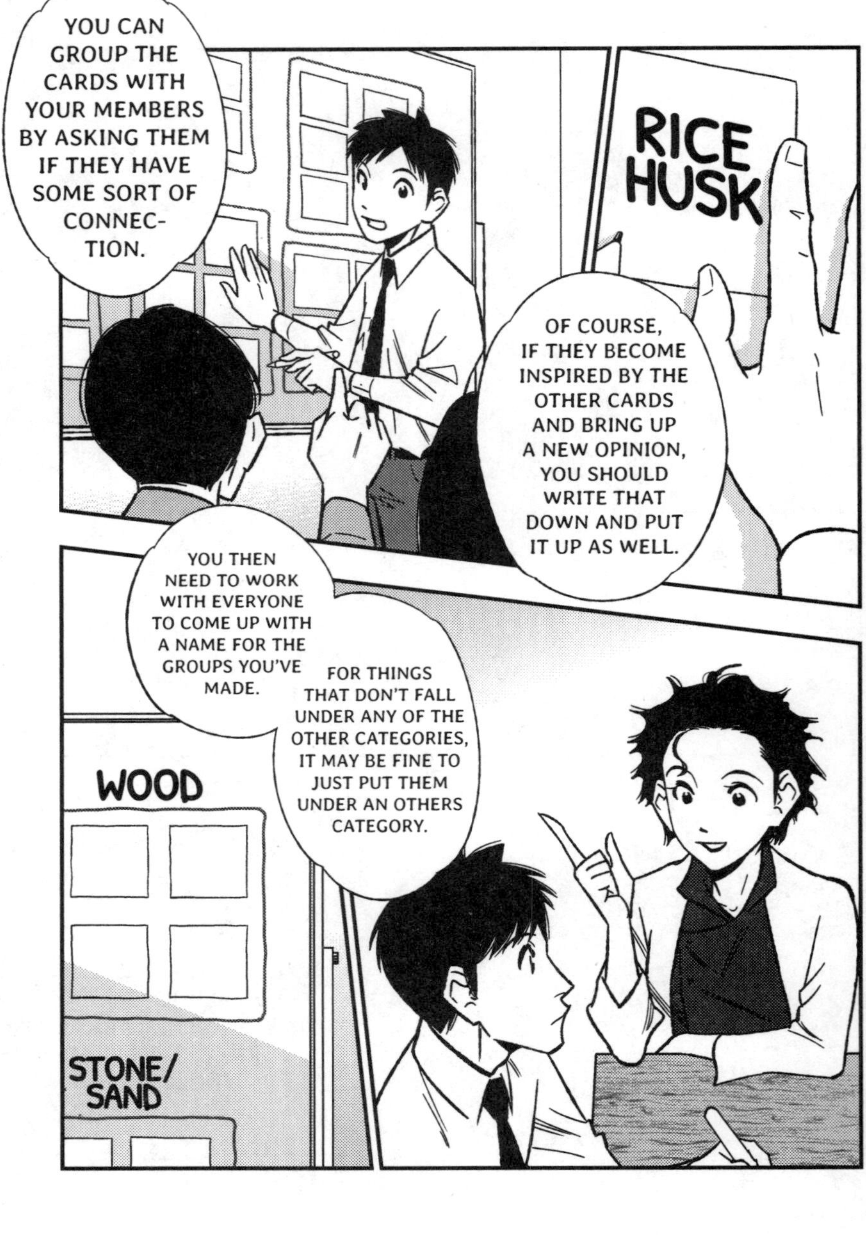
YOU CAN GROUP THE CARDS WITH YOUR MEMBERS BY ASKING THEM IF THEY HAVE SOME SORT OF CONNEC-TION.
RICE HUSK
OF COURSE, IF THEY BECOME INSPIRED BY THE OTHER CARDS AND BRING UP A NEW OPINION, YOU SHOULD WRITE THAT DOWN AND PUT IT UP AS WELL.
YOU THEN NEED TO WORK WITH EVERYONE TO COME UP WITH A NAME FOR THE GROUPS YOU'VE MADE.
FOR THINGS THAT DON'T FALL UNDER ANY OF THE OTHER CATEGORIES, IT MAY BE FINE TO JUST PUT THEM UNDER AN OTHERS CATEGORY.
WOOD
STONE/ SAND

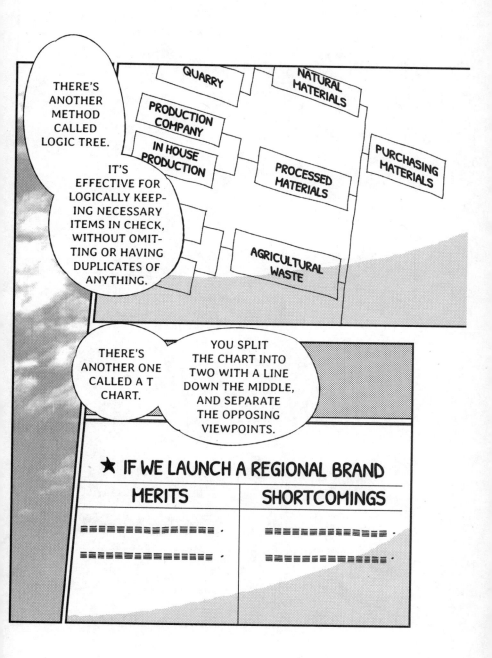

THERE'S ANOTHER METHOD CALLED LOGIC TREE.

IT'S EFFECTIVE FOR LOGICALLY KEEPING NECESSARY ITEMS IN CHECK, WITHOUT OMITTING OR HAVING DUPLICATES OF ANYTHING.

QUARRY

PRODUCTION COMPANY

IN HOUSE PRODUCTION

NATURAL MATERIALS

PURCHASING MATERIALS

PROCESSED MATERIALS

AGRICULTURAL WASTE

THERE'S ANOTHER ONE CALLED A T CHART.

YOU SPLIT THE CHART INTO TWO WITH A LINE DOWN THE MIDDLE, AND SEPARATE THE OPPOSING VIEWPOINTS.

★ IF WE LAUNCH A REGIONAL BRAND

MERITS	SHORTCOMINGS

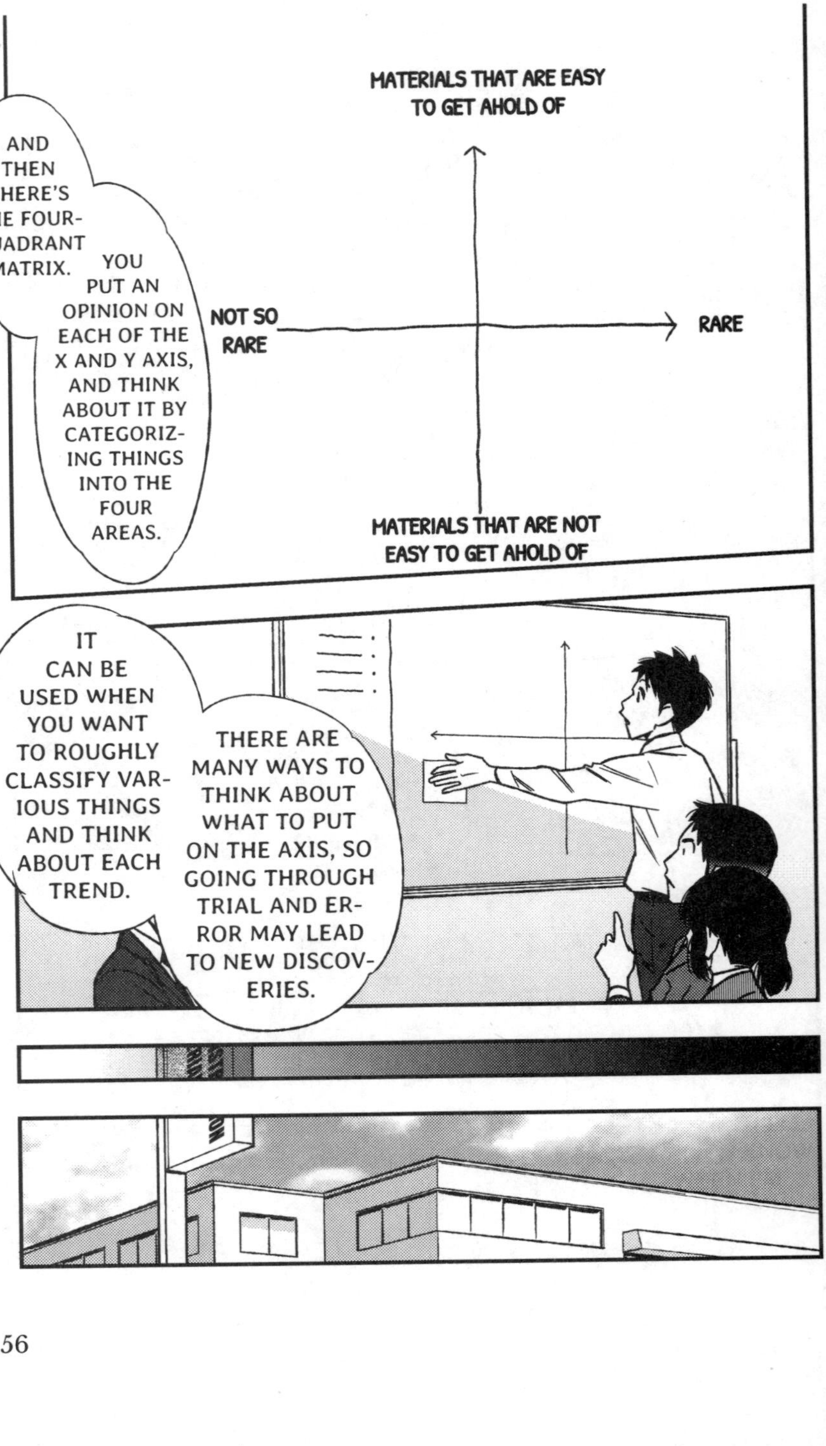
AND THEN THERE'S THE FOUR-QUADRANT MATRIX.
YOU PUT AN OPINION ON EACH OF THE X AND Y AXIS, AND THINK ABOUT IT BY CATEGORIZING THINGS INTO THE FOUR AREAS.
MATERIALS THAT ARE EASY TO GET AHOLD OF
NOT SO RARE
RARE
MATERIALS THAT ARE NOT EASY TO GET AHOLD OF
IT CAN BE USED WHEN YOU WANT TO ROUGHLY CLASSIFY VARIOUS THINGS AND THINK ABOUT EACH TREND.
THERE ARE MANY WAYS TO THINK ABOUT WHAT TO PUT ON THE AXIS, SO GOING THROUGH TRIAL AND ERROR MAY LEAD TO NEW DISCOVERIES.

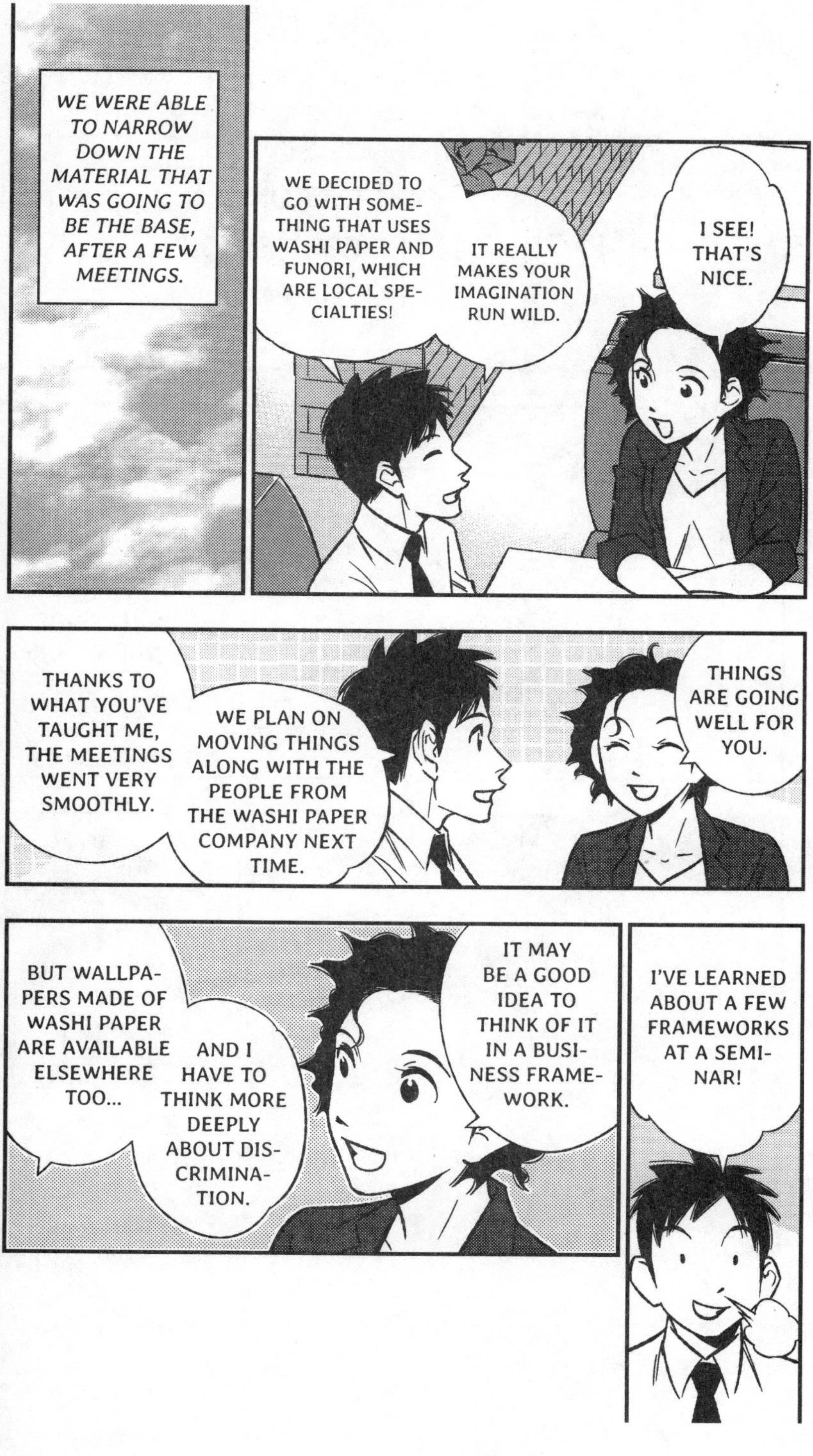
WE WERE ABLE TO NARROW DOWN THE MATERIAL THAT WAS GOING TO BE THE BASE, AFTER A FEW MEETINGS.
WE DECIDED TO GO WITH SOMETHING THAT USES WASHI PAPER AND FUNORI, WHICH ARE LOCAL SPECIALTIES!
IT REALLY MAKES YOUR IMAGINATION RUN WILD.
I SEE! THAT'S NICE.
THANKS TO WHAT YOU'VE TAUGHT ME, THE MEETINGS WENT VERY SMOOTHLY.
WE PLAN ON MOVING THINGS ALONG WITH THE PEOPLE FROM THE WASHI PAPER COMPANY NEXT TIME.
THINGS ARE GOING WELL FOR YOU.
BUT WALLPAPERS MADE OF WASHI PAPER ARE AVAILABLE ELSEWHERE TOO...
AND I HAVE TO THINK MORE DEEPLY ABOUT DISCRIMINATION.
IT MAY BE A GOOD IDEA TO THINK OF IT IN A BUSINESS FRAMEWORK.
I'VE LEARNED ABOUT A FEW FRAMEWORKS AT A SEMINAR!

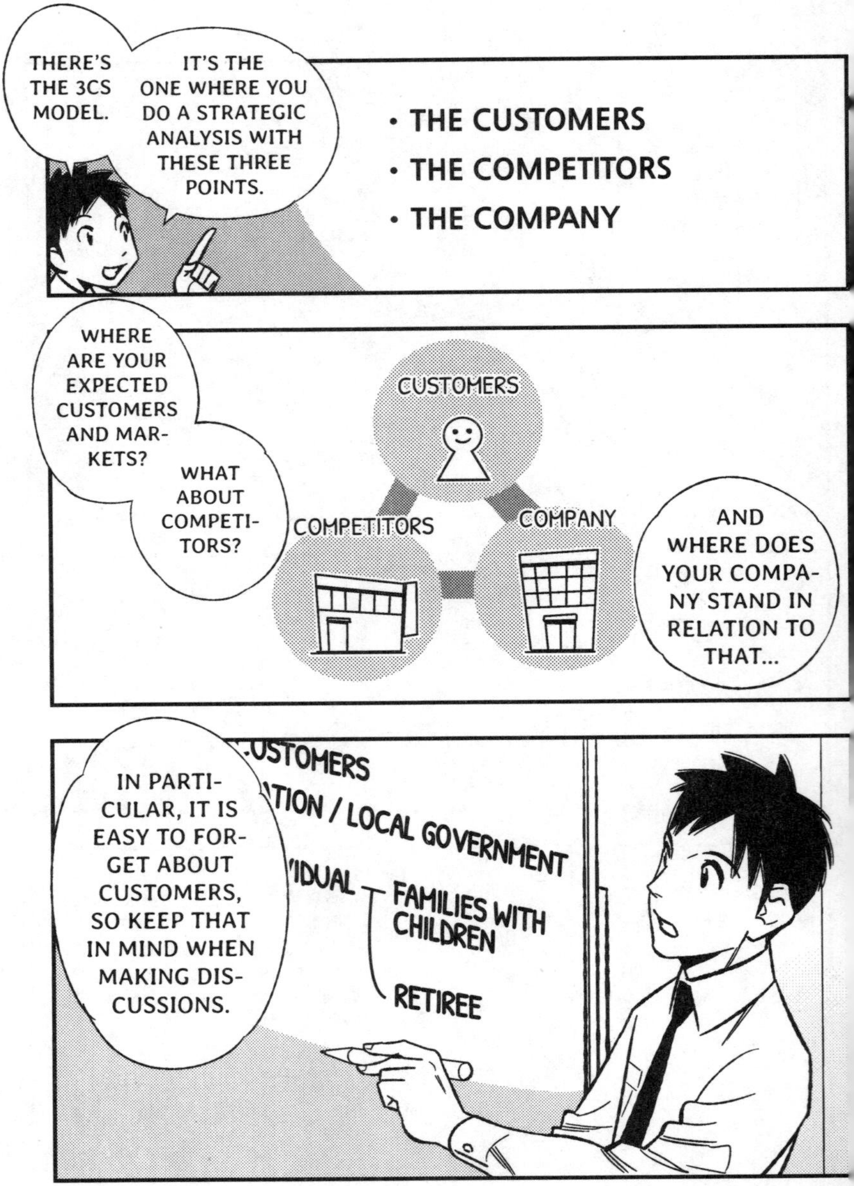
THERE'S THE 3CS MODEL.
IT'S THE ONE WHERE YOU DO A STRATEGIC ANALYSIS WITH THESE THREE POINTS.
• THE CUSTOMERS
• THE COMPETITORS
• THE COMPANY
WHERE ARE YOUR EXPECTED CUSTOMERS AND MARKETS?
WHAT ABOUT COMPETITORS?
CUSTOMERS
COMPETITORS
COMPANY
AND WHERE DOES YOUR COMPANY STAND IN RELATION TO THAT...
IN PARTICULAR, IT IS EASY TO FORGET ABOUT CUSTOMERS, SO KEEP THAT IN MIND WHEN MAKING DISCUSSIONS.
LOCAL GOVERNMENT
FAMILIES WITH CHILDREN
RETIREE

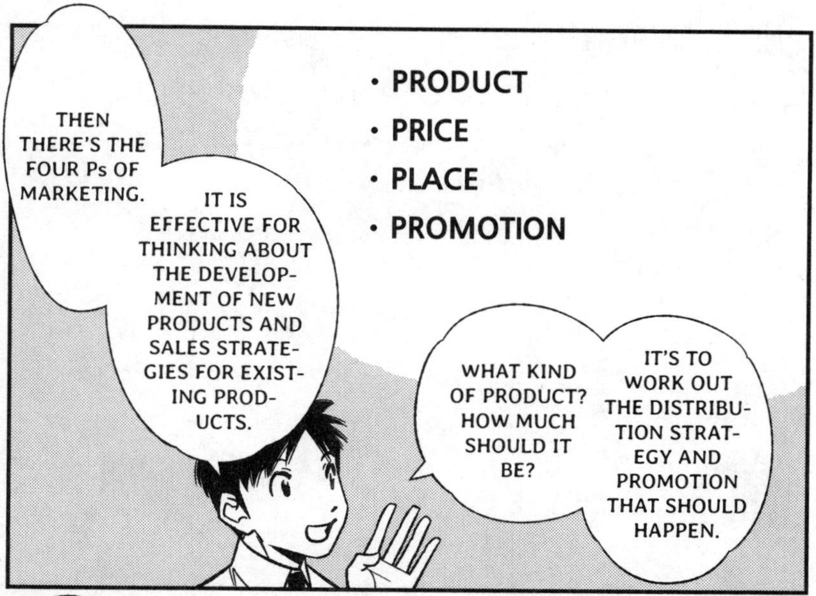
THEN THERE'S THE FOUR Ps OF MARKETING.
IT IS EFFECTIVE FOR THINKING ABOUT THE DEVELOPMENT OF NEW PRODUCTS AND SALES STRATEGIES FOR EXISTING PRODUCTS.
• PRODUCT
• PRICE
• PLACE
• PROMOTION
WHAT KIND OF PRODUCT? HOW MUCH SHOULD IT BE?
IT'S TO WORK OUT THE DISTRIBUTION STRATEGY AND PROMOTION THAT SHOULD HAPPEN.

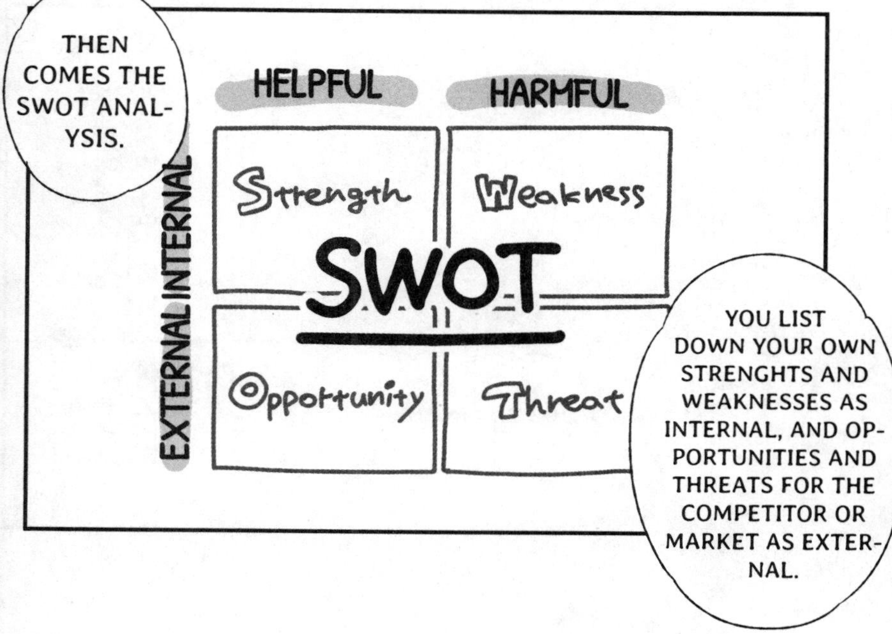
THEN COMES THE SWOT ANALYSIS.
HELPFUL
HARMFUL
INTERNAL
EXTERNAL
Strength
Weakness
Opportunity
Threat
SWOT
YOU LIST DOWN YOUR OWN STRENGHTS AND WEAKNESSES AS INTERNAL, AND OPPORTUNITIES AND THREATS FOR THE COMPETITOR OR MARKET AS EXTERNAL.

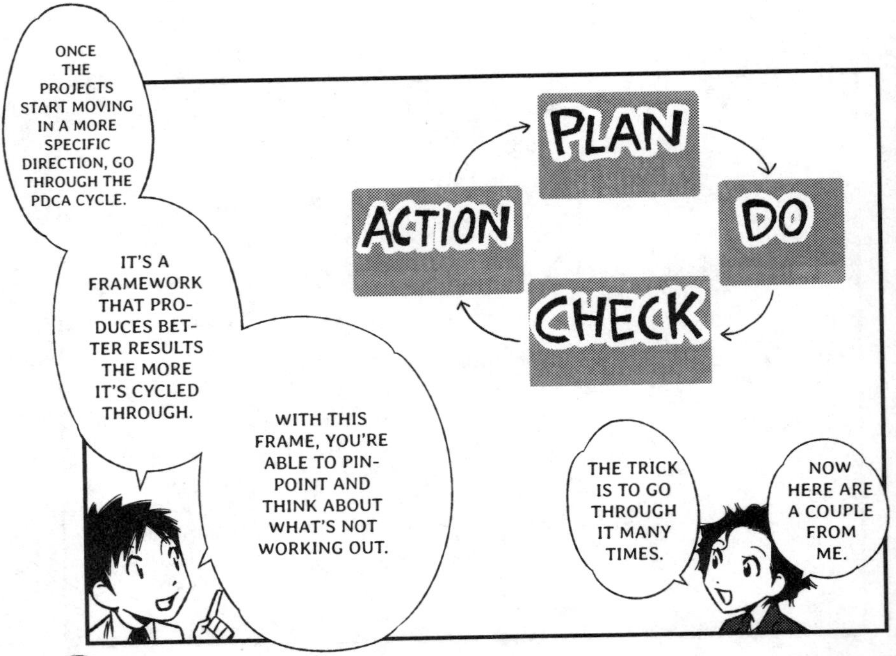
ONCE THE PROJECTS START MOVING IN A MORE SPECIFIC DIRECTION, GO THROUGH THE PDCA CYCLE.
IT'S A FRAMEWORK THAT PRODUCES BETTER RESULTS THE MORE IT'S CYCLED THROUGH.
PLAN
DO
CHECK
ACTION
WITH THIS FRAME, YOU'RE ABLE TO PINPOINT AND THINK ABOUT WHAT'S NOT WORKING OUT.
NOW HERE ARE A COUPLE FROM ME.
THE TRICK IS TO GO THROUGH IT MANY TIMES.

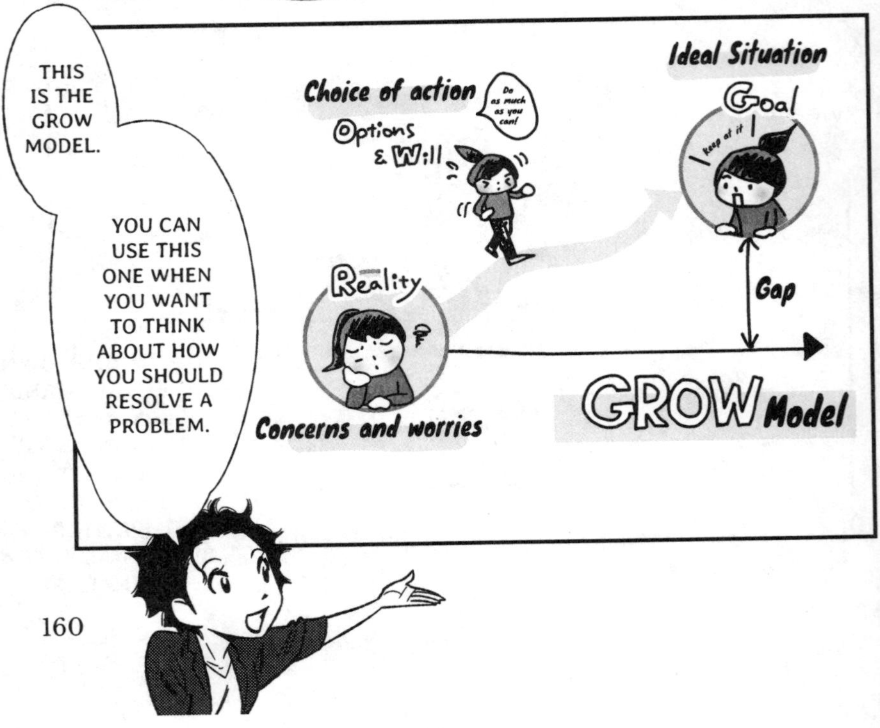
THIS IS THE GROW MODEL.
YOU CAN USE THIS ONE WHEN YOU WANT TO THINK ABOUT HOW YOU SHOULD RESOLVE A PROBLEM.
Ideal Situation
Goal
Keep at it
Choice of action
Options & Will
Do as much as you can!
Reality
Concerns and worries
Gap
GROW Model

USUALLY, IT IS COMMON TO DISCUSS MATTERS FROM THE GOAL...

...BUT IN THE CASE OF PROBLEM SOLVING, IT MAY BE EASIER TO START FROM UNDERSTANDING THE CURRENT SITUATION.

AFTER YOU UNDERSTAND THE CURRENT SITUATION, YOU NEED TO SET YOUR IDEAL. THEN YOU CAN COME UP WITH OPINIONS THAT CAN BRING YOU CLOSER TO YOUR GOAL.

THE POINT HERE IS TO PUT OUT AS MANY OPTIONS AS POSSIBLE.

TO DRAW OUT A VARIETY OF IDEAS FROM DIFFERENT VIEWPOINTS, IT WOULD BE EFFECTIVE TO SET A GOAL LIKE "LET'S COME UP WITH 30!" FOR EXAMPLE.

GOAL

LOTS!

ONCE YOU GET A LOT, YOU SHOULD GIVE THEM RATINGS ON EFFECTIVENESS AND FEASIBILITY.

EFFECTIVENESS	FEASIBILITY	
A	C	Option 1
B	B	Option 2
B	C	Option 3
C	A	Option 4

AFTER GATHERING EVERYONE'S OPINIONS, WHATEVER IS RATED HIGH ON BOTH THE EFFECTIVENESS AND FEASIBILITY IS THE BEST PLAN TO GO WITH.

LASTLY, HERE'S THE BUSINESS MODEL CANVAS.

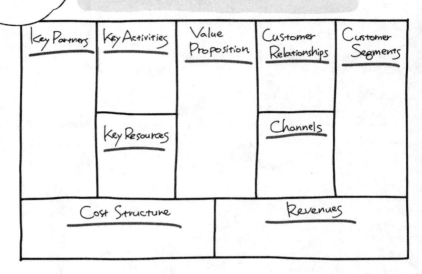

Key Partners	Key Activities	Value Proposition	Customer Relationships	Customer Segments
	Key Resources		Channels	
Cost Structure			Revenues	

THIS BUSINESS MODEL IS A USEFUL FRAMEWORK FOR THINKING ABOUT HOW TO MAKE MONEY.

BY FILLING IN THE BLOCKS WITH EVERYONE, YOU CAN DISCUSS ABOUT VARIOUS BUSINESS MODELS.

IT'S CONVENIENT TO PLACE STICKY NOTES ONTO A LARGE BOARD WITH THE FRAME DRAWN ONTO IT.

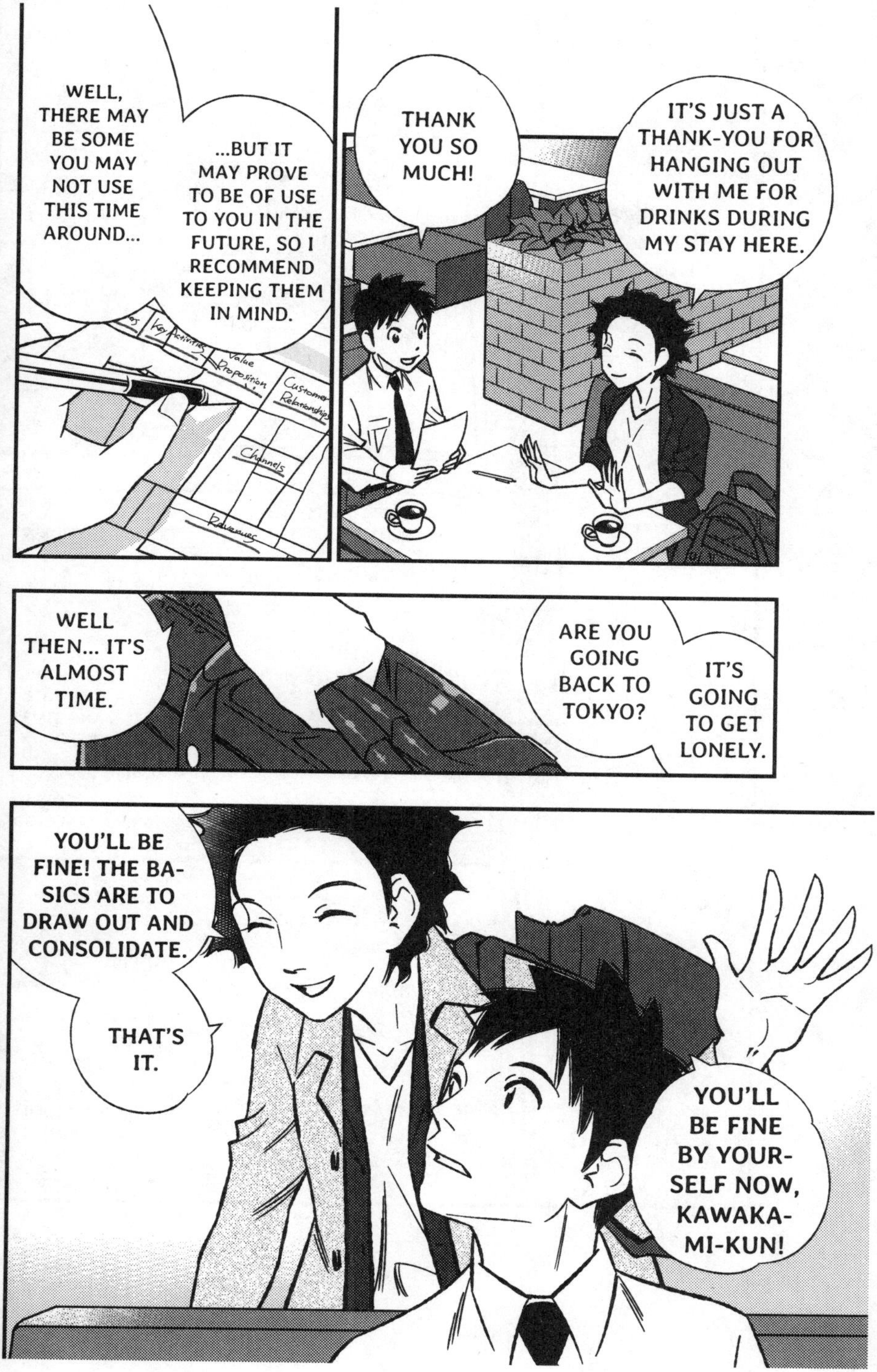

WELL, THERE MAY BE SOME YOU MAY NOT USE THIS TIME AROUND...
...BUT IT MAY PROVE TO BE OF USE TO YOU IN THE FUTURE, SO I RECOMMEND KEEPING THEM IN MIND.
Key Activities
Value Proposition
Customer Relationships
Channels
Revenues
THANK YOU SO MUCH!
IT'S JUST A THANK-YOU FOR HANGING OUT WITH ME FOR DRINKS DURING MY STAY HERE.
WELL THEN... IT'S ALMOST TIME.
ARE YOU GOING BACK TO TOKYO?
IT'S GOING TO GET LONELY.
YOU'LL BE FINE! THE BASICS ARE TO DRAW OUT AND CONSOLIDATE.
THAT'S IT.
YOU'LL BE FINE BY YOURSELF NOW, KAWAKAMI-KUN!

AND LIKE THAT, MAYU-MI-SAN WENT BACK TO TOKYO.

THE PROJECT TO DEVELOP A NEW BUILD-ING MATE-RIAL WENT SMOOTHLY.

WE'RE GETTING READY TO MAKE A TRI-AL PRODUCT.

I BECAME GREEDY AND STARTED WANT-ING TO EXPAND MY NETWORK. I EVEN PLANNED OUT AN EX-CHANGE MEET-ING.

Friend Book

FIRST, I NEED TO DECIDE ON A THEME, DATE, AND TIME... I'LL DECIDE ON THE LOCATION AFTER I SEE HOW MANY PEOPLE ARE INTERESTED.

SEE YOU!

B A M

ADING

RAMEN

FACILITATION

THE MIND MAP THAT MAYU-MI-SAN TAUGHT ME REALLY BRINGS THE MOOD UP, EVEN DURING FIRST MEETINGS.

164

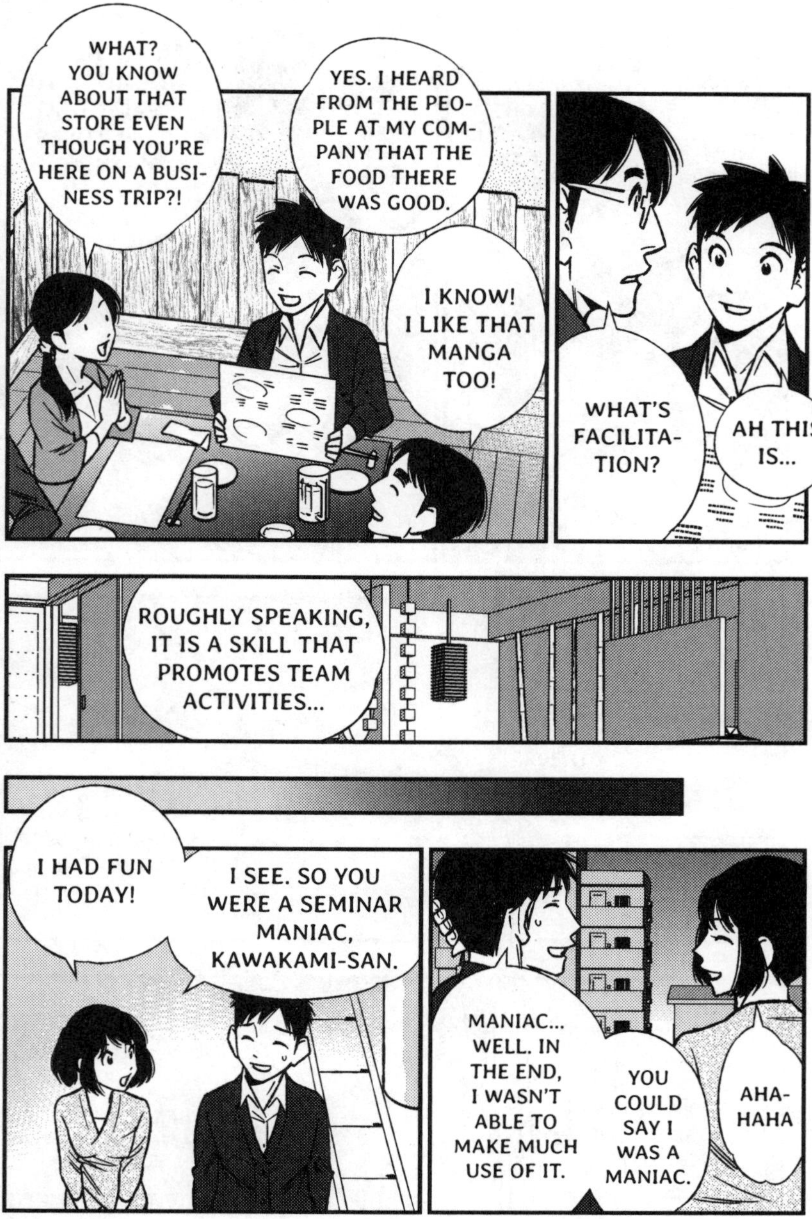
WHAT? YOU KNOW ABOUT THAT STORE EVEN THOUGH YOU'RE HERE ON A BUSINESS TRIP?!
YES. I HEARD FROM THE PEOPLE AT MY COMPANY THAT THE FOOD THERE WAS GOOD.
I KNOW! I LIKE THAT MANGA TOO!
WHAT'S FACILITATION?
AH THIS IS...
ROUGHLY SPEAKING, IT IS A SKILL THAT PROMOTES TEAM ACTIVITIES...
I HAD FUN TODAY!
I SEE. SO YOU WERE A SEMINAR MANIAC, KAWAKAMI-SAN.
MANIAC... WELL. IN THE END, I WASN'T ABLE TO MAKE MUCH USE OF IT.
YOU COULD SAY I WAS A MANIAC.
AHAHAHA

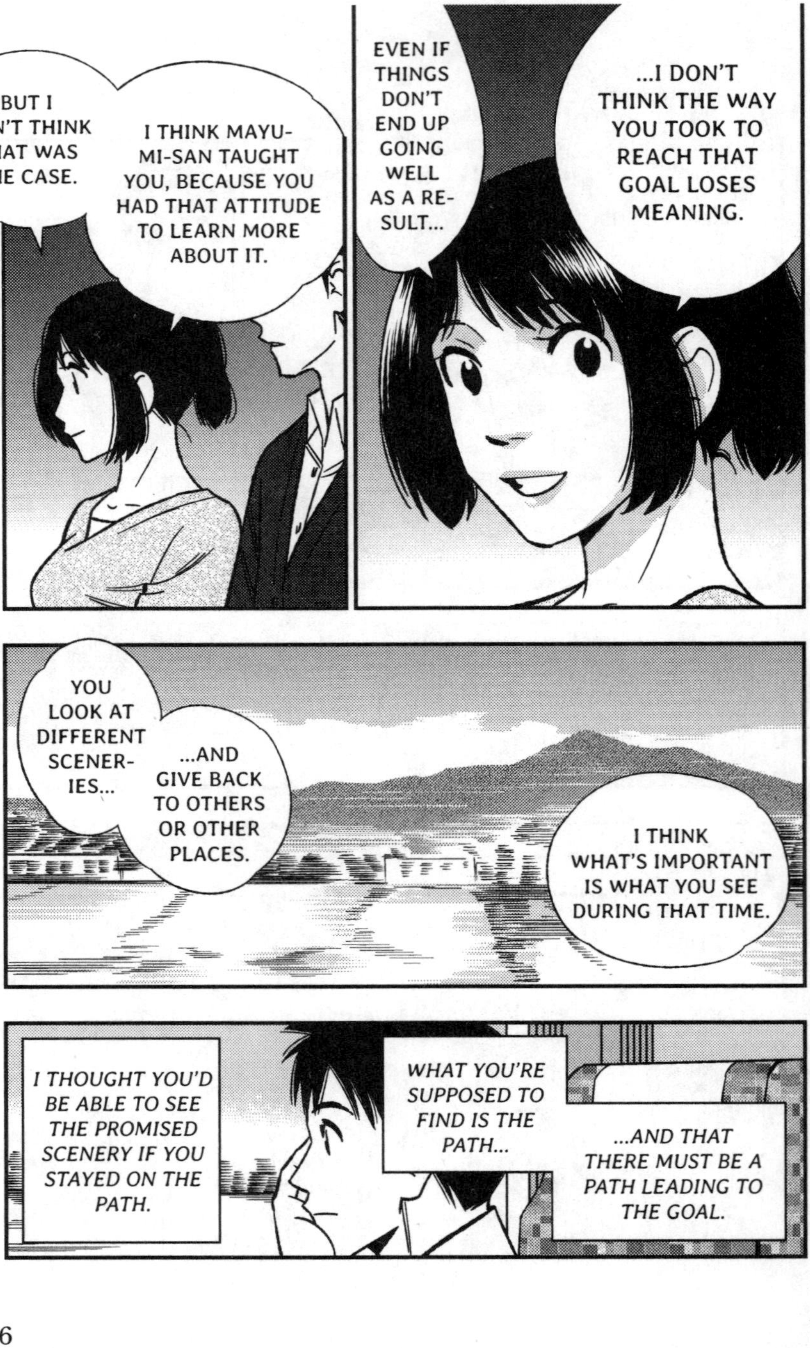
BUT I DON'T THINK THAT WAS THE CASE.
I THINK MAYU-MI-SAN TAUGHT YOU, BECAUSE YOU HAD THAT ATTITUDE TO LEARN MORE ABOUT IT.
EVEN IF THINGS DON'T END UP GOING WELL AS A RE-SULT...
...I DON'T THINK THE WAY YOU TOOK TO REACH THAT GOAL LOSES MEANING.
YOU LOOK AT DIFFERENT SCENER-IES...
...AND GIVE BACK TO OTHERS OR OTHER PLACES.
I THINK WHAT'S IMPORTANT IS WHAT YOU SEE DURING THAT TIME.
I THOUGHT YOU'D BE ABLE TO SEE THE PROMISED SCENERY IF YOU STAYED ON THE PATH.
WHAT YOU'RE SUPPOSED TO FIND IS THE PATH...
...AND THAT THERE MUST BE A PATH LEADING TO THE GOAL.

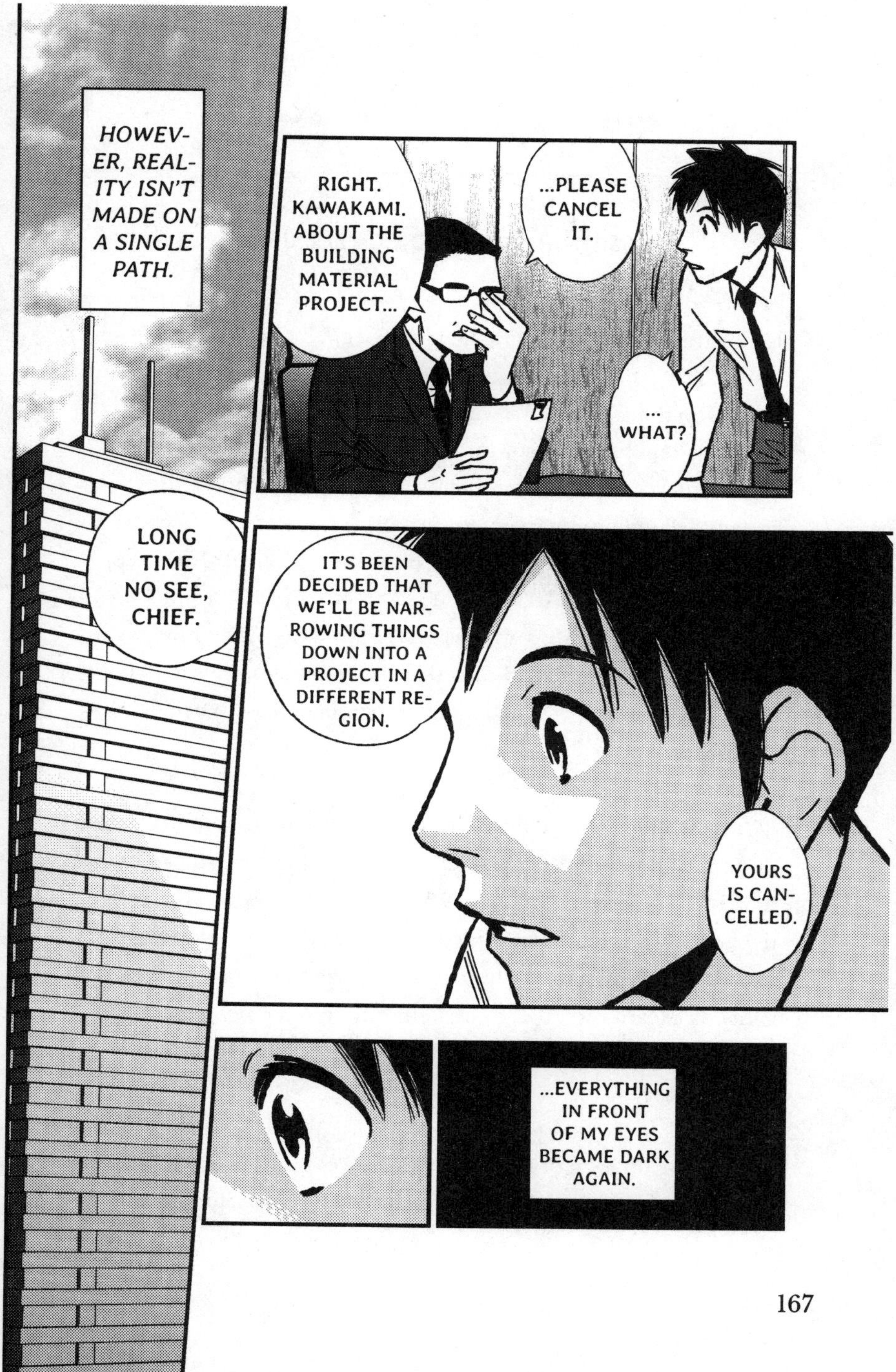
HOWEVER, REALITY ISN'T MADE ON A SINGLE PATH.
RIGHT. KAWAKAMI. ABOUT THE BUILDING MATERIAL PROJECT...
...PLEASE CANCEL IT.
... WHAT?
LONG TIME NO SEE, CHIEF.
IT'S BEEN DECIDED THAT WE'LL BE NARROWING THINGS DOWN INTO A PROJECT IN A DIFFERENT REGION.
YOURS IS CANCELLED.
...EVERYTHING IN FRONT OF MY EYES BECAME DARK AGAIN.

10 The Essentials for Project Leaders

If you are assigned project leadership, begin by determining two things. First, **the organization of group meetings.** Decide, to some extent, on the frequency of regular meetings, the framework for inter-departmental communication, and the methods for communicating internal problems. If you clearly outline the contents of upcoming meetings in advance, it can even become an effective deadline for tasks. If you plan for it, you can also create a time for openly discussing mistakes and other problems that are usually difficult to bring up. Design the contents of the meeting in order to get ahead of any issues that may come up. This is essential particularly for projects that involve members from outside the company.

It's also important to **assign a leader.** In cross-departmental projects and in projects made up of a team of experts, it can be difficult to determine who should take leadership and which department should be in charge. However, having too many captains can lead a ship astray. Is top management calling the shots? Is a team member going to be appointed a key person? Or are things going to be decided through a group discussion with everyone?

Depending on each organization and the content of each project, there will be various possible ways to structure decision making, but, in any case, try to do so as soon as possible. Keep in mind that once a project starts, unexpected things will happen and that team members who have to deal with such issues may get their hands extremely full and lose sight of their goals. At such times, it is paramount to schedule a meeting in order to look at the project from a wide angle—go over everyone's ideas, and assign roles and responsibilities. Leaders need to **create a space where people feel free to consult with them.**

There may be people who say one thing on the phone or during a private conversation and something else in a meeting or other official setting. Further, having too many individual consultations may lead to asynchronism between team members, so keep in mind to discuss important matters with the team, in front of everyone.

A project is but a dot on a long line called a business. Allow your experience and knowledge to become your leverage for your next project and lead to the development of future business.

In order to assemble a resolute, productive team that does not fear failure, you must first create a space where all team members can cooperate freely. For this very reason, the presence of a facilitative leader is paramount.

11 Broaden Your Horizons Through Gatherings

If you aim to become a facilitative leader, it's important to be aware of diverse opinions and ways of thinking and develop your adaptability. Meeting new people is the fastest way to broaden your views, so I suggest **attending various seminars and social events**. In fact, many business professionals, such as managers, shop owners, and self-employed individuals, visit social events and exchange information with a wide variety of people.

In addition to work functions, it's also wise to make use of morning meetings ahead of the workday, as well as lunch breaks. And if you want to meet and interact with new people, challenge yourself to **organize a social gathering**.

If you do a bit of research online, you'll find that many of these social gatherings are planned out regardless of the time of day. Beyond traditional social networking services such as Facebook and Twitter, make sure to look up various event planning websites. Once you become experienced, it's time for you to start planning your own event.

If you decide on a specific theme, it will be easy to appeal to the participation of members who have the same topic in mind, which will promote conversation. I recommend that you begin by deciding on a time and date and then decide on the venue based on the number of people who will attend. Find an organizational method that suits you and get started on your first event.

The trick to livening up a gathering of strangers is for everyone to get to know each other as soon as possible. For those unsure how to liven things up, I recommend drawing a mind map, which will surely serve that function.

The mind map was devised by educator Saito Takashi. To make a mind map, you begin by writing down things you love as specifically as possible; group participants and encourage them to show what they've written to each other and talk about it. While people can write however they feel like, and there's no limit in length, it's helpful to use terms that are as specific as possible.

You can either assign some time for people to write out their maps at the beginning of a meeting, or you can ask them to make them in advance.

Even when it's your first time meeting someone, or when they're from a different generation, or don't appear to be your type of person, after you share your mind maps you often find unexpected commonalities.

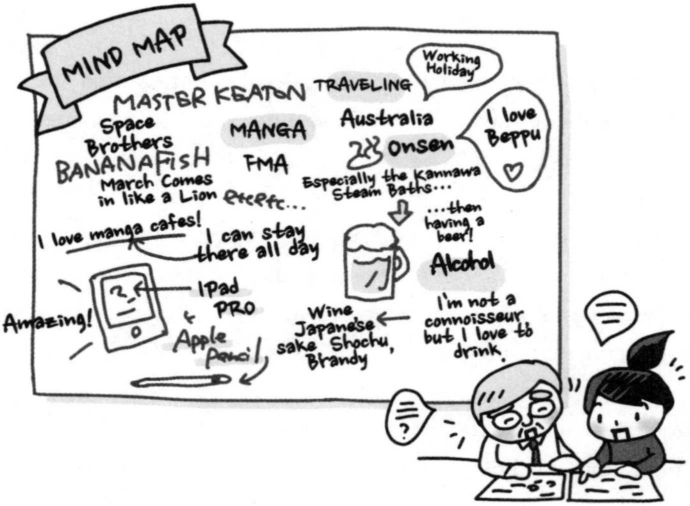
MIND MAP
MASTER KEATON
TRAVELING
Working Holiday
Space Brothers
MANGA
Australia
I love Beppu
BANANAFISH
FMA
Onsen
March Comes in like a Lion etcetc...
Especially the Kannawa Steam Baths...
...then having a beer!
I love manga cafes!
I can stay there all day
Alcohol
IPad PRO & Apple Pencil
Amazing!
Wine Japanese sake Shochu, Brandy
I'm not a connoisseur but I love to drink.

If people's tastes match, they'll easily engage in conversation, and even if they read something they have no clue about, it's a great opportunity to ask about it and talk from there. As such, mind maps are a wonderful and convenient tool. Of course, they can also be used in business meetings and company training.

I also recommend using the mind map to share things you want to do in the future or that you want to learn more about. Learning about one another's aspirations can facilitate creativity. So expand your world, and have fun doing so.

12 Knowing Is Only Half the Battle! Thinking in Frameworks

PRODUCT
PRICE
PLACE
PROMOTION
Customer
Competitor
Company
The 4Ps of Marketing 4P
3C Model
Use frameworks!

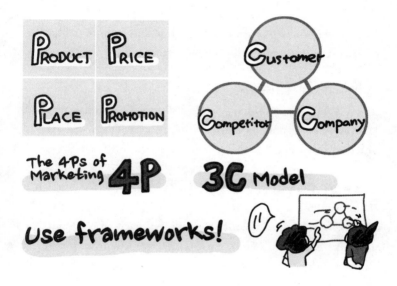

Frameworks are models you can use to help organize your thoughts. Implementing a framework into a discussion can lead you to obtain new perspectives.

① 3Cs Analysis

The 3Cs of strategic analysis stand for customer, competitor, and company. After determining what kind of customers and markets you envision for your company, as well as the nature of your competitors, discuss how your company stands in relation to them. Clearly define each element, and discuss how they relate to each other.

Bring this framework into your meetings, and get into the habit of analyzing your markets on a regular basis.

② The 4Ps of Marketing

The 4Ps stand for product, price, place, and promotion. Start off by analyzing these four elements. If you promote a deep discussion, you can work out an overall strategy that combines these four Ps.

③ SWOT Analysis

If you want to develop a strategy that can help your company overcome difficult situations, I recommend using the SWOT analysis framework. This method is effective when you want to analyze your current situation from multiple perspectives.

After analyzing your own strengths and weaknesses, you need to determine what opportunities and threats are around you. Since strengths and weaknesses are said to be internal factors, while opportunities and threats represent external ones, this method provides a multifaceted analysis both from within and outside your company. By developing and discussing those concepts, SWOT analysis can be used as a strategy-building tool.

Helpful
Harmful
Internal
External
Strength
Weakness
SWOT
Opportunity
Threat

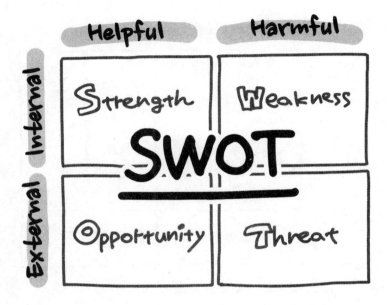

If it's difficult to think in terms of corporate strengths and weaknesses, it may be helpful to frame your discussion in comparative terms against competitors, or to clearly define your intended markets.

④ PDCA Cycle

This is the same framework that was introduced on page 119. This framework may prove necessary to check that a project is progressing smoothly.

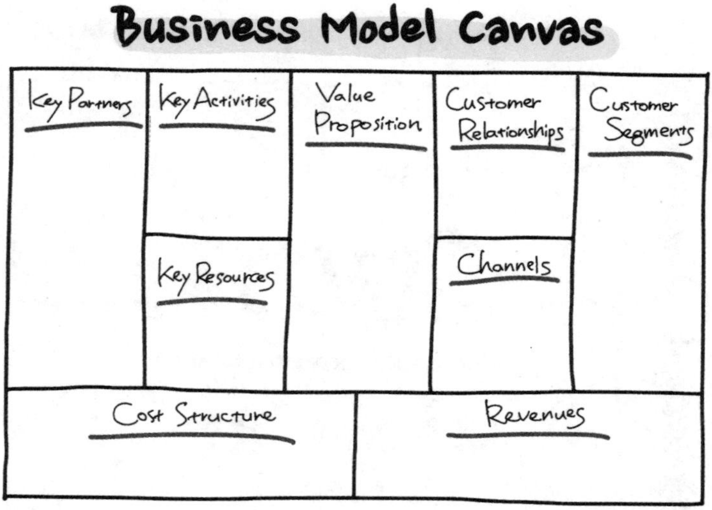

Business Model Canvas

Key Partners	Key Activities	Value Proposition	Customer Relationships	Customer Segments
	Key Resources		Channels	

Cost Structure	Revenues

⑤ GROW Model

This is the same framework that was introduced on page 139. Try using the GROW model in strategy meetings to tackle important issues and problems.

⑥ Business Model Canvas

This framework is convenient when you need to consider business models and profit structures.

First, draw nine large blocks on a whiteboard for each of the following categories: customer segments, value propositions, channels, customer relationships, revenues, key resources, key activities, key partners, and cost structures. By filling out each block as a group, your team will be able to hold discussions regarding various types of business models. It's convenient to fill your whiteboard using sticky notes.

You can also apply this framework to internal planning in order to take inventory of people's individual careers and review the role of each department.

Column ▶ **THE THREE THINGS "ADVISORS" DO**

Everyone knows people who are really easy to talk to, even upon first meeting. Somehow, it's easy to express your opinions and confide your concerns to them. I will teach you the three points of the communication by subtraction technique that these people use in order to act as advisors.

1) Know That the Other Person Is the Main Character
Your coworkers' problems are their own. They are the ones to resolve them, so you don't need to pressure yourself into coming up with a solution. If we relax and listen to them, they'll relax as well. Problems can be better understood by talking, and solutions may naturally come

up just by doing so. Even if you don't arrive at an answer, the sense of relief that comes from someone listening to them will be comforting.

2) Create a Safe Space
Conversations stay between you and them. You may think this is obvious, but have you never spoken about someone else's matters in front of others, even if it was without ill intent?

Even if you aren't using them to speak ill of others, do not share matters your coworkers confided in you. Keep them to yourself.

3) Listen to Others Without Judgment
To many people, an advisor is someone who will be neutral when listening to them. They don't judge whether their actions are good or bad, and simply listen. Of course, if there's something you want to tell them, you can, but the timing with which you do so is important. If they feel that they won't be criticized or ridiculed regardless of what they say, they will be able to open up about their concerns and personal weaknesses. If you want to be a good listener, keep in mind to openly lend an ear and save your opinions for later.

Various people go to advisors for help with their problems and to relieve their stress. Even if you can't talk about what others confide in you, the things you hear can contribute to your own wisdom and gradually expand your views and values. Advisors use the communication by subtraction technique to bring happiness to those around them and to themselves. If you strive to be like that, be aware of these three aspects starting today.

EPILOGUE

The Facilitation Mindset

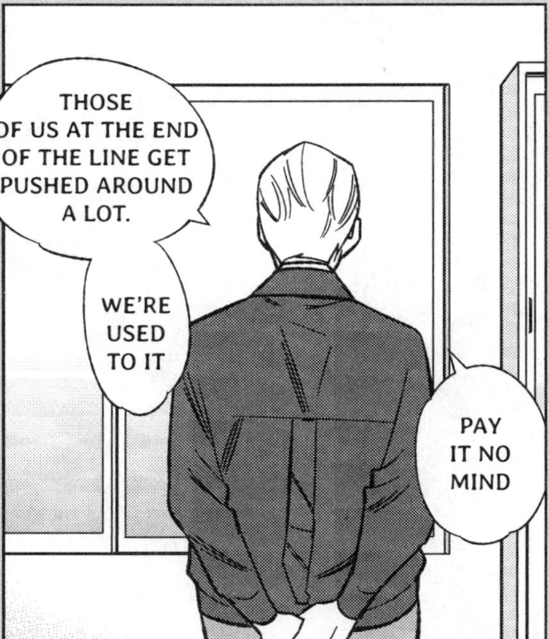
THOSE OF US AT THE END OF THE LINE GET PUSHED AROUND A LOT.
WE'RE USED TO IT
PAY IT NO MIND

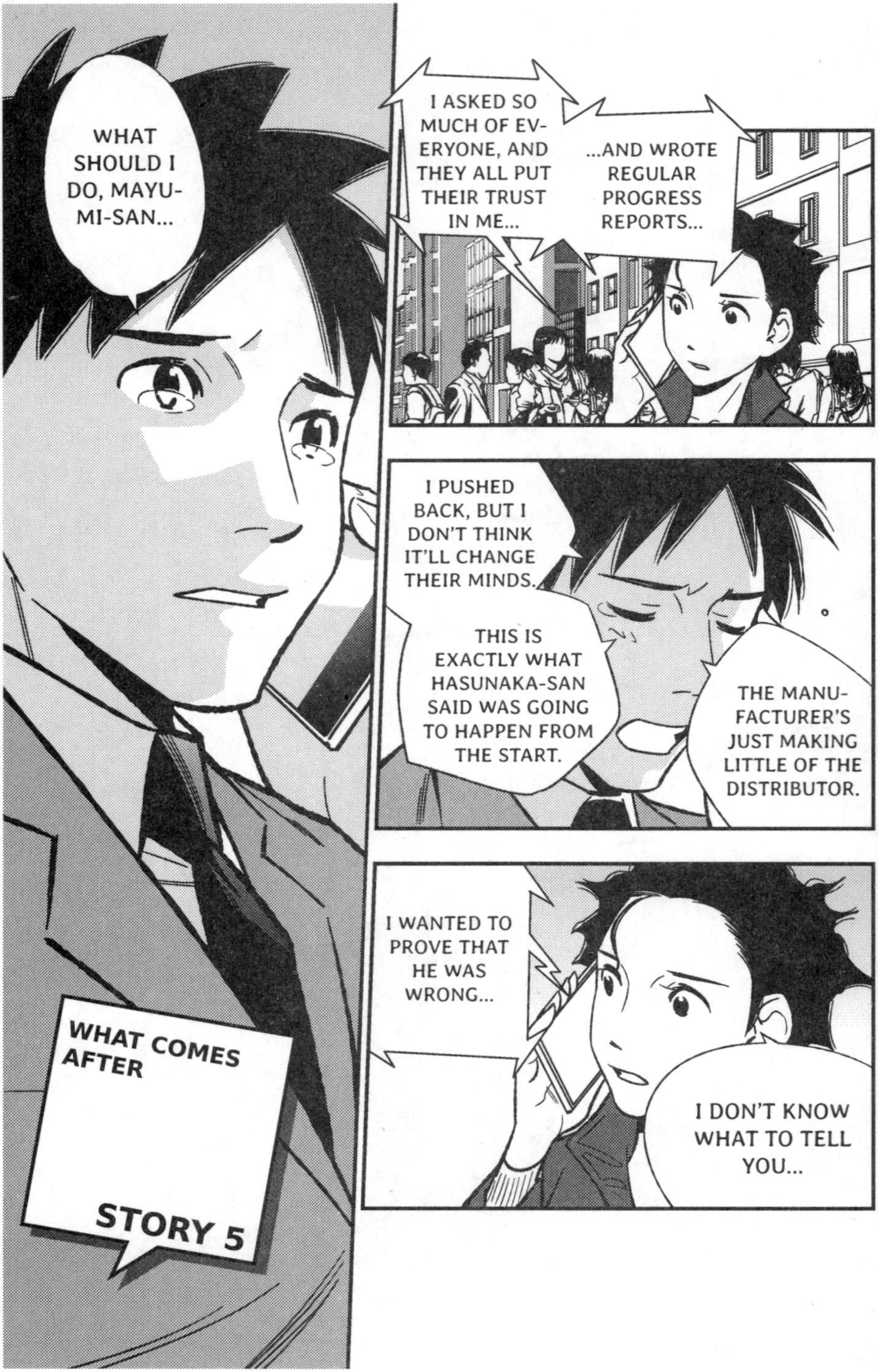
WHAT SHOULD I DO, MAYU-MI-SAN...
WHAT COMES AFTER
STORY 5
I ASKED SO MUCH OF EV-ERYONE, AND THEY ALL PUT THEIR TRUST IN ME...
...AND WROTE REGULAR PROGRESS REPORTS...
I PUSHED BACK, BUT I DON'T THINK IT'LL CHANGE THEIR MINDS.
THIS IS EXACTLY WHAT HASUNAKA-SAN SAID WAS GOING TO HAPPEN FROM THE START.
THE MANU-FACTURER'S JUST MAKING LITTLE OF THE DISTRIBUTOR.
I WANTED TO PROVE THAT HE WAS WRONG...
I DON'T KNOW WHAT TO TELL YOU...

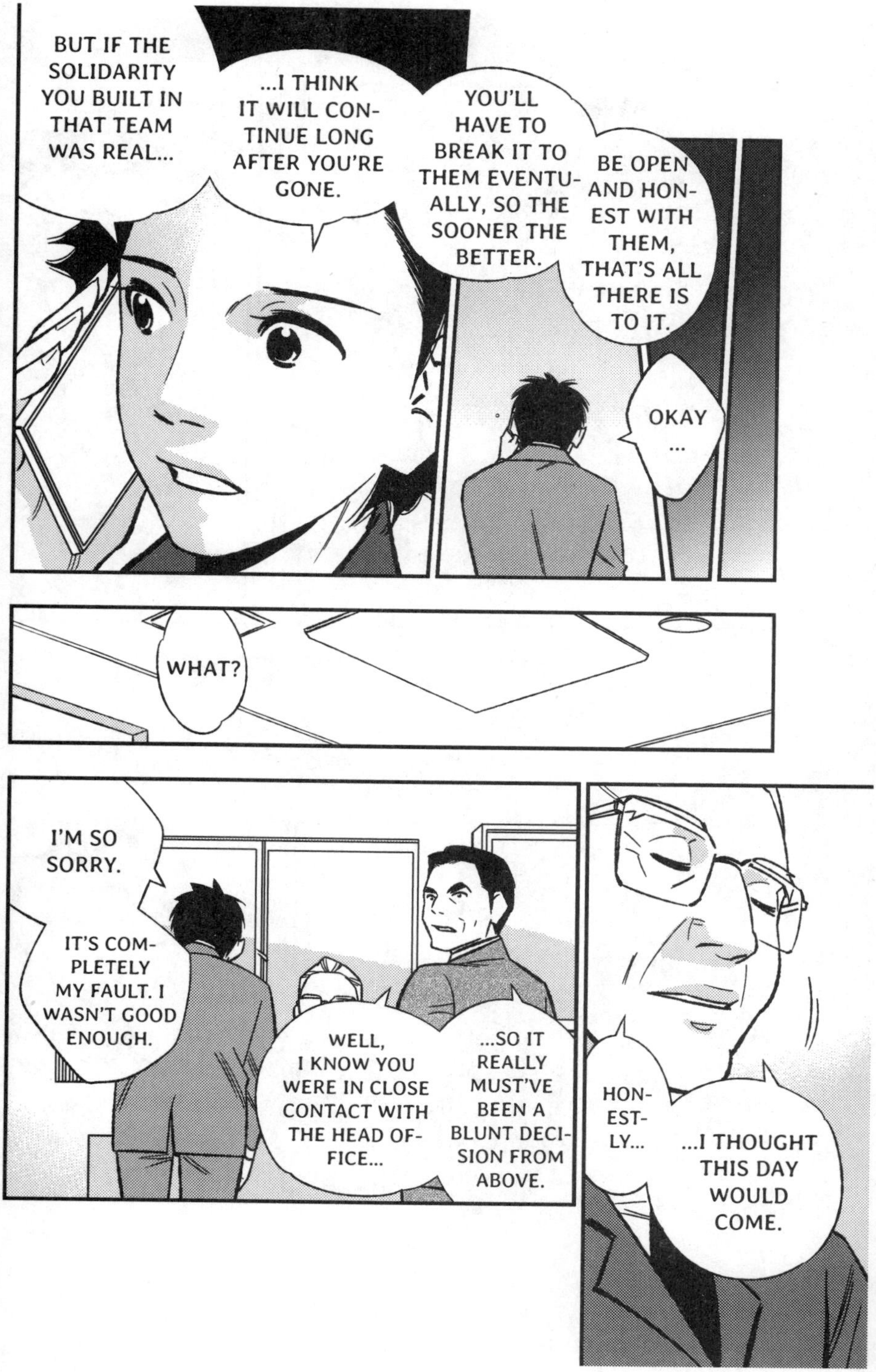
BUT IF THE SOLIDARITY YOU BUILT IN THAT TEAM WAS REAL...
...I THINK IT WILL CONTINUE LONG AFTER YOU'RE GONE.
YOU'LL HAVE TO BREAK IT TO THEM EVENTUALLY, SO THE SOONER THE BETTER.
BE OPEN AND HONEST WITH THEM, THAT'S ALL THERE IS TO IT.
OKAY ...
WHAT?
I'M SO SORRY.
IT'S COMPLETELY MY FAULT. I WASN'T GOOD ENOUGH.
WELL, I KNOW YOU WERE IN CLOSE CONTACT WITH THE HEAD OFFICE...
...SO IT REALLY MUST'VE BEEN A BLUNT DECISION FROM ABOVE.
HONESTLY...
...I THOUGHT THIS DAY WOULD COME.

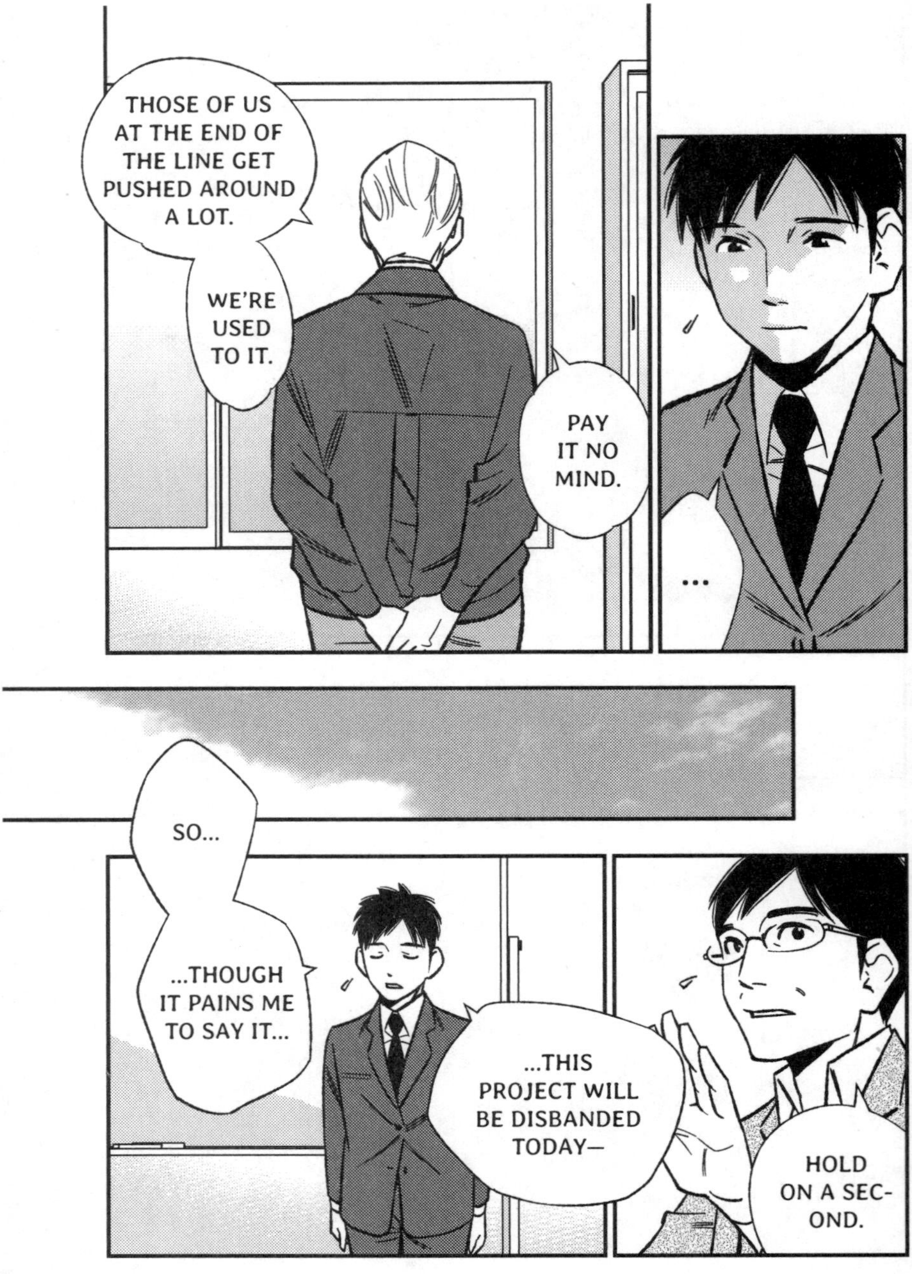
THOSE OF US AT THE END OF THE LINE GET PUSHED AROUND A LOT.
WE'RE USED TO IT.
PAY IT NO MIND.
...
SO...
...THOUGH IT PAINS ME TO SAY IT...
...THIS PROJECT WILL BE DISBANDED TODAY—
HOLD ON A SEC-OND.

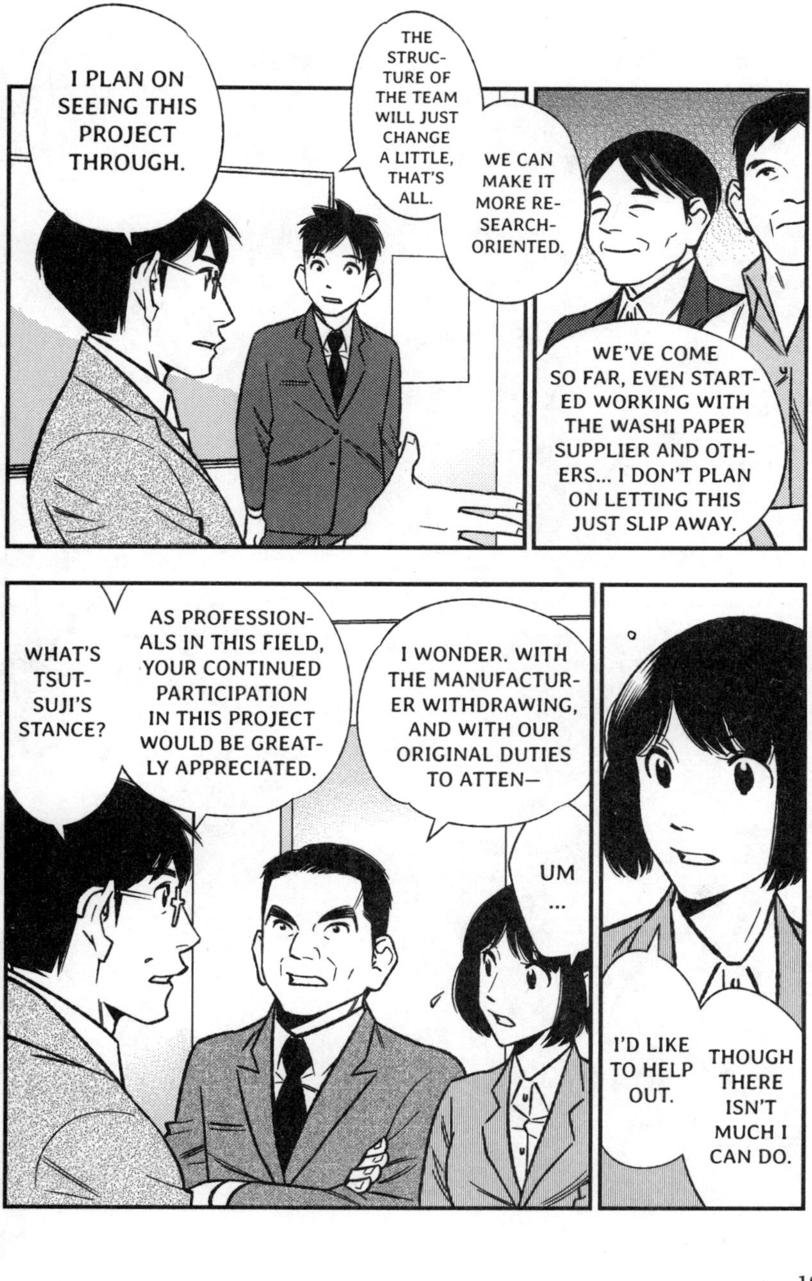
I PLAN ON SEEING THIS PROJECT THROUGH.
THE STRUCTURE OF THE TEAM WILL JUST CHANGE A LITTLE, THAT'S ALL.
WE CAN MAKE IT MORE RESEARCH-ORIENTED.
WE'VE COME SO FAR, EVEN STARTED WORKING WITH THE WASHI PAPER SUPPLIER AND OTHERS... I DON'T PLAN ON LETTING THIS JUST SLIP AWAY.
WHAT'S TSUTSUJI'S STANCE?
AS PROFESSIONALS IN THIS FIELD, YOUR CONTINUED PARTICIPATION IN THIS PROJECT WOULD BE GREATLY APPRECIATED.
I WONDER. WITH THE MANUFACTURER WITHDRAWING, AND WITH OUR ORIGINAL DUTIES TO ATTEN—
UM...
I'D LIKE TO HELP OUT.
THOUGH THERE ISN'T MUCH I CAN DO.

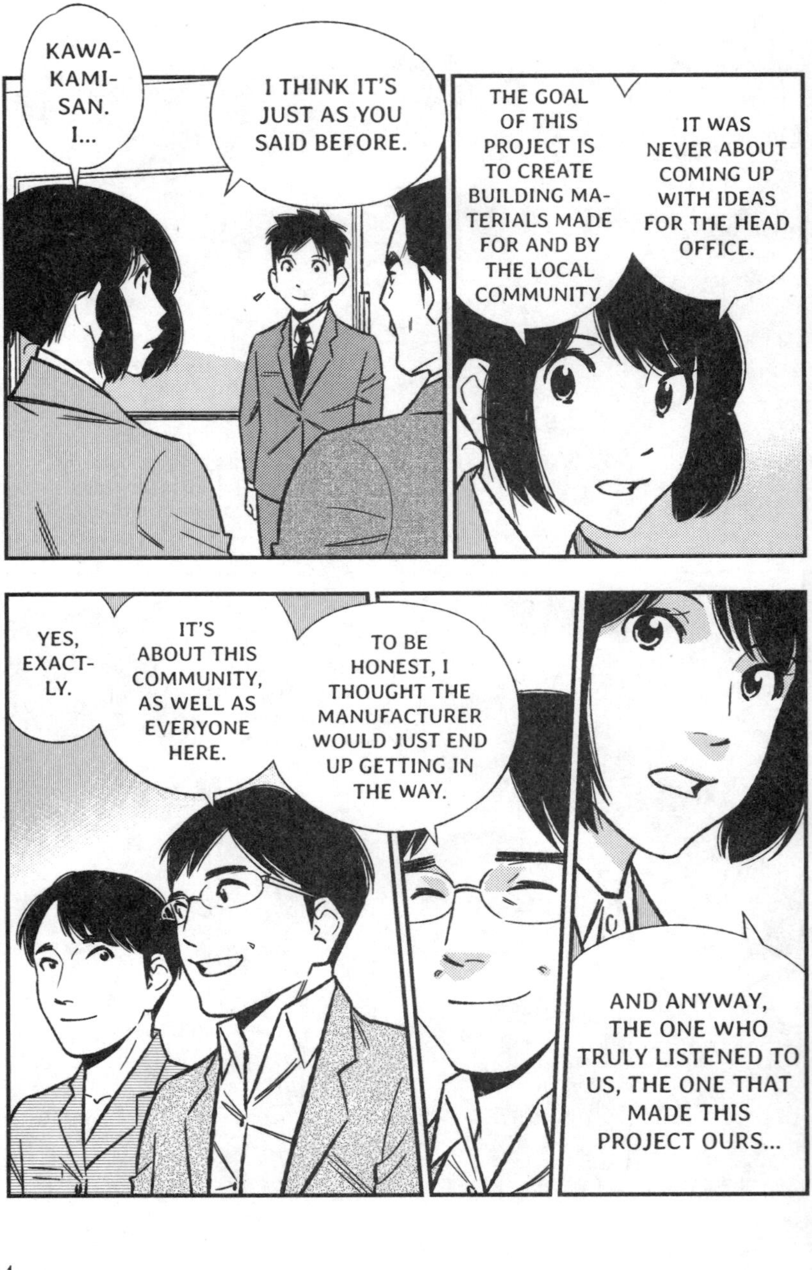
KAWA-KAMI-SAN. I...
I THINK IT'S JUST AS YOU SAID BEFORE.
THE GOAL OF THIS PROJECT IS TO CREATE BUILDING MA-TERIALS MADE FOR AND BY THE LOCAL COMMUNITY.
IT WAS NEVER ABOUT COMING UP WITH IDEAS FOR THE HEAD OFFICE.
YES, EXACT-LY.
IT'S ABOUT THIS COMMUNITY, AS WELL AS EVERYONE HERE.
TO BE HONEST, I THOUGHT THE MANUFACTURER WOULD JUST END UP GETTING IN THE WAY.
AND ANYWAY, THE ONE WHO TRULY LISTENED TO US, THE ONE THAT MADE THIS PROJECT OURS...

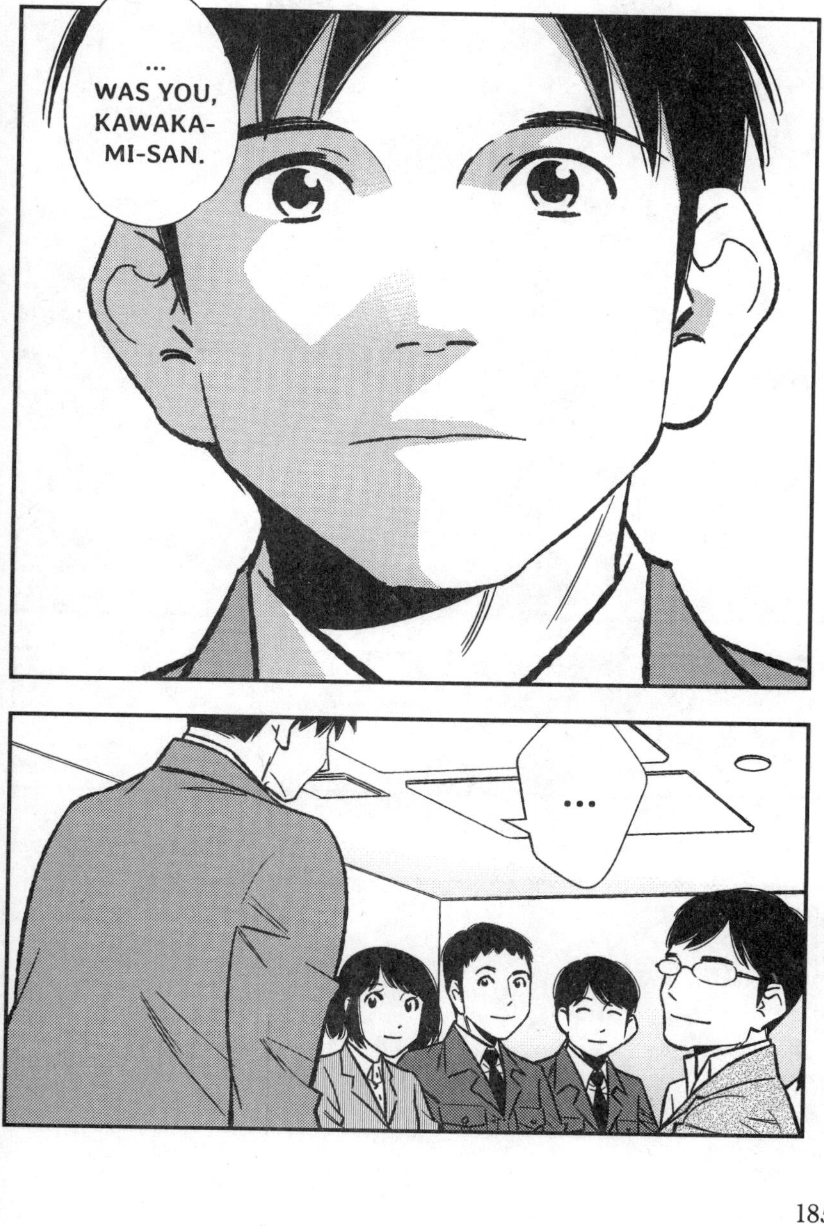
... WAS YOU, KAWAKA-MI-SAN.
...

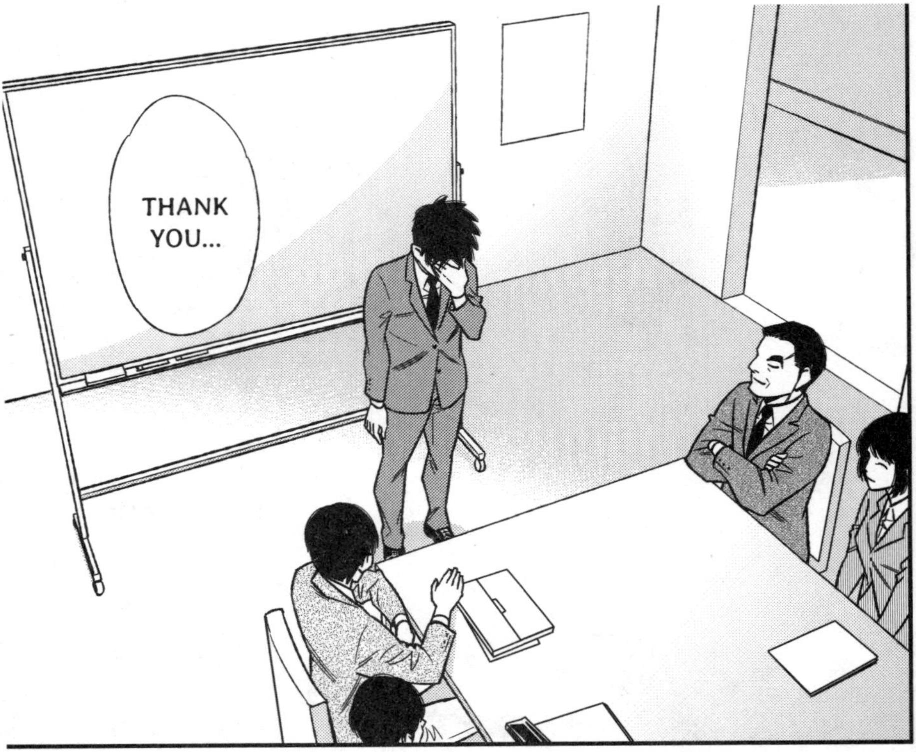
THANK YOU...

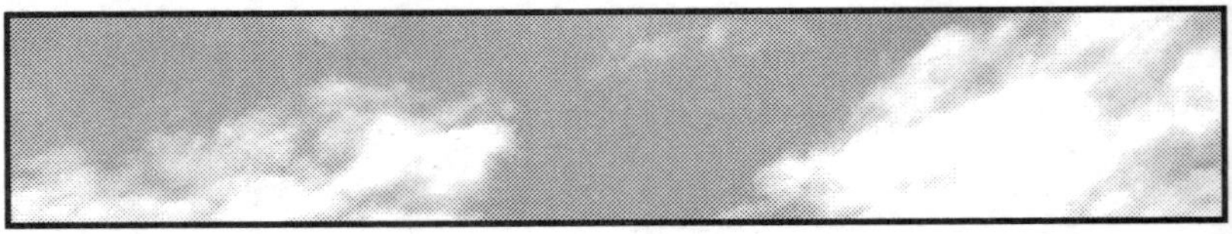

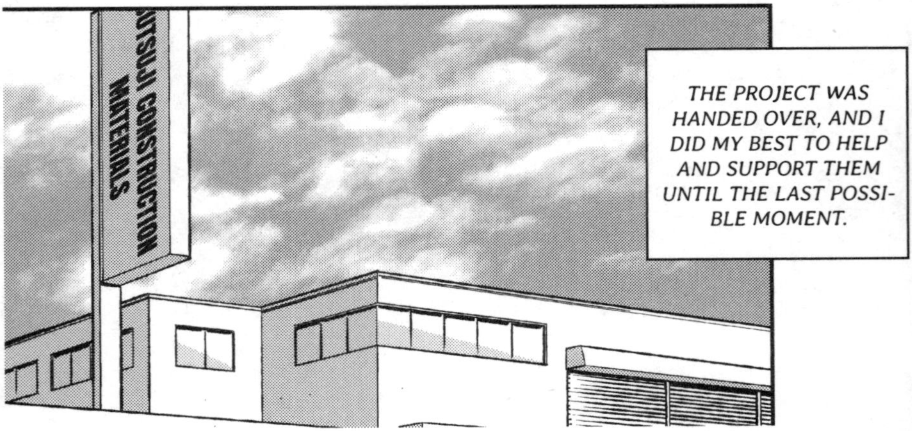
CONSTRUCTION
MATERIALS
THE PROJECT WAS HANDED OVER, AND I DID MY BEST TO HELP AND SUPPORT THEM UNTIL THE LAST POSSI-BLE MOMENT.

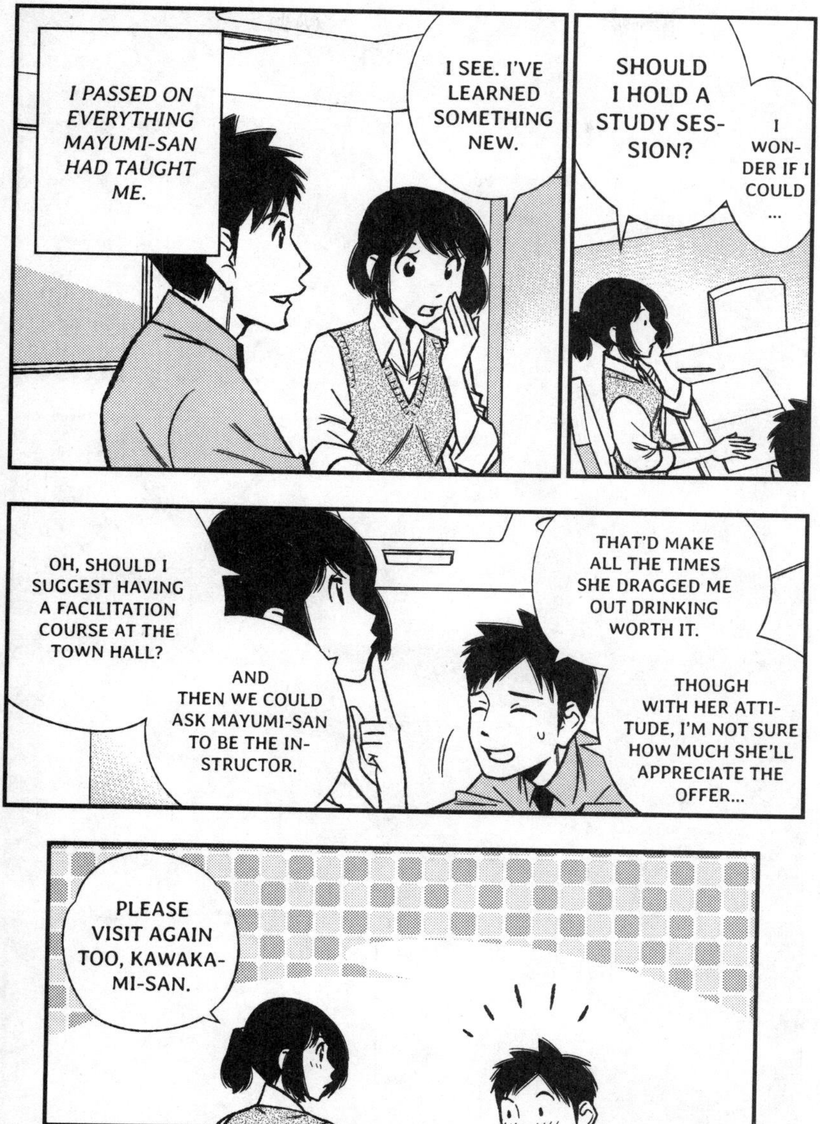
I PASSED ON EVERYTHING MAYUMI-SAN HAD TAUGHT ME.
I SEE. I'VE LEARNED SOMETHING NEW.
SHOULD I HOLD A STUDY SESSION?
I WONDER IF I COULD ...
OH, SHOULD I SUGGEST HAVING A FACILITATION COURSE AT THE TOWN HALL?
AND THEN WE COULD ASK MAYUMI-SAN TO BE THE INSTRUCTOR.
THAT'D MAKE ALL THE TIMES SHE DRAGGED ME OUT DRINKING WORTH IT.
THOUGH WITH HER ATTITUDE, I'M NOT SURE HOW MUCH SHE'LL APPRECIATE THE OFFER...
PLEASE VISIT AGAIN TOO, KAWAKAMI-SAN.

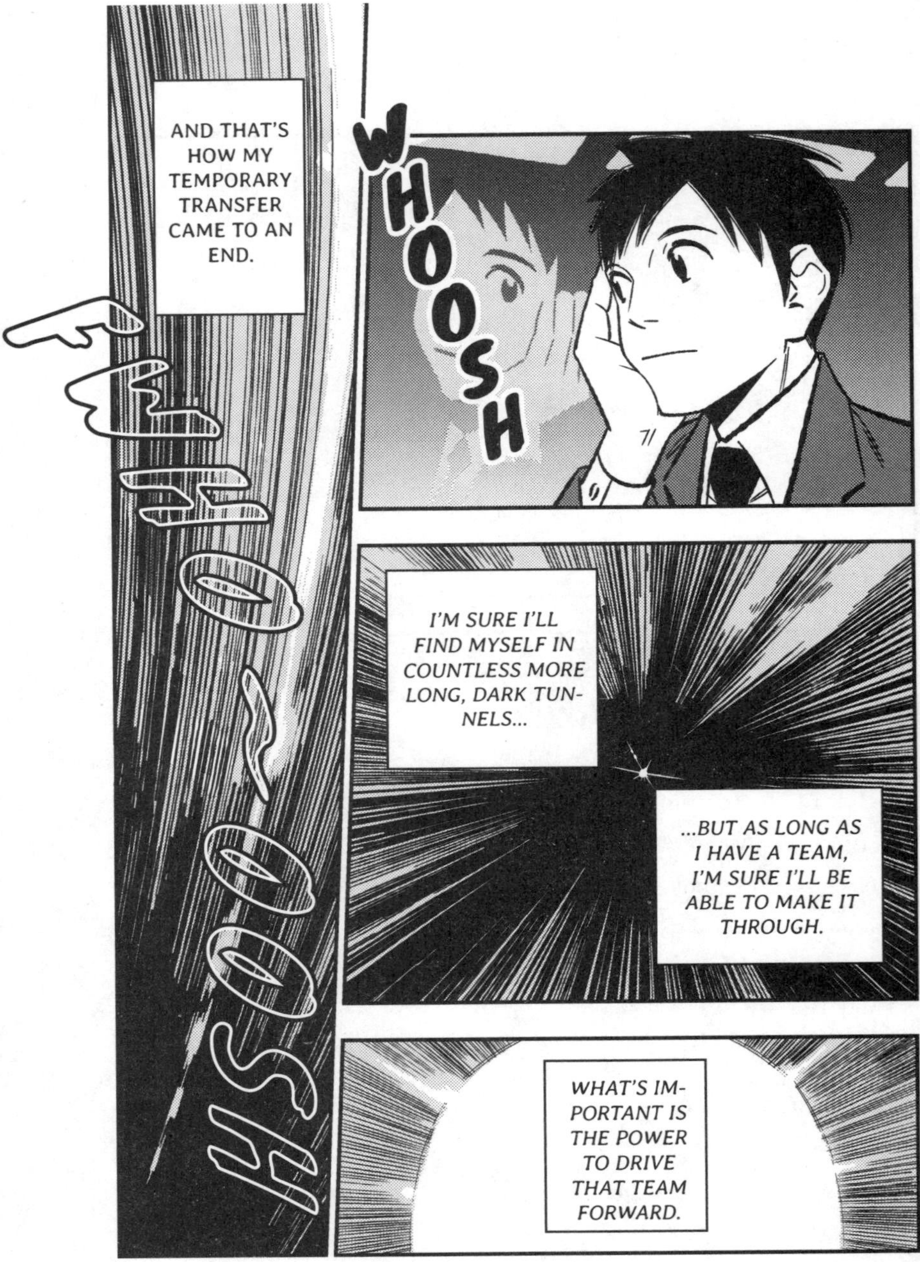
AND THAT'S HOW MY TEMPORARY TRANSFER CAME TO AN END.
WHO~OOSH
WHOOSH
I'M SURE I'LL FIND MYSELF IN COUNTLESS MORE LONG, DARK TUNNELS...
...BUT AS LONG AS I HAVE A TEAM, I'M SURE I'LL BE ABLE TO MAKE IT THROUGH.
WHAT'S IMPORTANT IS THE POWER TO DRIVE THAT TEAM FORWARD.

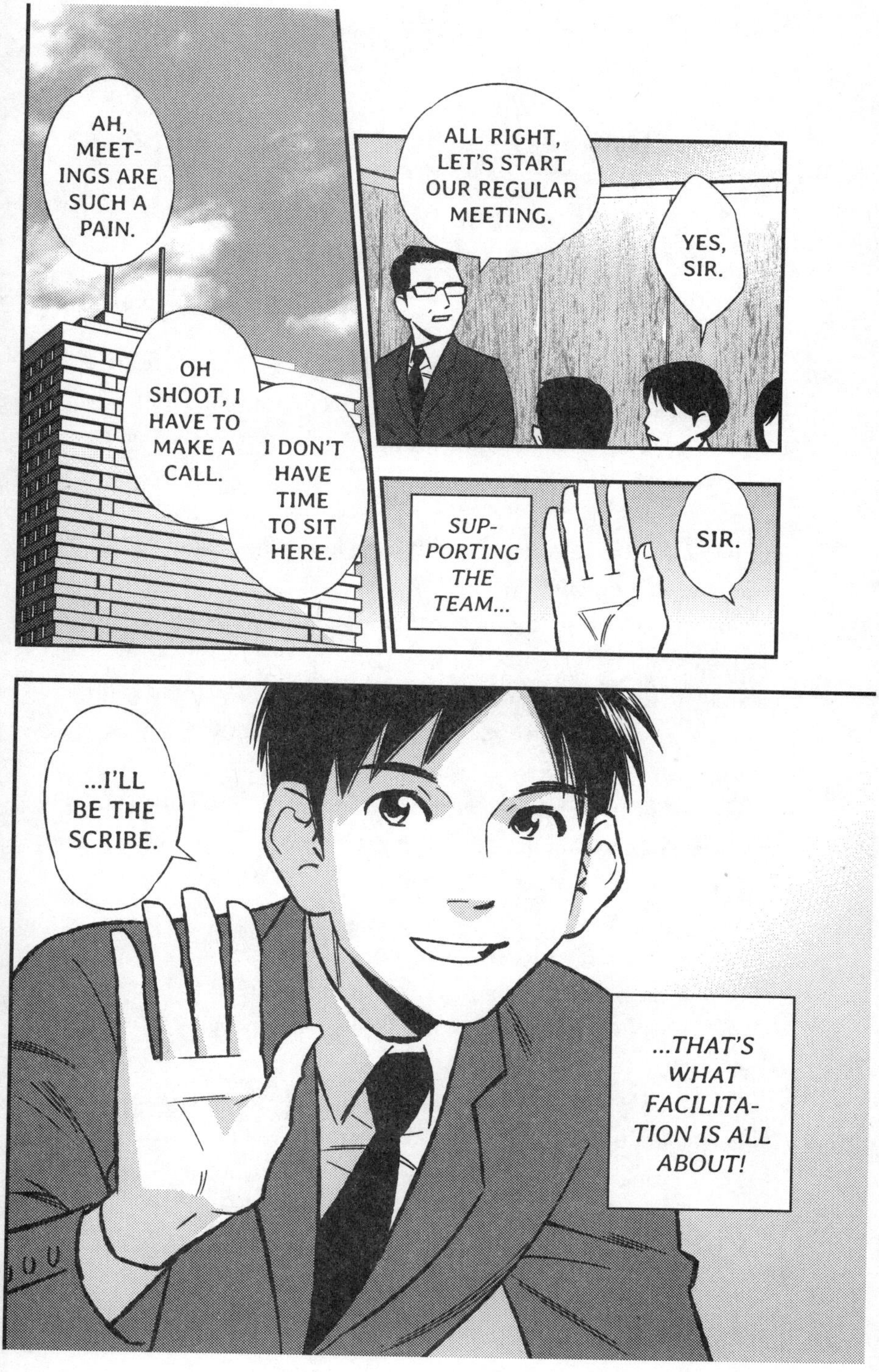
AH, MEETINGS ARE SUCH A PAIN.
OH SHOOT, I HAVE TO MAKE A CALL.
I DON'T HAVE TIME TO SIT HERE.
ALL RIGHT, LET'S START OUR REGULAR MEETING.
YES, SIR.
SIR.
SUPPORTING THE TEAM...
...I'LL BE THE SCRIBE.
...THAT'S WHAT FACILITATION IS ALL ABOUT!

13 A Team Is a Group of Individuals. Don't Forget to Give Individualized Support

Up until now, I've talked a lot about facilitation techniques for running a team, but one thing that you can't forget is that a team is a collection of individuals. I will be listing four tips on how to support your team members individually, while not neglecting the group as a whole.

○ **Individualized Support Tip #1: Get to know each team member individually.**
Leaders who look out for their team members and communicate well are trusted and respected. That's why the first thing you should do when dealing with new team members is to get to know them. For example, have you ever asked your team what they as individuals would like their leader to know? In order to provide each member with the best work environment, opportunities, and advice, it's important to be familiar with members from various perspectives and deepen your understanding of them.

○ **Individualized Support Tip #2: Look closely.**
In addition to getting to know your team members, you should be familiar with the various ways of effectively observing them.

Look at the whole team to get a big picture, examine those that pique your interest, care for the members you want to nurture as they change and evolve, keep an eye on those who are likely

190

to cause problems and determine what the problem is, and watch over members who aren't feeling well and encourage their recovery.

You'll need to use these different methods of observation depending on the situation and person you'll deal with. By doing so, the world you observe will change.

In order to bring the best performance out of each team member, you'll first need to observe.

○ **Individual Support Tip #3: Engage in strategic communication.** They don't look motivated. They look on edge today.

If you watch your team members carefully, you'll sometimes notice negative moods.

Finding them demotivated may put you on edge as well; this is where you need to take a deep breath.

They may be simply feeling unwell or have something else to worry about. If something feels off, go and speak to them. If you make assumptions based only on surface factors, you won't be able to provide adequate support, so it's important to grasp what kind of situation they are in. You can express your emotions after that; if you plan on approaching them, take a moment to breathe and set up a plan in advance.

1. **What's the purpose of interacting with them?**
2. **What do you want to draw out of them?**
3. **What questions would work best in order to draw that out of them?**

After you've answered these three, strategically converse with the team member in question.

You may find moments when you feel irritated by your team members' performance to be particularly difficult. At such times, answer these three questions in a calm and neutral manner, and strategically inspire your team members to engage with their work.

An ordinary conversation should then turn into a rather productive one.

○ **Individual Support Tip #4: Be positive, especially toward difficult members.**
There may be difficult members within your team. In such cases, don't try to come up with a quick solution, and tell yourself that forming a relationship with them will take time.

It's important to know what they value and what they feel to be an issue, and it may be effective to change your approach based on their social style.

On top of that, I recommend discovering and informing your team members about their strong points.

You will be able to gradually develop a positive image of such people by making an effort to observe their qualities, even if you might feel reluctant to do so.

Interacting with a variety of people will inevitably bring you growth as a facilitative leader. If you find things are stuck at work, talk it out with someone, remember to communicate, and develop your individual support skills.

Summary Lesson

Be Aware of Your Own Challenges

(1) Your Questioning Ability and the Fundamentals of Inspiring

"I lend an ear to so many people around me that it all becomes too much. What should I do?"

You've probably found yourself in the midst of conflicting opinions and ended up overwhelmed. This may be a common headache for those who lean toward the amiable type.

When I see people who get stressed from hearing too many opinions, I find myself thinking that there are many who are dragged down by their emotions.

For example, if someone comes up and tells them there's no point in what they're doing, such people may become anxious about how to proceed or worry that they communicated poorly. They may stress that their work is not appreciated or feel anxious about being criticized.

But in reality, there should be some sort of basis behind words such as "there's no point in doing that." You need to not allow yourself to be pulled down by negative emotions; figure out that basis, and discuss it.

Hearing other people's opinions can be great for the self. However, it's necessary to clearly state what that opinion is, as well as the basis behind it. If you're going to listen to what people have to say, you should be acutely aware of all sides of a conversation.

For example, whether something tastes good or bad is a matter of opinion.

In response to a confrontation of opinions, like someone thinking an item tastes good, while someone else believes it tastes bad, beyond acknowledging everyone's thoughts, you need to properly structure and ask questions such as the following:

- Who is the target audience for this product?
- Who is saying that it's good and that it's bad?
- How did these opinions come about?

It is because people don't ask these sorts of questions that they get caught up in and struggle to resolve uncompromising arguments.

"What should I do if the above technique conflicts with my workplace environment?"

Whenever you try something new, your workplace will generally oppose it. It's important to assume from the start that you'll find resistance when trying something new.

I think we fundamentally want to live in a way that's convenient for us. If things are going well, we won't want to change them, since if we make changes, new problems might come up. I think it's understandable that people oppose new ideas at first, because they don't want that to happen.

If you simply suppress dissenting opinions and force your own agenda from the top down, your workplace won't function smoothly. That's why it's so important to **create an atmosphere where anyone can freely express themselves**. A facilitator's listening attitude greatly influences the atmosphere of the workplace. How the facilitator responds to different remarks, how they listen, and how they communicate shape a workspace's atmosphere. For example, toward any given plan, there will be positive, negative, and unclear opinions.

In such a situation, if you validate positive opinions but question negative ones and dismiss unclear ones, you've created an atmosphere where people feel admonished for voicing opposition and judged for asking questions and ultimately end up feeling like they can only agree.

By equally acknowledging agreeing and dissenting opinions, and appreciating any questions, you can create an atmosphere that allows people to freely express their opinions. If you don't consciously create such inclusive environments, people will keep to themselves. Even if they do, they will still hold concerns and anxieties, so it's important to bring them out and deal with them.

It's okay to be in a place where some people feel that they can't honestly agree with a plan to the fullest but are still willing to try it, and not aim for a situation where everyone agrees 100%. I'm sure you want to avoid situations where conflict and discontent crop up in the workplace even though no one voices opinions during meetings. Conferences and meetings are held to resolve conflicts and move things forward, so it's important to create a space where people can express their own opinions properly.

What you really want to grasp is what their intent is in the first place. Initiatives and plans are means to reach a goal, so if people aren't clear about what they are aiming for, the discussion won't move forward.

Communicate the aim of plans handed down from the top, and make sure that each member understands their own role, along with everyone else's. If the organizational structure isn't yet clearly understood, it's important to begin by pinning it down.

There are many skills and methods for successfully running a meeting, but that base mindset is fundamental. If you don't have solid foundational ideas such as **"Always be conscious of your goal," "It's OK to have conflict,"** and **"Listen to all opinions and their basis,"** no matter what you do, it won't go well.

As for meeting skills, my questions tend to be one-note, so discussions don't really develop.

"I see. They certainly won't develop that way."

But it's amazing that you were able to realize that you were using the same questions all the time. If you hadn't noticed, you wouldn't have been able to improve on it.

As mentioned in the column on page 38, "The Four Stages of Leveling Up," stage 1 is the stage of dissatisfaction with the other participants. You feel like they have no opinions or ideas to contribute.

You feel there's something wrong with them, but that attitude won't lead to their personal growth or self-improvement. In order to progress from that stage, you need to realize the issue you are facing. That realization will be your first step.

"When I asked an advisor, they told me that it's important to ask 'Why?' What are your thoughts on that?"

Oh! Wonderful! I fully agree with that person.

However, if you ask "Why?" too much, some people will find it difficult to engage in the conversation, so be careful. It's useful to add to the types of questions and phrases you use. Some examples are "Why do you think so?" or "What are some examples?"

And so by listening to your team members, you'll start to build a **database of opinions and of the bases behind them**. You'll become aware that when dealing with a certain type of project, a certain kind of problem tends to come up, and certain types of complaints typically arise. I'm sure that you come across this kind of wisdom that is accumulated through experience throughout your workplace.

As this knowledge accumulates, you will be able to formulate hypotheses and make progress without having to ask the team members about every detail.

Practicing facilitation on a daily basis and compiling ideas from different people will naturally improve your work skills. You can learn a lot from your workplace and everyone's opinions, and develop your ability to find **commonalities** among disparate opinions.

By collecting ideas through questions you formulate via the frameworks I've introduced, it will become easier for you to organize your thoughts. I recommend practicing facilitation as a way to level yourself up as well.

"I tend to just ask yes-or-no questions. How can I change that?"

There's a time and a place for yes-or-no questions. But if you are using them all the time, then it may be best to consciously fix that.

I usually use open-ended questions to gather various opinions and strengthen my personal database. By doing so, your creative juices will start flowing, and you'll be able to **hypothesize** the cause of a problem and its potential solutions. Even for consultations from team members or clients, if beyond listening you also ask clear questions, you'll be able to provide a quick resolution.

"What should I do if I'm not good at asking questions in general?"

This might mean you're too worried about coming off as rude or offending others by asking certain questions.

In this case, I feel it is best for you to organize the main points you should ask about and set up a framework inside yourself. For example, if someone comes up to you to consult about starting a business, you should start off by asking them these customary questions: What are your strengths? What are your weaknesses? Who is the competition? Who are the customers?

Then you should move on to some questions that are a bit more difficult to ask, such as: How much do you want your sales to be? What kind of profit do you want to make? How much money do you have? Even if these questions are difficult to ask, you need to make things clear and prepare a framework that includes those important elements.

Rather than coming up with an original framework by yourself, it would be better to use an existing, go-to framework based on the subjects you're dealing with.

If you ask questions based on the framework I introduced on page 173, you will be able to **substantiate your questioning**, i.e., say that "I'm asking this because we need to consider X element," rather than simply "I'm asking because I want to."

I would especially like for those who are not keen to actively take the initiative to interact with others and to take advantage of these tools while doing so.

"Is it really all right to approach people like that?"

Yes, it's fine! Of course, I'm not telling you to forcefully approach them, but depending on the person, it may be necessary to make them aware that the success of a certain job will lead to the happiness of many people involved.

Amiable types in particular may feel apologetic **about making others work.**

Thinking and acting within discussions is good for the team members, the company, and society. I want you to keep that in mind. When you need to make a certain project succeed, you need to consider what are the necessary requirements to make it succeed, and how you need to get everyone to think in order to meet those requirements. Asking questions is then really important to get them to think that way.

Moreover, the questions facilitators ask are not for themselves.

The questions are for **the person who's being asked and the people around them**. I think it's important for you to understand that and employ questions accordingly.

"What are the differences between questions for myself and questions for others?"

I would say the main purpose of questions for yourself would be to gather information.

You can also clear up doubts and ask for ideas. These questions are for your gain, for what you want. On the other hand, facilitators consciously use **questions for the benefit of others.**

- Consider what was asked;
- Commit it to memory;
- Find an opportunity to speak up about it;
- Gain a new perspective;

- Expand your ways of thinking;
- Come up with ideas;
- Become aware of your biases;
- And remember that true knowledge is recognizing that you know nothing.

Asking questions can have many benefits. The purpose of the question for the other party is to promote thinking and to create **awareness** of various issues. Furthermore, by thinking and putting ideas into words by yourself, you will be able to **bring out your independence.**

In the first place, the purpose of collecting information is for the person who asked to think about solving their own problem. It's for them to collect information and think of what to do. In a situation where information only gathers around you, you'll be stuck thinking by yourself. Instead, if you want to think of the problem together with everyone and come up with a satisfactory answer, you need to share the problem at a meeting where everyone gathers. You'll need to **ask questions that encourage discussion.** What kind of thinking do you want the members to have? What direction do you need the team to move in?

(2) **Designing a Meeting**

"I'm troubled because there's a member on my project team who takes up a lot of work."

Ah... I feel like I'm being described... (lol)

I'm like this as well, but those who take up too much work **may not understand what they're doing specifically.** Rather than taking on too much work, they may be in a situation where they don't know who to ask. They may not be understanding what work they're doing or how much they've done. If you don't know, you won't be able to ask. Also, timing may play a part in this. In the midst of being overwhelmed by work every day, even if they want to involve someone at the last minute in a project that has an approaching deadline, they may not have time to teach or ask for help.

In fact, they may want everyone to be considerate and take the initiative to work. They may be waiting to hear, "Do you need help?" or "I'll take care of this." I often hear complaints from leaders who want others to use their heads and work. Of course that would be ideal, but a reason why that may not happen is because both you and those around you may not know specifically what kind of work they're doing.

And so I believe it's important to hold regular meetings to confirm what kind of work they're doing. I also think it's **necessary to hold meetings to check** the progress of projects.

As mentioned on page 168, in the section titled "The Essence of a Project Leader," when a project starts, it's important to **design how you'll communicate** from the kickoff to the post-review meeting.

In the first place, communication through language is prone to misalignment. Even if you use the same words, the image that comes to mind is not necessarily the same.

Have you ever had times where you asked someone to do something and felt relieved since they accepted the task, but had a completely different result come out, or it didn't meet your expectations? This is because we often don't realize the potential that our own image is different from the other person's image.

It's too late if you realize that things are wrong when the deadline approaches. If you don't want to feel regrets, it would be smoother to proceed with projects under the assumption that teamwork is meant to have misalignments. Once the project starts, make sure to check the progress as soon as possible. If you're able to find the misalignment and fix it there, it won't be too late.

So even if the other person is doing something that is different from what you were imagining, there's no need for you to feel down about it. I recommend thinking that you're lucky to find out the differences between each other.

However, remaining misaligned will just lead to problems later, so you need to align things properly here. Just asking them, "Why is it like this?" will make them feel condemned, and lead to both of you to just butt heads over your respective opinions. So it is important to take a stance to listen to what the other person has to say.

It is precisely because there is an environment in which both sides can calmly express their opinions that positive discussions are born.

"I'm troubled by my leader who switches up what they are saying often..."

Hm. That certainly does happen... (lol)

Members may complain, saying, "What's going on!" even though they were doing exactly what they were told to do. And the project would stop moving forward.

I often talk to both managers and team leaders and members on site, but when I listen to both stories, in the end, **there's a difference in what they're seeing.** The on-site members look at the site. People like leaders who pull the team along tend to look at the surroundings or the external parts of the project. Of course, there are differences in individuals here, and there are many who are able to balance things well and see things from both sides.

When I hear the stories of both sides of teams that say things aren't running well for them, they tend to have a difference in what they're seeing.

Especially when the leader is looking at the external environment, such as the position of the project within the company, the results that must be produced internally, and the degree of appeal, they will be sensitive to changes in the situation. They may come down to the decision that things must now be this way, since the situation changed. I believe that things turn odd because they try to fix the project's path while believing that everyone understands the situation, or that it's weird if they don't understand.

In the manga too, when Kawakami-kun is blindsided by his superior's decision, he becomes dispirited, and that's exactly what that feels like. If you feel helpless in the face of arbitrary decisions from above, workplace morale will drop. Nonetheless, these situations do come up to different extents on a regular basis. That is why it is important for team members to maintain a close interest in a leader's vision, their values, their decision-making, and in the kind of issues they are aware of, among other matters.

208

Of course, this responsibility falls equally on leaders. Promoting the exchange of visions is key to a strong and agile team. Also, those who are aware of their teammates' character can create opportunities to be open with and reconcile a team's differences. I would be happy for everyone reading this book to begin to apply such skills.

(3) Learn to Handle Differences

You've grasped your team's diverse nature, but you're worried about how to lead such an eclectic group of people.

Indeed, if you aim to lead a diverse team, it's important to fashion **your own style of leadership**.

There are people out there who aren't necessarily leaders and that people flock to anyway. There are various reasons why people stay close to others, such as their personality, their drive, and how fun they are. I don't think people have to be a certain way for others to gravitate to them. This being the case, you should be aware of what your own traits are and forge a leadership style that makes the most of your strengths.

Social style theory, introduced on page 126, is also useful when searching for your own personality. Each style comes with **positive and negative** aspects, and I'll introduce each in the following section.

● Driving

Driving types are the kind who don't beat around the bush, and they are at home with the **top-down style of leadership**. This type is a perfect fit for situations that demand agility and initiative, such as starting a business or dealing with emergencies, but on the other hand, they fall short at paying due consideration to coworkers. It's important to convey feelings of gratitude to one's team members on a regular basis. If you think this is something you struggle with, appoint an **attentive staff** member to advise you.

● Expressive

Expressives are adept at getting everyone onboard through **engaging leadership styles**. Their personal drive is amazing, but they struggle with planning ahead and forecasting, and so they stumble often. They may be fine with that themselves, but their coworkers may feel differently, and so it will sometimes be necessary for them to create detailed plans. Don't hate the details, and get a **team member who is good with numbers and project planning** on your side.

● Amiable

Amiable types excel at getting the motivation to do their best out of their team members. This type of leader **pays due consideration to and closely watches** their team members. Thoughtful attentiveness is important, but on the other hand, listening to your team members' feelings and opinions too much can lead to indecisiveness. It would be a shame if you were to be labeled an indecisive leader, so develop your **decision-making skills**, even from small things in your daily life.

Also, to prevent stress from overthinking, I recommend finding an advisor you can rely on and going for consultations early on.

● Analytical

Analyticals are the type of leaders who **master their field of expertise and lead by example**. They lead their team cooly, working at their own pace and with accuracy. They are skilled at work that focuses on planning, where it is important to adhere to a determined course of action, such as in factory environments. However, though they may share their knowledge, they rarely talk about their own feelings and thoughts, which may leave some members feeling displeased or uneasy. Keeping in mind that a team needs energy and initiative, keep a **bright and energetic** member of your team by your side.

If you want to lead a team with diverse members, you need to **adapt yourself to each individual.** There will be team members who want to be informed of your vision, just as there will be those who won't care about it and only want specific instructions. There will be team members who want to get along and have fun with their coworkers, just as there will be those who only want to simply get the job done. However, there are people for whom handling all this diversity by themselves becomes too much.

"I'm sure there are people who won't want to handle all of that by themselves."

That's why it is so important to have a partner with whom you can bring out each other's strengths and complement your efforts. After concluding what kind of leadership style you excel at and where you fall short, you might find yourself wondering who to compensate for your shortcomings with or what kind of systems to implement. But with so many different team members, don't you find yourself feeling that the sky is the limit?

"Are you saying, then, that rather than doing everything on your own, it's also important to make use of those around you?"

Exactly. Of course, as a leader, one must pull their own weight, but trying to do everything yourself is **simply overwhelming**. Be aware of your and your team members' strengths and differences, and leverage them to move your team forward. Facilitation skills are very useful to this end.

For example, writing on a whiteboard isn't just for record keeping. In fact, **the whiteboard acts as a receiver**. The facilitator isn't the one that collects all opinions, the whiteboard is. If you write it on the whiteboard, an individual idea can become the team's shared opinion, and you can bring about a situation where everyone accepts an idea that came up on the spot.

"So whiteboards serve not only to focus people's gazes and keep record, but also to catch ideas."

Yes, that's right. It's difficult for an individual facilitator to catch diverse ideas on their own. That's why you write them on the whiteboard so that the whole team can see them and grapple with them collectively.

If you do so, you will be able to equally discuss both veterans' and newcomers' ideas alike. Don't note that person A said this, or person B said that. Write ideas on the board without noting the name of the person who came up with them.

Do that, and you'll find that you're able to discuss **the opinions of the whole**, not just individuals. If you grant everyone the chance to voice their opinion and consolidate everything on a whiteboard, you can avoid a situation in which only the opinions of the vocal minority are heard. Get everything drawn up first, and you can probe for everyone's reasoning after the fact.

"If everyone's opinions are treated equally, how should I go about making a decision? In my experience, it often does end up being the case that the vocal minority decides the outcome."

If your team accepts decisions made in this fashion, and if your workplace runs smoothly as a result, then I don't think it's a problem. If everyone is in agreement, and you find your team saying things such as, "Sounds good, let's go with that," I think it's fine if the decision is made solely by the leader, or if the most vocal participants drag everyone else along to their conclusion. It becomes a problem if no one then acts on that decision. I think that before agonizing over that decision process, it's important to first take a look at the conduct of your coworkers and the condition of your workplace.

For example, let's imagine a five-person team made up of persons A, B, C, D, and E. I don't think it would ever be the case that all five of these people have exactly the same influence over the team when they speak.

This is because position, experience, expertise, intelligence, and so on, all vary greatly from person to person.

It can even be the case that role-wise, person A is officially the leader, but in reality, person D speaks loudly and often and is so influential that they are the real leader for all intents and purposes.

Even so, if the team and workplace are running smoothly, then person A is a lucky leader. This is often the case when a team member perhaps has a more influential voice, but the leader is better at team management—maybe the type of management that pulls the strings from behind the scenes, like any good politician. In fact, young leaders who are good at dealing with their older subordinates, and female leaders who lead male teams, tend to skillfully bring out the strengths of their team members in such a way that the team actually functions better as a result. Team members may find that they're able to work more comfortably, and it's less strain on you, the leader. In any case, a team can't go on with an exhausted leader, and if both the team and the leader are exhausted, then there's no hope whatsoever.

The important thing is to first decide **who will decide, and how they will decide**. If you don't figure these points out before you start making decisions, it can be tricky to consolidate everything and come to a succinct conclusion.

If you want to decide democratically, I recommend using the effectiveness and feasibility analysis framework that I introduced between pages 141 and 162, to make decisions based on how fundamentally effective a proposition is instead of just using the majority vote. This method allows you to decide by going through each opinion one by one and rating them with A, B, or C, based on their effectiveness and feasibility. For example, in order to liven up the workplace, a work function may be graded A for effectiveness, but may only be a C in terms of feasibility because of everyone's differing shifts. If you start by trying to tackle the opinions that seem to be most effective and feasible first, you'll find that the options you should be prioritizing become obvious. In order to form a strong team by taking advantage of the different qualities of its constituent members, **you to need start by enjoying each of those differences**.

If you want to enjoy them, you need to realize your preferences, such as how you like things to be, and how you prefer things to be done. On top of that, if you have the knowledge and know the skill set to do your job well, and if you train those skills on a regular basis, you'll find that your surroundings will start to change for the better, too.

"I'm glad you're here."
"I want someone like you on my team, too."

I sincerely hope that the number of wonderful facileaders who will receive such words will increase, and from the bottom of my heart, I'm rooting for you all to rise to the challenge!

About the Author
Masumi Tani

Coach and facilitator. ONDO Co., Ltd. Representative Director. Born 1974 in Kagawa Prefecture. Graduated from Kagawa University. Became independent in 2005 after working in sales at a building materials trading company and in sales at an IT company. Part-time lecturer at Waseda Business School and Okayama University. NPO International Coach Federation Japan Branch Advisor. NPO Japan Coach Association Shikoku Chapter Advisor.

Specializes in business coaching and facilitation. She creates about 200 practical learning opportunities per year, through coaching training and corporate coaching at companies, universities, government offices, etc. In 2015, she received the Waseda University Teaching Award, which is given to teachers who conduct excellent lectures. She has also contributed articles to magazines and websites, accepted requests for interviews, and more.

This book also contains bits from *Facilitation Skills for Leaders!*, *Coaching Skills for Leaders!* (Subarusha), *Communication Skills That Will Go Well If You Know Their Type* (Sougo Horei Publishers | Coauthor: Edagawa Yoshikuni),

"Understanding the importance and recognition of practice when coaching" (Dissertation. Practicing management, Volume 51, 2014. Coauthor: Sugiura Masakazu), and the illustrations for *For People Who Think MBAs Are Basically People and the Organization* (Douyukan).

ONDO Co., Ltd.
http://www.ondo.company